Heaven Has a Wall

Heaven Has a Wall

Religion, Borders, and the Global United States

ELIZABETH SHAKMAN HURD

The University of Chicago Press
Chicago and London

The University of Chicago Press, Chicago 60637
The University of Chicago Press, Ltd., London
© 2025 by The University of Chicago
All rights reserved. No part of this book may be used or reproduced in any manner whatsoever without written permission, except in the case of brief quotations in critical articles and reviews. For more information, contact the University of Chicago Press, 1427 E. 60th St., Chicago, IL 60637.
Published 2025

34 33 32 31 30 29 28 27 26 25   1 2 3 4 5

ISBN-13: 978-0-226-84118-2 (cloth)
ISBN-13: 978-0-226-84120-5 (paper)
ISBN-13: 978-0-226-84119-9 (e-book)
DOI: https://doi.org/10.7208/chicago/9780226841199.001.0001

Library of Congress Cataloging-in-Publication Data

Names: Hurd, Elizabeth Shakman, 1970–, author.
Title: Heaven has a wall : religion, borders, and the global United States / Elizabeth Shakman Hurd.
Description: Chicago ; London : The University of Chicago Press, 2025. | Includes bibliographical references and index.
Identifiers: LCCN 2024052589 | ISBN 9780226841182 (cloth) | ISBN 9780226841205 (paperback) | ISBN 9780226841199 (ebook)
Subjects: LCSH: Religion and politics—United States. | Political culture—United States. | United States—Emigration and immigration—Public opinion. | National security—United States—Public opinion. | United States—Public opinion.
Classification: LCC BL2525 .H874 2025 | DDC 261.7—dc23/eng/20241203
LC record available at https://lccn.loc.gov/2024052589

For the border crossers

The American homeland is the planet.

9/11 COMMISSION REPORT

Contents

Introduction   Where People Come to Press Close to the Other Side 1
Chapter 1   Creating: The Liturgy of Asylum 26
Interlude I   *Border/less* 48
Chapter 2   Enforcing: National Security 59
Interlude II   *Unbordered: Land without Law* 77
Chapter 3   Suspending: AmericaIsrael 92
Interlude III   *Crossing* 122
Chapter 4   Refusing: Holy Death in the Borderlands 128
Interlude IV   *Walking: Pilgrimage to Magdalena* 155
Conclusion   The Ideal Border 168

Acknowledgments 179
Sources 183
Index 211

INTRODUCTION

Where People Come to Press Close to the Other Side

FIGURE 1. *Border Dynamics 2003*. Taller Yonke (Guadalupe Serrano and Alberto Morackis), University of Arizona Public Art Collection (Tucson).
Photo by author.

In January 2020, I visited the US-Mexico borderlands as a part of a trip to northern Sonora with Border Community Alliance, a civil society group based in Tubac, Arizona. We crossed into Mexico at Nogales, a city bisected by the border and often called Ambos Nogales ("both Nogales" in Spanish) for that reason. I was, at first, struck by a sense of inevitability and banality at the border. A lone US border official waited quietly at the unassuming Morley Gate pedestrian-only border crossing, leaning off his bike and staring up at a cloudless sky. My traveling companion, a fellow US citizen, and I were able to cross back and forth at will between the US and Mexico as if passing through a metro station. At the end of our trip to Sonora, after crossing over to the US to check into a hotel and prepare for our return to Tucson, we returned to Mexico for happy hour at La Roca, a landmark bar nestled into a picturesque cliff face steps from the border. A century ago, Mexican Nogales was a boomtown and haven for Americans seeking to escape Prohibition—including Al Capone, Charlie Chaplin, Bing Crosby, and Clark Gable. Celebrities also frequented the Agua Caliente casino in Tijuana, where in the 1920s, according to the Chamber of Commerce, "modern gaiety finds expression in a setting of Old World luxury and splendor."[1] It is said that at least one binational bar let American patrons drink as long as they stood on the Mexican side of the room.[2] For those on both sides, the border was largely irrelevant until the 1950s or 1960s, at least in some locations. Residents neither saw the border nor experienced it as an obstacle. As Maria Eugenio Trillo, a resident of El Paso's Segundo Barrio at the time, explained to a journalist: "There was never a physical division at that time between the two countries, other than the river."[3]

This is not the case in the twenty-first century.[4] At Morley Gate, while searching for the nineteenth-century border marker on the Mexican side, my

---

1. Cited in Vanderwood, Juan Soldado, 146. On July 4, 2020, sixty-five thousand Americans in 12,654 cars visited Tijuana to celebrate US Independence Day. San Diego ran out of gas and by evening only emergency vehicles could obtain fuel (92).

2. There were watering holes along the US-Canada border during Prohibition as well. I came across a dilapidated two-story building in Vermont-Quebec, bisected by the border, in which, during that era, liquor could be legally bought and consumed on the Canadian side. The abandoned structure used to be a store, with exterior doors on each side of the line and a connecting door inside (Center for Land Use Interpretation, "The Forty-Fifth Parallel").

3. Maria Eugenio Trillo as told to Timmons, "Trump's Wall," 18. "In the binational context of border towns," writes Rachel St. John, "society was divided by neither national citizenship nor the boundary line, but by class and racial-ethnic categories that took their meaning from the context in which they were used" (*Line in the Sand*, 88).

4. The 1969 launch of Nixon's Operation Intercept, led by G. Gordon Liddy and former Maricopa County sheriff Joe Arpaio, marks a turning point (Timmons, "Trump's Wall").

friend and I noticed two men who, we assumed, lacked permission to enter the United States. They were gazing patiently through the border fence onto International Boulevard in Nogales, Arizona. Were they waiting for someone? I was reminded of journalist and poet Amelia Urry's remark, "Nogales is a place where people come to press close to the other side."[5]

There were other signs of the border's weightier presence. Within sight of Morley Gate, on the US side, a store called Nogales Tactical set a different tone. A block from the border, Nogales Tactical sells tactical gear and accessories for official as well as self-appointed border enforcers. Window displays leave little doubt as to what is for sale (combat gear) and who the intended customers are (American border defenders). The store's website boasts, "Nogales Tactical is proud to serve the men and women of public safety and homeland security. Nogales Tactical specializes in tactical accessories, uniforms, and boots for Customs and Border Patrol, Local Police Departments, EMS, Firefighters, Military and Security." The sense of a no-holds-barred militarized defense of the border, of America, and, more quietly, of whiteness was frightening. It brought to mind Harel Shapira's description of the Minutemen border militia group's perception of the US-Mexico border.[6] Their opening ceremonies, or "muster," he observes, "help constitute the border as a stage—a sacred and damaged one—and consequentially frame the practices that take place there as patriotic endeavors, involving notions of danger and sacrifice, where lost masculinity can be reclaimed."[7]

Most Americans think the border should be secured. Borders are necessary and perhaps inevitable; as the neighbor in Robert Frost's poem "Mending Wall" famously claimed, "good fences make good neighbors."[8] Public resources dedicated to border enforcement reinforce this consensus. US annual budgets for immigration and border enforcement have grown more than eightyfold since 1978, totaling nearly $25 billion for US Customs and Border Protection (CBP) and Immigration and Customs Enforcement (ICE) in President Biden's 2024 budget. This was an increase of almost $800 million

---

5. Urry, "Come and See Me." On the border's blending of "enticements to passage and stern prohibitions" see also Yeh, *Passing*.

6. For a perceptive ethnography of the Minutemen in southern Arizona in the early 2000s, see Shapira, *Waiting for José*, where the author concludes that "illegal immigration matters to the Minutemen, but it matters first and foremost because through it these men have created a culture, a camp, a set of heroes, a set of enemies, an entire social world, through which their post is extended, resurrected, and in the case of some, invented" (158).

7. Shapira, *Waiting for José*, 54.

8. Frost, "Mending Wall," 404.

over the 2023 level.⁹ In every year since 2016, the US government has spent more on border and immigration enforcement than on all other federal law-enforcement agencies combined.¹⁰ US borders are more than a line in the sand, a wall in the desert, or an airport checkpoint. They are a web of militarized and racialized enforcement regimes blanketing the world.¹¹ This was palpable at Nogales Tactical and in the CBP advertisements posted around American Nogales. The authors of the *Report of the National Commission on Terrorist Attacks upon the United States* (*The 9/11 Commission Report*) expressed a similar sentiment: "The American homeland is the planet."¹²

One can physically see and cross the US-Mexico border in Nogales. At Morley Gate, it is easy to cross on foot. The border here has a sense of finality and fixity in space and time. Legally speaking, however, the border extends deep into the interior of the United States. As defined by US law, most Americans reside in the border zone, a place where special rules apply and rights are different. CBP does not need a warrant to board vehicles and vessels and search for people without immigration documentation "within a reasonable distance from any external boundary of the United States." These "external boundaries" include international land borders but also the entire US coastline. As Laila Lalami observed, "the border is all around us, and it's growing."¹³

The laws governing US borders are part of, and at the same time partly distinct from, other US legal regimes. The American Civil Liberties Union (ACLU) describes the one-hundred-mile border jurisdiction zone (figure 2) in the US as "Constitution-free." Most of the ten largest cities in the US, including New York, Los Angeles, and Chicago, are in the border zone, as is the entire state of Florida.¹⁴ This capacious border zone is part of the border magic described in this book.

Just as US borders are internalized, so are they also externalized. Guatemalan border agents such as the Chorti are, in the words of journalist Todd Miller, "as much members of the U.S. border guard as the Border Patrol agents patrolling the deserts of Texas and Arizona."¹⁵ US CBP has attaché offices in

---

9. White House, "Fact Sheet."
10. Grandin, *End of the Myth*, 263.
11. Miller, *Empire of Borders*.
12. 9/11 Commission, *9/11 Commission Report*.
13. Lalami, "Border Is All around Us."
14. American Civil Liberties Union, "Customs and Border Protection's (CBP's) 100-Mile Rule"; American Civil Liberties Union, "Know Your Rights."
15. Miller, *Empire of Borders*, 47.

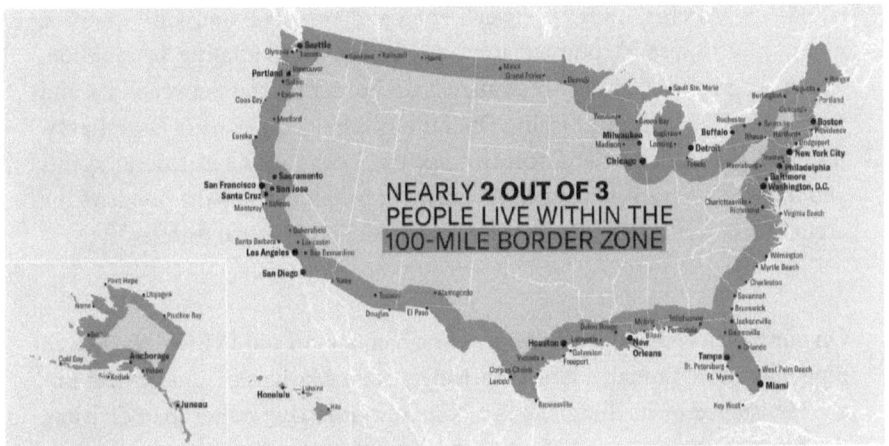

FIGURE 2. The one-hundred-mile border zone.
Copyright 2018 American Civil Liberties Union. Originally posted by the ACLU at https://www.aclu.org/news/immigrants-rights/your-rights-border-zone.

twenty-three countries around the world.[16] Homeland Security Investigations (HSI, ICE's International Operations wing) has ninety-three offices located in fifty-six countries.[17] Between 1997 and 2001, Operation Global Reach, an $8.2 million Immigration and Naturalization Service (INS) initiative, established forty overseas offices and trained forty-five thousand officials in Africa, Asia, and Latin America.

The mission to globalize and fortify US borders has grown exponentially since 9/11. Resources dedicated to border security have increased at a breakneck pace in this century; between 1993 and 2020, the number of US Border Patrol agents quintupled from just over 4,000 to just under 20,000.[18] Since 9/11, Congress has spent over $100 billion on immigration and border control.[19] CBP's annual budget has increased from $5.9 billion to nearly $17 billion since it began operations as part of the Department of Homeland Security

---

16. CBP attachés are posted in US embassies and consulates and serve as the chief of mission's Customs and Border Protection in-house specialists.

17. International Operations is the largest international investigative arm of the Department of Homeland Security (DHS) (US Immigration and Customs Enforcement, "International Operations").

18. Statista, "Agent Staffing of the U.S. Border Patrol from FY 1992 to FY 2020."

19. Kang, INS on the Line, 173.

(DHS) on March 3, 2003.[20] Between 2006 and 2013, ICE and CBP awarded ninety-nine thousand contracts to private corporations totaling $45.2 billion, which is equal to the total accumulated US border budget between 1975 and 2002.[21] US CBP Air and Marine Operations Assets, the world's largest aviation and maritime law-enforcement agency,[22] employs 1,800 federal agents and mission support personnel. A statement from their website previews the argument of this book: "The border is not merely a physical frontier."[23]

*

On our final day in Nogales, my traveling companion and I visited the newer, reputably more humane, and surprisingly artsy Mariposa Land Port of Entry. Envisioned by its designers as a point of connection rather than division, the fifty-four-acre site outside Nogales won the 2016 American Institute of Architects (AIA) National Institute Honor Award after a $250 million renovation led by designer Jones Studio and the engineering firm Stantec.[24] Stantec's website boasts, "We always design with community in mind." Principal designer Eddie Jones found inspiration in the 2003 poem "Border Lines" by Arizona Poet Laureate Alberto Ríos. The poem, inscribed in a glass partition within the queueing lanes in the visitor lobby, concludes: "Let us turn the map until we see clearly:/The border is what joins us,/Not what separates us."[25] Jones Studio describes their vision:

> Influenced by the smooth, continuous lines of a railroad yard and the contrasting vision of a desert oasis, the site design wraps the port's utilitarian needs of vehicular and pedestrian processing around a lush central garden for port staff and visitors. Pedestrians are led towards the center of the site along a quiet shaded path to continue their passage north.... The central spine of the port is the Oasis, a desert garden running the length of the site that provides respite from the harsh climate and the stress of border protection. Each path

---

20. American Civil Liberties Union Michigan, "Border's Long Shadow."
21. Miller, "Walls Must Fall."
22. The agency works in the Baltics, Mexico, and the Middle East, offering what is known as "domain awareness capacity," or real-time actionable information (Miller, *Empire of Borders*, 181).
23. US Customs and Border Protection, "Air and Marine Operations Operating Locations."
24. The AIA award was among the nineteen received by the Mariposa LPOE, ranging from "Exposing the Best in Concrete" from the International Concrete Repair Institute, Arizona chapter to LEED—Gold Certification from the US Green Building Council.
25. Ríos, "Border Lines."

crosses the threshold of the new port marking the entry into the country: a canopy of color—red, white, and blue—stretching 1000 feet across the site.[26]

Wandering through the complex, we were struck by the artwork in the long approach to the facility. Adult- and child-sized footprints of migrants are embedded in the tilt-slab, bullet-proof concrete walls, as if a parent and child had walked together sideways across the walls and then up and out of the facility (figure 3). It was eerie and also oddly humanizing. Maria Salinger, a public artist and architect with Jones Studio, came up with the idea of the footprints. With all those bare concrete walls, Eddie Jones explained, "we needed to tell a story." They used real shoe soles to make the molds used to imprint the footprints on the walls. The fact that concrete was cast on site and poured horizontally in tilt-slab construction made it easier. When I asked Jones where the people who made the footprints were meant to be going, he told me, "They're on a journey."[27]

Surprisingly, more tomatoes pass through Mariposa than people. Hailed as the "Port of the Future," this crossing is the main entry point for an estimated 60 percent of all winter produce consumed in the United States. Allison Moore of the Fresh Produce Association of the Americas puts this number in perspective: "We have four billion pounds of produce that passes through here annually. In tomatoes alone, if you put a year's worth of crossings end-to-end, you'd circle the earth nine times in tomatoes."[28] The total value of exports and imports passing through Mariposa each year is nearly $35 billion. As of 2022, nearly $1 million in bilateral trade takes place across the US-Mexico border *every minute*, or roughly $1.8 billion per day, at some fifty-six points of entry.[29] When it comes to goods, Nogales Tactical is nowhere to be found. The border is open.

The Mariposa Port of Entry speaks to a contrasting feature of US borders that is central to this book: the American aspiration to transcend borders, supersede laws, and encompass the world. While Americans support tight border controls, they also refuse to be constrained by borders. Americans can do anything: build the Panama Canal, bring freedom and democracy to the Middle East, conquer outer space, innovate our way out of climate crisis, and make crossing the border at Mariposa as pleasant as a trip to an art museum

26. Jones Studio, "Mariposa Land Port of Entry."
27. Conversation with Eddie Jones, August 29, 2024. See also Jones, "There's No Invasion at Our Southern Border."
28. Allen, "State-of-the-Art Border Crossing Opens in Arizona."
29. Green, "US Exports More to Mexico Than to all EU Countries Combined."

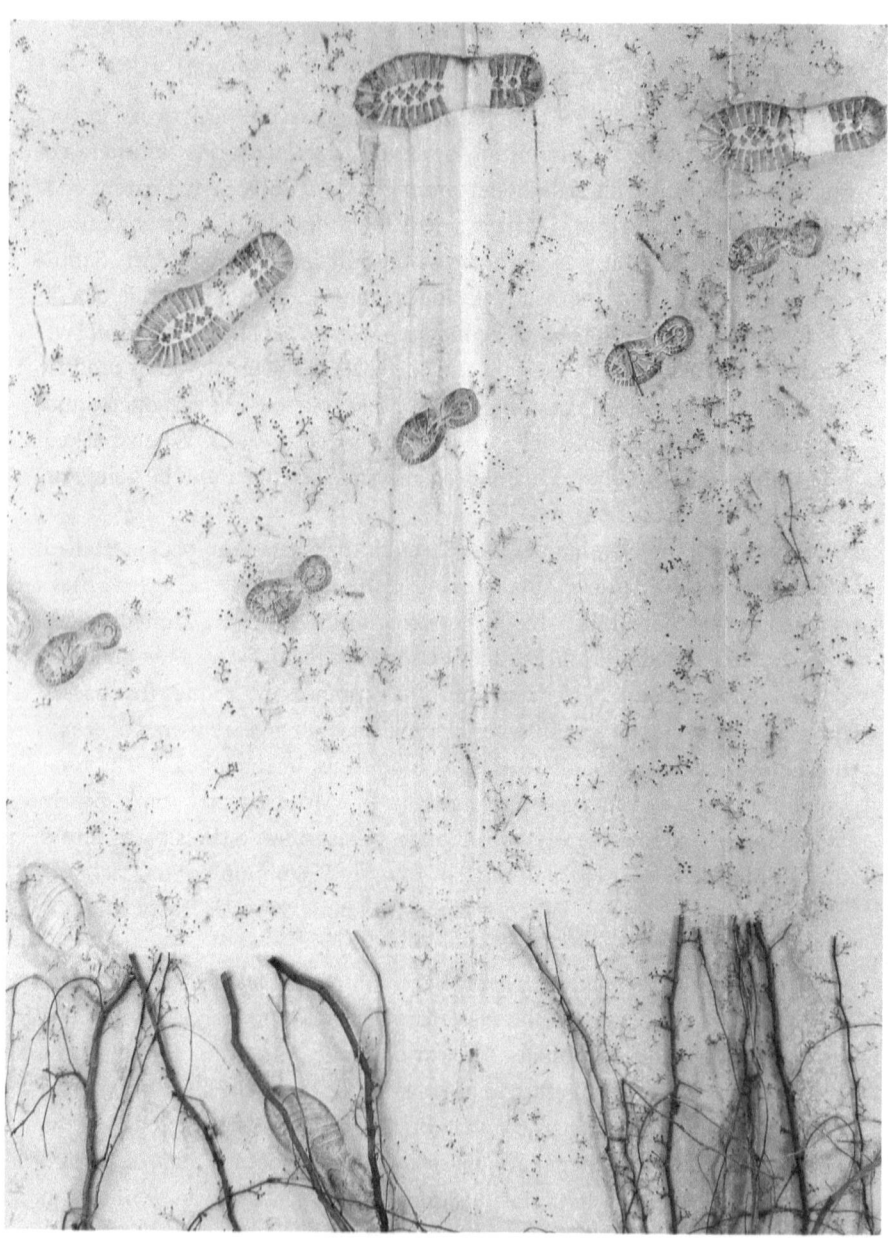

FIGURE 3. Mariposa port of entry, 2020. Photo by author.

with a whimsical rock garden and a soothing fountain. Adults and children stroll in and out, continuing together on their journey through the garden path and border passage. Mariposa even has an innovative rainwater harvesting system that captures runoff and stores it in a million-gallon underground tank; according to Jones, "Once we connected the system, the first monsoon totally filled it, and it's never been empty since.... All this beautiful landscaping survives on rainwater in the desert."[30] Even the name Mariposa, which means "butterfly" in Spanish, connotes lightness, freedom, and openness. Butterflies cross borders effortlessly.[31]

In practice, however, butterflies too are threatened by border fortification. The most diverse butterfly sanctuary in the country, the National Butterfly Center, is located on the border in Mission, Texas, where it faces desecration by wall and fence construction. The construction was facilitated by a 2018 Supreme Court ruling that allowed the Trump administration to waive twenty-eight federal laws, including the Native American Graves Protection and Repatriation Act and the American Indian Religious Freedom Act, to begin work on thirty miles of border wall in the valley passing through the center. Known as the Real ID waiver after the 2005 legislation by that name,[32] it allows for the waiver of laws protecting clean air, clean water, public lands, and endangered wildlife.[33] "Never before has the government circumvented

---

30. Karaim, "Mariposa Land Point of Entry."

31. In Mexican Spanish, *mariposa* can also refer to LGBTQ+ individuals. See the work of the Tucson-based advocacy group Mariposas sin Fronteras ("Butterflies without Borders"), a community "dedicated to supporting both incarcerated and recently released from detention LGBTQIJ+ migrating folks with material, legal, and medical resources" (https://astraeafoundation.org/stories/mariposas-sin-fronteras/).

32. The REAL ID Act was passed as part of the Emergency Supplemental Appropriations for Defense, the Global War on Terror, and Tsunami Relief. Section 102 "amends the Illegal Immigration Reform and Immigrant Responsibility Act of 1996 to authorize the Secretary of Homeland Security, in the Secretary's sole discretion, to waive all laws as necessary to ensure expeditious construction of certain barriers and roads at the U.S. border. Prohibits courts, administrative agencies, and other entities from reviewing the Secretary's decision or from ordering relief for damages alleged to have resulted from such decision" (Real ID Act of 2005). In January 2008, DHS promulgated the final regulations, which contain 280 pages of explanation as well as responses to over twenty-one thousand comments.

33. Laws waived include the National Environmental Policy Act; the Endangered Species Act; the Clean Water Act; the National Historic Preservation Act; the Migratory Bird Treaty Act; the Migratory Bird Conservation Act; the Clean Air Act; the Archeological Resources Protection Act; the Paleontological Resources Preservation Act; the Federal Cave Resources Protection Act; the Safe Drinking Water Act; the Noise Control Act; the Solid Waste Disposal Act; the Comprehensive Environmental Response, Compensation, and Liability Act; the Archaeological and Historic Preservation Act; the Antiquities Act; the Historic Sites, Buildings, and Antiquities

so many of its own laws to build and govern the virtual and physical border wall," notes Felicity Amaya Schaeffer.[34]

The same construction project has severely reduced the flow of water to Quitobaquito Springs in Arizona's Organ Pipe Cactus National Monument, one of the only aboveground water sources in the Sonoran Desert. The Quitobaquito area is associated with a prehistoric trade route known as the Old Salt Trail, with artifacts found in the area dating back sixteen thousand years.[35] Sacred to the Hia C-ed O'odham and Tohono O'odham peoples, the springs are home to the Sonoyta mud turtle and other endangered species. The Hia C-ed and Tohono O'odham are two of forty-five recognized and unrecognized Indigenous nations whose territory spans the US border with Mexico or Canada.[36] Twenty-six US tribal nations recognized by the federal government are living in the US-Mexico borderlands. A smaller number of Indigenous peoples' land and presence is shared across the US and Mexico, including the Tohono O'odham, the Yaqui (Yoeme), the Cocopah, the Kumeyaay, the Pai, the Apaches, the Tigua (Tiwa), and the Kickapoo.[37]

To the north, the US-Canada border stretches 3,987 miles across North America. Six tribes recognized by the US government straddle the border, and many others have homelands in the US-Canada borderlands.[38] Borders are blurry in these places. The town of Pittsburg, New Hampshire, sits on land that was once contested between the French and the Abenaki and then the British and the Americans. The 1783 Treaty of Paris, which ended the American Revolution, left the Quebec-New Hampshire border ill-defined, and in 1832 residents declared independence from Great Britain and the United

---

Act; the Farmland Protection Policy Act; the Coastal Zone Management Act; the Federal Land Policy and Management Act; the National Wildlife Refuge System Administration Act; the National Fish and Wildlife Act; the Fish and Wildlife Coordination Act; the Administrative Procedure Act; the River and Harbors Act; the Eagle Protection Act; the Native American Graves Protection and Repatriation Act; and the American Indian Religious Freedom Act (Center for Biological Diversity, press release).

34. Schaeffer, *Unsettled Borders*, 1.

35. National Park Service, "Quitobaquito Springs"; Congressional Research Service, "574 Federally Recognized Indian Tribes in the United States."

36. Schaeffer, *Unsettled Borders*, 57.

37. Schaeffer, *Unsettled Borders*, 2.

38. Marchbanks, "Borderline." Federal recognition or federal acknowledgment formalizes a government-to-government relationship between the United States and a particular tribe, engendering certain rights and protections for the tribe, among them limited sovereign immunity and powers of self-government. As of February 2023, there were 574 federally recognized Indian tribes in the United States (347 within the forty-eight contiguous states and 227 in Alaska) (Congressional Research Service, "574 Federally Recognized Indian Tribes in the United States").

States, founding the short-lived sovereign Republic of Indian Stream.[39] Today the CBP station uses a Canadian area code because American telephone lines do not reach the border.[40] The blurriness of borders extends to economic relations. In 2022, President Biden signed a presidential determination permitting the use of Defense Production Act (DPA) Title III authorities to strengthen the US industrial base for large-capacity batteries. It invoked Canada as a *domestic* source.[41]

US-Canada water borders are relatively lightly patrolled, and the border is often imperceptible.[42] If you want to go trout and walleye fishing on Saganaga Lake, just outside of the Boundary Waters Canoe Area Wilderness (US) and Quetico Provincial Park (Canada) in northern Minnesota/southern Ontario and are traveling on a US passport, you will need a "Remote Area Border Crossing Pass" to cross the border. But once you are on the lake, it can be difficult to say exactly when you've crossed because the border zigzags around little islands through the middle of the enormous body of water. Only a map can tell you which islands are in Minnesota and which are in Canada. The border exists but it is beside the point.[43] The fish, and their pursuers, cross it at will.[44]

---

39. "The Republic lasted only three years and was followed by five more of 'occupation' by New Hampshire, while letters were dispatched between Washington and London. In 1840, the Indian Streamers incorporated under New Hampshire as Pittsburg, and, finally, in 1842, the Webster-Ashburton Treaty specified that Halls Stream was in fact the border, whereby Great Britain relinquished its claim to the Connecticut headwaters. Between 1843 and 1847, an official survey was conducted, then renewed in 1908, using up-to-date geodetic methods, by the newly created International Boundary Commission" (Morley, "Walking New Hampshire's Northern Border"; see also Doan, *Indian Stream Republic*).

40. Morley, "Walking New Hampshire's Northern Border."

41. White House, "Memorandum on Presidential Determination." The determination provides the Department of Energy with "the authority to utilize the DPA to accelerate domestic production of five key energy technologies: (1) solar; (2) transformers and electric grid components; (3) heat pumps; (4) insulation; and (5) electrolyzers, fuel cells, and platinum group metals" (US Department of Energy, "President Biden Invokes Defense Production Act").

42. On the Canadian border see Porter Fox's travelogue, *Northland*. Areas of tension between the United States and Canada include fishing rights, oil-drilling rights, and navigational rights.

43. In contrast with other US waters where borders are rigidly enforced. On a single day in January 2023, the US Coast Guard's fleet of ships off the Florida coast collectively detained more than one thousand migrants, and from July 2021 to September 2023, the number of unaccompanied children held by the Coast Guard spiked, a nearly tenfold increase over the prior two years (Wessler, "Border Where Different Rules Apply"). The Coast Guard is an arm of DHS.

44. While this border fluidity exists for these anglers, that is not the case for most border crossers; human smuggling across the US-Canada border is increasingly common. In January 2022 a family that was being smuggled to the United States from Gujarat via Canada, including

Border Religion

US borders offer up a paradox. They have a capacity to be both present and absent. They are avowed and deferred. Open and closed. They are a "substantial yet porous object" whose "boundaries are clear yet also open."⁴⁵ The US is defined simultaneously by ferocious bordering practices and a willingness to defy borders in the name of something greater than itself. This paradox cannot be explained away by material interests. The experience of the border speaks to something more: it is a site of retrenchment and transcendence. It involves erasure and enforcement. It demands the suspension of the law as well as its vigorous prosecution. At the heart of this paradox is the conviction that borders must be rigorously defended even as America is celebrated as borderless and all encompassing. Borders are technocratic fantasies and places of extreme violence. They are efforts to escape the ordinary. They exist within and beyond the law. "In contrast to the emphasis on a historic homeland that would define European nations," writes historian Rachel St. John, "Americans embraced the notion that their national boundaries would continue to expand to incorporate ever more land and people under the umbrella of republican government."⁴⁶ Philosopher Jean Baudrillard describes this expansionist tendency as a "hyperreality": "America is neither dream nor reality. It is a hyperreality. It is a hyperreality because it is a utopia which has behaved from the very beginning as though it were already achieved."⁴⁷

The border paradox resists resolution even as it incessantly demands it.⁴⁸ News from the border drives the news cycle and floods the airwaves. Discussions echo through American courtrooms, classrooms, and congressional hearing rooms. Border law and policy motivate protests and grassroot movements,⁴⁹ from private paramilitary groups like the Minutemen to legal reform advocates and those calling for borders to be abolished.⁵⁰ Civil, immigrant, and Indigenous rights' advocates file lawsuits and raise funds. Nationalists organize border patrols and argue with humanitarian activists in the desert.⁵¹ Advocacy groups are stretched to the limit as US borders are

---

children aged three and eleven, froze to death in a blizzard while attempting to cross into Minnesota from Ontario (Kubzansky, "Man Accused of Human Smuggling").

45. Bender, "America Is Hard to See," 97.
46. St. John, *Line in the Sand*, 17.
47. Baudrillard, *America*, 28.
48. Blankholm, *Secular Paradox*, 66; on the secular paradox see 142.
49. Sostaita, "Water, Not Walls."
50. Walia, *Undoing Border Imperialism*.
51. Paramilitary groups such as the Minuteman have been active in the borderlands since

transformed into sites of humanitarian and natural disaster.[52] Experts invoke border enforcement in discussions of defense and security, built infrastructure and biometric technologies, and humanitarian and climate crises. Religious groups spearhead humanitarian relief, harkening back to the Sanctuary movement of the 1980s.[53] Academic and policy discussions of refugees, migration, and religion are flourishing.[54] Scholars debate the finer points of border history; one prominent historian describes the wall as a monument to the final closing of the American frontier.[55] Though some contend that US territorial expansion has seen its day, others see America's boundless frontier manifesting in new ways: in the US commitment to technological innovation over territorial expansion and in American efforts to innovate our way out of the climate crisis.[56]

Despite the flurry of attention surrounding US borders, few have considered borders as sites not only of regulation, violence, and control but also of redemption, enchantment, boundless expansion, and salvation. These are religious as well as political concepts.

There is something sacred about borders.[57] They are religious in Kathryn Lofton's sense of "enshrining certain commitments stronger than almost any other acts of social participation."[58] As Lofton explains, "religion isn't only something you volunteer to join, open-hearted and confessing. It is not only something you inherit, enjoined by your parents. Religion is also the thing into which you become ensnared despite yourself."[59] Borders are religious in the sense that they reckon with human limits. They are sites at which the

---

the 1980s (Felbab-Brown and Norio, "What Border Vigilantes Taught U.S. Right-Wing Armed Groups").

52. In southern Arizona, see for example Kino Border Initiative, Borderlinks, Border Angels, Border Network for Human Rights, the Florence Immigrant & Refugee Rights Project, Casas Alitas, and the Immigration Law Project at the University of Arizona.

53. Machado, Turner, and Wyller, *Borderland Religion*; Sostaita, *Sanctuary Everywhere*; Cunningham, *God and Caesar at the Rio Grande*.

54. Meyer, *Refugees and Religion*; Mavelli and Wilson, *Refugee Crisis and Religion*; Jansen, Celikates, and de Bloois, *Irregularization of Migration*.

55. Grandin, *End of the Myth*.

56. Immerwahr, *How to Hide an Empire*; Sideris, "American Techno-Optimism."

57. Borders also evoke elements of what Robert Bellah described as civil religion: "a collection of beliefs, symbols, and rituals with respect to sacred things and institutionalized in a collectivity" (Bellah, "Civil Religion in America," 40), reminding us that the term is Rousseau's from chapter 8, book 4 of *The Social Contract* (Bellah, "Civil Religion in America," 43).

58. Lofton, *Consuming Religion*, 6.

59. Lofton, *Consuming Religion*, xi.

limits of the human become apparent.[60] They are religious in the sense of having a capacity to summon a sacred American nation without necessarily summoning "religion."[61] To enter into the religiosity of borders conceived in this way it is helpful to start with material and other exchanges that are *not* usually considered problematic: tomatoes, tourists, butterflies, and so on. The "religious," we quickly find, is not the only place we find the sacred. The sacred is expressed in ways that exceed the logics of the modern construct of religion. It has been captured in notions such as the *mysterium tremendum et fascinosum* (mystery that repels and attracts), the *homo sacer* (in Roman law, he who is banned but cannot be sacrificed), and all that which is honored through borders, such as clean/dirty, permitted/taboo, and sacred/profane.[62] It is in objects too, as Mateo Taussig-Rubbo finds in property recovered from the rubble of 9/11.[63]

The slipperiness of borders shapes some of the most urgent political developments of our time. The border's capacity to be simultaneously fluid and firm, present and absent, lawful and lawless, sacred and secular disrupts social scientific and governmental efforts to describe, delineate, and control border spaces. The border paradox manifests in the politics of race, immigration, asylum, foreign policy, and national security. It shapes the adjudication of asylum. It authorizes national security to operate simultaneously within and beyond the reach of the law. It buoys US support for the State of Israel in ways that have yet to be fully understood. It enables the off-site detention of "enemy combatants." It energizes stand-offs and sparks fear among US law enforcement as they face down countersovereigns who refuse American borders of all kinds. It traverses presidential administrations and confounds partisan divides, galvanizing unlikely alliances between liberals and conservatives.

That the border is a zone of legal exception is not a new insight.[64] Rachel St. John notes that as early as the 1920s the border had become a "complicated system of relational space" that "could either be fluid or firm."[65] In her history of the INS, the predecessor to the US Citizenship and Immigration

---

60. Scherer, *Beyond Church and State*, 172, referencing philosopher Stanley Cavell's understanding of religion.
61. Bender, "America Is Hard to See," 94.
62. Thanks to Ben Schonthal.
63. Taussig-Rubbo, "Sacred Property," 325.
64. On the militarization and racialization of the US border historically, see Rosen, *Border Law*.
65. St. John, *Line in the Sand*, 196. On the criminalization of migrant labor in contrast to the lack of restrictions on transnational capital movement, see Chacón, *Border Crossed Us*.

Service, ICE, and CBP, S. Deborah Kang describes the border as "an impermeable sovereign boundary, a permeable socioeconomic zone, and a vast policing jurisdiction."[66] Because the INS was exempt from the Administrative Procedures Act (APA) of 1946, Kang notes, the agency was "unconstrained by the procedures stipulated by the APA and judicial review of its administration practices and internal adjudication," thus becoming "an 'outlaw' in American legal culture."[67] In his autobiographical account, former Border Patrol agent Francisco Cantú describes the US-Mexico border as "a vast zone of exception, a place where laws and rights are applied differently than in any other part of the nation."[68] The one-hundred-mile aforementioned "Constitution-free" border jurisdiction zone includes roughly one-third of the United States and nearly two-thirds of its population.[69] It includes the entire state of Michigan, which has had the fastest rate of growth of any Border Patrol Sector in the country. The number of agents in Border Patrol's Detroit Sector grew from 35 agents in 2000 to 404 agents in 2019, a 1,054 percent increase.[70] The ACLU explains:

> The Fourth Amendment of the U.S. Constitution protects Americans from random and arbitrary stops and searches. According to the government, however, these basic constitutional principles do not apply fully at our borders. For example, at border crossings (also called "ports of entry"), federal authorities do not need a warrant or even suspicion of wrongdoing to justify conducting what courts have called a "routine search," such as searching luggage or a vehicle. Even in places far removed from the border, deep into the interior of the

---

66. Kang, *INS on the Line*, 3. Kang focuses on the agency as law*making* rather than merely law enforcing. The INS, she explains, was sentenced to "administrative death" after *The 9/11 Commission Report* found that if immigration laws had been strictly enforced, fifteen of the nineteen terrorists would have been barred from entry. Federal officials split the INS into three agencies: "US Citizenship and Immigration Services (USCIS), which focuses on providing services such as naturalization and work visas; US Immigration and Customs Enforcement (ICE), which combined the forces of the Customs and Immigration bureaus and conducts immigrant removals at and between the nation's ports of entry as well as from the nation's interior; and US Customs and Border Protection (CBP), which consolidated several agencies, including the border immigration inspection force, the Border Patrol, the US Customs Service, and agricultural inspections, to conduct enforcement operations on the international boundary" (Kang, *INS on the Line*, 172–73).
67. Kang, *INS on the Line*, 4, citing Salyer, *Laws Harsh as Tigers*, xiv.
68. Cantú, *Line Becomes a River*, 258.
69. Apuzzo and Schmidt, "U.S. to Continue Racial, Ethnic Profiling." "Agent power was limited by no constitutional clause. There was no place patrollers couldn't search, no property belonging to migrants they couldn't seize" (Grandin, *End of the Myth*, 250).
70. American Civil Liberties Union Michigan, "Border's Long Shadow."

country, immigration officials enjoy broad—though not limitless—powers. Specifically, federal regulations give U.S. Customs and Border Protection (CBP) authority to operate within 100 miles of any U.S. "external boundary."

The exceptions continue. DHS considers itself exempt from the Fourth Amendment, and the government has exempted both CBP and DHS from restrictions on racial profiling that are imposed on other federal departments.[71] One DHS official explained, "We can't do our job without taking ethnicity into account," prompting the *New York Times* to report that "department officials argued that it was impractical to ignore ethnicity when it came to border enforcement."[72] The organization People Helping People documented a pattern of profiling people of color at Border Patrol interior checkpoints,[73] invoking a long history of white supremacy in the patrol.[74] Founded in 1924 as part of the Immigration Act, the patrol in those days, as described by historian Greg Grandin, was "a frontline instrument of white supremacist power"[75] and "a vanguard of race vigilantism."[76]

US borders are about more than making laws, building barriers, and rationally managing flows of goods and people. Borders involve reaching beyond the collective self, transcending constraints in the search for an American utopia. Borders are also liminal spaces and places. The act of crossing them is imbued with magic and fear. Walls, lines, doorways, and arches are dangerous places to be human. Should one look backward? To whom should one give one's real name? Can one go back after crossing?[77] The title of this book, *Heaven Has a Wall*, alludes to the idea that borders are religious as well as political objects.[78] Moving beyond a conventional focus on religious

---

71. Miller, *Empire of Borders*, 126. See US Department of Justice, "Guidance for Federal Law Enforcement."

72. Apuzzo and Schmidt, "U.S. to Continue Racial, Ethnic Profiling."

73. Check Point Monitoring Report, "People Helping People in the Border Zone," October 26, 2014, cited in Miller, *Empire of Borders*, 203.

74. "DHS's current department-wide guidance on discriminatory profiling fails to cover religion, even as targeting of Muslims has been at the center of concerns about discriminatory profiling. That same guidance gives frontline agents discretion to inappropriately consider race, ethnicity, religion, national origin, and nationality" (Panduranga and Patel, *Stronger Rules against Bias*).

75. Grandin, *End of the Myth*, 163.

76. Grandin, *End of the Myth*, 250. For critiques of these practices see Walia, *Undoing Border Imperialism*; Espejo, *On Borders*; Shachar, *Shifting Border*.

77. Mohsin Hamid's novel *Exit West* (New York: Riverhead Books, 2017) features magical doors in place of borders. Thanks to Iza Hussin.

78. See also Paul Kahn on US sovereignty as "incomprehensible if stripped of its theological origins" (Kahn, *Political Theology*, 140).

traditions, practices, and beliefs and their influence on collective life, I turn to border history, national security, and immigration politics and foreign policy. Religion is embedded in the matrices of all these phenomena. It cannot be set apart as a distinct object. At the same time, and even as I question fixed boundaries between religion and politics, sacred and secular, and theory and theology, this book is not only for scholars of religion and politics. It is for anyone interested in borders and in the American national project. I especially want to speak to readers who see their own ways of life as less dogmatically religious than others and as therefore promising more inclusive forms of politics and public life.[79] This is common among liberal academics. Religion, they say, is something to be kept in its place, out of politics and public life. If only those to the political and religious right would outgrow their dogmatic expressions of religiosity and the distorted forms of politics they engender, it is said, the US would regain its naturally emancipatory and progressive bearings.

I propose an alternative. US (religious) politics, including border politics, are neither private nor the exclusive domain of political or religious conservatives. Modernity is not a post-religious achievement. The oft-presumed dichotomy between secular modernity and its theological past is a false one.[80] In Eric Santner's words, "There is more political theology in everyday life than we might have ever thought."[81] The political is an already-religious space that need not be feared or overcome but understood.[82]

The Magic of Borders

In his magnum opus, *The King's Two Bodies*, Ernst Kantorowicz traces the transferences and exchanges of properties between church and state, and the

---

79. For an example, see Posner, "Army of Prayer Warriors."
80. Yelle, *Sovereignty and the Sacred*, 36.
81. Santner, *Royal Remains*, 46. Similarly, for Kahn, "the state is not the secular arrangement that it purports to be" *Political Theology*, 18.
82. E.S. Hurd, *Politics of Secularism*. I am inspired by the work of Talal Asad, described here by Chidester: "A distinctively Protestant rendering of religion, defining religion as separate from and independent of the power of the state, has been crucial in the history of Euro-American negotiations over the relation between religious meaning and political power. But Asad went further by suggesting that this notion of religion as an autonomous cultural system converged with the contemporary interests of secular liberals in confining religion and liberal Christians in defending religion within modern societies. Asad's critique, therefore, was not merely about the validity of Geertz's definition; it was also about the politics of defining religion as an autonomous cultural system" (Chidester, *Empire of Religion*, 308).

gradual emergence of what he calls a secular *corpus mysticum*. The latter, he explains, "came to be less and less mystical as time passed on, and came to mean simply the Church as a body politic or, by transference, any body politic of the secular world."[83] Kantorowicz is best known for distinguishing between "the king's two bodies": a mortal "body natural" and an immortal "body politic." The king's immortal political body passed on through succession after the mortal body's natural death. Theorists and theologians debate whether and how this immortal aspect of the king's body carried over and was transformed in the transition from monarchy to popular sovereignty. What happens to these "royal remains" under regimes of popular sovereignty? For Kantorowicz, one author explains, "the sacred second body of 'the people' has never been *solely* concentrated in the figuration of presidents and other charismatic leaders, but also diffused throughout the body politic in a way distinct to the modern era." This uncertainty surrounding the location of the king's second body "provides us with a framework with which to illuminate aspects of political modernity that are left in the background, or even denied, in theories of differentiation and disenchantment (and their Marxist variants)."[84] Borders are among them. How the US treats its borders can be understood in part as an effect of the "secular *corpus mysticum*."

This brings us to *The Royal Remains*. Narrowing the focus of Kantorowicz's sweeping account of medieval political theology, Eric Santner homes in on the changing status of the cultural locations of the royal remains—or what he calls "the flesh"—as it accompanied the passage from royal to popular sovereignty.[85] He tracks the separation of the flesh from the king, and its entrance, "like a strange alien presence," into the "body of the people."[86] He agrees with Kantorowicz that "the complex symbolic structures and dynamics

83. Kantorowicz, *King's Two Bodies*, 192, 206, especially chap. 5, "Polity-Centered Kingship: *Corpus Mysticum*"; Santner, *Royal Remains*, 37.

84. Reed, "King's Two Bodies."

85. Santner, *Royal Remains*, 31. "What I hope, above all, to have made clear, is that the persistence of the metaphor of the political body, of 'corporate' conceptions of community and belonging, cannot be fully understood without grasping the nature of the substance that always seems to threaten the integrity and 'organicity' of its composition and that . . . represents a dimension of, as Esposito has put it, 'unbearable excess.'" This "surplus immanence" is the subject of *Royal Remains* (30); it is "that 'thing' in the king that cannot be contained in his natural life and body but only—and indeed *only barely*—in a second one" (12).

86. "The real object of the new physics of power is not simply the body or life but rather the flesh that has become separated from the body of the king and has entered, like a strange alien presence, into that of the people" (Santner, *Royal Remains*, 12).

of sovereignty . . . in the context of medieval and early modern European monarchies do not simply disappear from the space of politics once the body of the king is no longer available as the primary incarnation of the principle and function of sovereignty; rather, these structures and dynamics—along with their attendant paradoxes and impasses—'migrate' into a new location that thereby assumes a turbulent and disorienting semiotic density previously concentrated in the 'strange material and physical presence' of the king."[87] In other words, assuming that the king's two bodies mutated into the people's two bodies, Santner's task is to grapple with the materiality of the "sublime somatic substance" that made this migration and mutation possible. His interest is in the material science of sovereignty. After the fall of the king, sovereignty became incarnated in the flesh, referring not only to the corporeal matter beneath the skin but to the "semiotic—and somatic—vibrancy generated by the inscription of bodies into a normative social space."[88] Santner strives to capture the pressures and stresses of this "creaturely life." The flesh, he explains, is a "mode of *exposure* that distinguishes human beings from other kinds of life;" an exposure to "an ultimate lack of foundation for the historical forms of life that distinguish human community."[89] Though not the focus of my argument, this notion of a semiotic and somatic vibrancy generated by the inscription of bodies into a normative political and social order resonates in the collective experience of US borders described in this book. Borders and border work embody the symbolic structures and dynamics of sovereignty discussed by these political theologians. A material science of sovereignty offers resources for reflecting on the popular resonance of the Muslim ban, for example, among certain groups of Americans.

Border policy and politics also may be understood as an effect of state power that borrow "from the church the sign of the sovereign as sacred," as Winnifred Fallers Sullivan puts it in her powerful updating of Kantorowicz in *Church State Corporation*.[90] Borders express the charisma of the collective. They transcend the logic of secular rationality. They traverse sacred and secular, confounding claims to separation and differentiation at every turn. Part of their efficacy lies in their capacity to shift registers. Borders are a crucial figure in the interplay

---

87. Santner, *Royal Remains*, 33.
88. Santner, *Royal Remains*, 4.
89. Santner, *Royal Remains*, 5.
90. Sullivan identifies a "profound interchangeability among the church, the state, and the corporation—the state and the corporation borrowing from the church the sign of the sovereign as sacred" (*Church State Corporation*, 121, 94).

between American political order and the drive to reach beyond it. They express a human need to affirm and to transcend, to reach for "something more." To study US borders is to acknowledge with Robert Yelle that "what we call 'religion' or the 'sacred' encompasses the dynamic interplay between a normative order and the drive to go beyond this order, either to escape or to legitimate it."[91] Borders take part in a modern spiritual economy in which "human beings aim at something more than reason and legality alone."[92] They are magical spaces not only in politics but also in liturgy, poetry, art, and folklore.[93] They contain and invite transcendence. They entice and prohibit.

Borders also invoke human limits, as mentioned. Another resource underlying my thinking in this book is the immanent philosophy of Gilles Deleuze and Félix Guattari.[94] These philosopher-theologians emphasize human capacities to affect and to be affected. Probing the limits of the human and of human knowledge, they stress human embeddedness in and indebtedness to forces and factors that sit beyond our control and apprehension.[95] Their critique of modern subjectivity, their decentering of the subject, offers a glimpse of the human as a fluid, contingent, and perhaps unfamiliar figure, especially held up against the image of the rational individual that anchors analytical philosophy and most mainstream social science. In *A Thousand Plateaus*, Deleuze and Guattari articulate what Nikolas Rose describes as "the most radical alternative to the conventional image of subjectivity as coherent, enduring, and individualized." In this rendering, humans "are more multiple, transient, non-subjectified than we so often are made to believe; further, at least at certain moments, they suggest that we can act upon ourselves to inhabit such non-subjectified forms of existence."[96] In Deleuze and Guattari's memorable words, "You are a longitude and a latitude, a set of speeds and slownesses between unformed particles, a set of non-subjectified affects. You have the individuality of a day, a season, a year, a life (regardless of its duration)—a climate, a wind, a fog, a swarm, a pack (regardless of its regularity)."[97]

---

91. Yelle, *Sovereignty and the Sacred*, 8.

92. Yelle, *Sovereignty and the Sacred*, 184.

93. See, for example, Khosravi and Keshavarz, "Magic of Borders."

94. See Deleuze and Guattari, *Thousand Plateaus*; Deleuze and Guattari, *What Is Philosophy?*.

95. On the participation of the nonhuman and its implications for our understanding of agency, see Jane Bennett's concept of "vital materiality" in *Vibrant Matter*. For a profile of Bennett see Meis, "Philosopher Who Believes."

96. Rose, *Inventing Our Selves*, 170.

97. Deleuze and Guattari, *Thousand Plateaus*, 262. Rose elaborates: "These non-subjectified forms they term 'haeccities'—modes of individualization which are not those of a substance, a

What does this have to do with borders? These philosopher-theologians are productively indifferent to how and whether religion should relate to political and legal order.[98] Operating with different assumptions about the experience of being human, they take for granted critiques of attempts to treat religion as an autonomous system that stands apart from its surroundings.[99] They work out of a different ontology, that is, a different set of fundamental assumptions about the nature of being. These critiques of the concept of religion are well developed, including in my own earlier work.[100] In their wake, secularism appears as a tired yet insistent impulse "to continually ask what religion is and where it belongs."[101]

This is not a question asked in this book. Instead, I dive into a series of messy jumbles of religiosities, legalities, and modalities of stateliness and statelessness—and the spaces and senses in which they cannot be separated—in search of a capacious phenomenology of US borders. I find that the US produces and sustains a national collective self in large measure through its treatment of borders. This takes multiple forms: the US simultaneously posits and transcends its own borders. It evokes an incomplete and impossible incorporation of the sacred in its processes of bordering. And it performs a series of public rituals, including collective material manifestations of sacred presences. This American border religion comes with an array of beliefs and practices, including a reverence for national security, a liturgy of immigration, and an eschatological foreign policy. Each of these themes is developed in the chapters to come.

Chapter Previews

The book has four chapters and four interludes. They need not be read sequentially, and one need not have an interest in political theory or political theology to find them relevant. Each chapter focuses on an aspect of US borders and borderlessness: creating, enforcing, suspending, and refusing. The interludes present stories of border ambiguation: bordered/borderless,

---

person, a thing, or a subject but of a season, a winter, an hour, a date—'relations of movement and rest between molecules or particles, capacities to affect and be affected'" (*Inventing Our Selves*, citing Deleuze and Guattari, *Thousand Plateaus*, 262).

98. For an example of the circularity of these debates, see Brown, *Debating Yoga and Mindfulness*.

99. Chidester, *Empire of Religion*, 308.

100. Hurd, *Politics of Secularism*; *Beyond Religious Freedom*.

101. Howe, *Landscapes of the Secular*, 6. On the emergence of the concept of religion, see Nongbri, *Before Religion*.

unbordered, crossing, and walking. This dual format allows me to experiment with different modes of introducing the paradoxes of US borders while offering instructors options in how to work through these materials with different audiences.

Chapter 1, "Creating," is a study of the creation and crossing of borders via the liturgy of religious asylum. In the United States, religious asylum is premised on an exceptional American capacity for salvation and redemption. Americans see themselves as living out a unique national project that offers an opportunity for anyone willing to experience free religion through individual choice.[102] Religious asylum is an act of grace offered by the American people to protect others' religious freedom. Borders play a complex role in this process. The durability and appeal of the asylum regime hinges on a collective affirmation of an essential distinction between Americans and others. The liturgical performance of asylum conjures, and ferries the asylum seeker across, a tenuous border that can only be sustained by continual scrutiny, performance, repetition, and reenactment. It is a public ritual. The politics of asylum is politico-theological, then, but not in the sense of marking an inheritance of Protestant Christian forms in modern politics. Rather, it commingles the sacred and secular in an overarching faith in the realization of freedom and grace through conversion to Americanness. Redemption is imagined as something having issued from deeper than the state and society, depending on, and conjuring, a truth and goodness that transcends state or society. The true spirit of American sovereignty as guarantor of religious freedom comes into view in this process, despite the brokenness of asylum courts and flaws and failings of the asylum system as a whole. The repeated invocation of a free American subject and its juxtaposition with an unfree non-American other in the liturgy of asylum affirms the boundary between true American religion and its lesser contenders, even as it also draws the successful individual claimant across that boundary. To traverse the American border successfully requires claimants to attest to the universality of the American project.

The first interlude, "Border/less," turns to a historical illustration of the border paradox—the simultaneous positing and transcending of borders—in the nineteenth century. I contrast the increasing fortification or "securitization" of US borders during this period for the Indigenous O'odham people, who have lived for thousands of years along both sides of what is now the US-Mexico border, with the experience of borderlessness for nineteenth-century US ranchers who could avail themselves of the legal fiction of Mexican

---

102. Mullen, *Chance of Salvation*.

corporate nationality to circumvent laws against foreign ownership of land near the newly inaugurated US-Mexico border. Taking advantage of this legal exception allowed these investors to establish lucrative transnational ranches that ignored or defied the border altogether, even as that same border was becoming increasingly restrictive for Indigenous peoples striving to maintain their ancestral ties across the line.

Once created, borders need to be enforced. That is the job of national security and the subject of chapter 2, "Enforcing," on US foreign and immigration policy. On the surface, US national security policy separates religion from politics and law. As in other forms of secularist politics, however, this claim to separation requires a continuous reassertion of the tenuous line between religion and other domains.[103] These attempts to corral and contain religion distract us from the religious aspects of national security that are the subject of this chapter. Focusing on the controversy surrounding Proclamation 9645, also known as the "Muslim ban," I evaluate the aspirational, though never actual, segregation of religion from national security in the 2018 US Supreme Court decision in *Trump v. Hawaii*, which upheld the ban. In that decision, the majority confined *religion*, legally speaking, in order to create space for an all-encompassing political theology of national security. In the United States, it is national security, and not only religion, that is vested with the power to transcend human limitations in the name of order, control, and social harmony. National security is bounded and boundless. It enjoys broad and bipartisan appeal. It is sacred. The means invoked to defend it form the substance of the exception. They authorize the simultaneous enforcement and suspension of the law. US borders were "secured," and the Muslim ban enforced, in the name of this untouchable figure of sovereign authority.

A second interlude, "Unbordered," examines (non)borders between the United States and Cuba in the region surrounding the US military base at Guantánamo. The United States does not claim sovereignty over Guantánamo, but it does claim complete jurisdiction and total control over the base and its inhabitants. This paradox ensures that the exact location, forms of attachment, and modes of enforcement of US borders around the base remain hazy and uncertain. Borders between the United States and Cuba on the island are present and absent. Posited and transcended.

Chapter 3, "Suspending," turns to relations between the United States and Israel. Here I use the border as a heuristic to explore the cultural foundations and affective politics of US support for Israel. I suggest that the border between the US and Israel is both posited and suspended. I refer to the latter with

---

103. Agrama, *Questioning Secularism*; Beaman, *Transition of Religion*.

the shorthand "AmericaIsrael." The idea of Israel and the idea of America act as interwoven expressions of redemption. Standing apart from what is designated as religion, AmericaIsrael summons a sacred supra-nation.[104] It invokes an easy, almost heroic overcoming of borders such that at points to criticize Israel is to criticize the US. As such, AmericaIsrael helps explain efforts to criminalize the Boycott, Divestment, Sanctions movement and to collapse the distinction between anti-Zionism and anti-Semitism. AmericaIsrael also invokes darker dynamics of racialization and anti-Semitism. Notably, it speaks to an unwillingness to incorporate an inassimilable Jewish racial and religious other into a purportedly Christian nation. The image of Jewish Americans as outsiders is familiar in American politics. The fallout from, as well as frontal challenges to, AmericaIsrael intensified in the wake of the Israeli invasion of Gaza in 2023. Cracks in a fragile consensus have widened into unbridgeable chasms.

A third interlude, "Crossing," tells the story of my own border crossing at an airport in Chicago where biometric facial recognition technologies are replacing human beings at points of entry. I describe a conversation I had during an interview with a border agent who had recently visited the US-Mexico border in Texas. His assertion that media reports about detained children kept in cages that summer near the border "were all lies" contrasted with a series of revelations in a report about the dismal detention conditions for families in Texas issued by his employer, DHS, a few days prior to the interview.

Chapter 4, "Refusing," brings the discussion full circle with the introduction of a figure who offers spiritual resources to those who refuse American borders. La Santa Muerte, or Holy Death, is an agent of borderlessness and a countersovereign. She incites panic among US law enforcement, who claim that the outlaw saint inspires demonic forms of devotion that incline her followers toward criminality. Her illicit blurring of boundaries and recourse to archaic forms of religiosity is said to heighten devotees' susceptibility to the dark temptations of the drug trade. Anxieties about the effects of the saint's presence have led to clumsy attempts on the part of law enforcement to manage her alleged incursions on public order, good religion, and (white) civilization. I describe the rebel saint's insurgent borderless religion and its commercialization, investment in lawbreaking, and practice of outlaw sovereignty, as well as the backlash against it. Defying borders of all kinds, Santa Muerte transcends her assigned roles as a demonized icon of death or pitiable pseudo-saint of the dispossessed. She is a real presence in the borderlands and beyond.

---

104. Bender, "America is Hard to See," 94.

A final interlude, "Walking," reflects on the pilgrimage to Magdalena, a traditional practice that predates, and quietly refuses, the US-Mexico border. The border not only divides US-based pilgrims from their destination in Magdalena, Mexico, but it also divides the Tohono O'odham Nation in two. The pilgrims' dedication to walking brings to life the contrast between more fluid understandings of the geography of the region and the enclosure and claiming that has come to define US borders. The latter has intensified in recent decades as militarization of the Tohono O'odham reservation continues: in 2019, CBP paid a US subsidiary of the Israeli military contractor Elbit Systems $26 million to build surveillance towers on the reservation. The pilgrims' refusal to participate in American border religion and enactment of a form of shadow sovereignty challenges US authority in unexpected ways.

"The Ideal Border," a final interlude of sorts, concludes by exploring the meanders of the Rio Grande/Rio Bravo del Norte and the futile attempts by border enforcers on both banks of the river to control and channel it.

*

In a searing indictment of the US government's mistreatment of undocumented migrant children, *Tell Me How It Ends*, Valeria Luiselli reflects on her experience as an immigrant advocate and writer: "There are things that can only be understood retrospectively, when many years have passed and the story has ended. In the meantime, while the story continues, the only thing to do is to tell it over and over again as it develops, bifurcates, knots around itself. And it must be told, because before anything can be understood, it has to be narrated many times, in many different words and from many different angles, by many different minds."[105] This book tells a story of US borders: where they appear to be; where they are; their limitations, provocations, and paradoxes; and the multiple registers in which they compel, elude, and fail to convince. I take for granted the simultaneity of the political and religious in US borders, not as an exception to other formations of political modernity, but as constitutive of it. If, as Ian Hacking proposes, new modes of description create new possibilities for action,[106] then this book is an invitation to see the border's locations, powers, and limits anew.

---

105. Luiselli, *Tell Me How It Ends*, 96–97.
106. Ian Hacking, "Making Up People," in *Historical Ontology*, 108.

CHAPTER 1

Creating

The Liturgy of Asylum

FIGURE 4. Museo de Derechos Humanos, Santiago de Chile, 2023. Photo by author.

Performing Asylum

Iranian American novelist Dina Nayeri received asylum in the US in the late 1980s at the age of nine after her mother credibly established to US authorities that the family had converted to Christianity. In an interview, Lulu Garcia-Navarro of National Public Radio asked Nayeri to describe the experience from her perspective as a child:

LGN: You focus on how the asylum process tests believability. You know, I've covered refugee resettlement, and I know that it is an incredibly arduous process. And this process can be derailed at any point if you are found to be not credible. That's the actual language that they use.

DN: Yeah.

LGN: Do you remember your interview for resettlement in the US? Can you take me back to that day?

DN: Yeah. You know, the memory is very, very foggy, because we had so many different kinds of interviews during that time. But I do remember the one. This interview, myself, my brother, and my mother were all in the room. And my mother was being questioned by a woman, by an asylum officer. And it had already been explained to me that being a Christian convert in Iran was enough to qualify us for asylum. So the only question was were we really Christians in Iran? Did this one woman believe that we had converted truly in our hearts? And my mother, of course, had converted, and she was truly a Christian—a very faithful one. And she knew the Bible backwards and forwards. She had this Bible that she had underlined, and she used a different color every year that she read through the entire thing. And so yeah, she knew her stuff. And then at one point, this woman turned to me and asked a very simple Bible question. It was one of the Bible stories, like Jonah or some such. And the answer came easy to me, but only later did I realize that it mattered what the children said. Because it showed to her whether or not my mother had actually educated her children in her new faith, which is a sign of whether or not you believe.

LGN: How old were you?

DN: I was nine years old.

LGN: Yeah.

DN: But I think the real nervousness over it—the real worry—came with the waiting for a letter that told us whether or not we had been accepted. And that time, I think, was excruciating. And it was particularly excruciating for my mom, I know, because it was her performance that really mattered.[1]

Claiming asylum in the United States is a performative act. The ritual of asylum creates a border between Americans and others while also ferrying

---

1. Garcia-Navarro, "In America, We Trust the Wrong People."

the successful asylee across that border. I describe this as being "liturgied into citizenship." In this chapter I invite readers to consider asylum seeking and claiming as a liturgical practice that "enacts or produces that which it names:"[2] a particular religious understanding of Americanness, and a border between free Americans and unfree others.

Politically and theologically, the asylum process involves simultaneously violating and asserting a boundary. The process invites in successful asylees while it reaffirms the boundary between Americans and others. The liturgical performance of asylum conjures, and ferries the asylum seeker across, a tenuous border that can only be sustained through continual scrutiny, performance, repetition, and reenactment. It is a public ritual. The border is not there, and the difference is not preexisting. Rather, the liturgy imposes a border between true American political religion and its foreign contenders, even as it also draws select individuals across that boundary. The liturgy disciplines and subjectifies through its demands for true confession, as in Dina Nayeri's experience, and in its baptism of seekers as Americans.

I begin by introducing the asylum regime and critiques of it for those less familiar with its workings. The laser-like focus on the legal aspects of the regime in much of the literature, including verification and truth telling, diverts attention away from its performative dimensions.[3] The final section turns to the performative process through which asylees are "liturgied into citizenship."

Religious Asylum 101

Under US law, individuals who flee their countries because they fear persecution can apply for asylum, and if it is granted, they are given protection and the right to stay in the United States.[4] The UN Refugee Agency, or UNHCR, defines asylum as "a form of protection which allows an individual to remain in the United States instead of being removed (deported) to a country where he or she fears persecution or harm."[5] Asylum is a discretionary remedy, meaning it

---

2. Judith Butler argues that "within speech act theory, a performative is that discursive practice that enacts or produces that which it names" (*Bodies That Matter*, 13).

3. Didier Fassin notes of the asylum process that "the whole question to be ultimately determined is thus, for the officers, rapporteurs and magistrates, whether or not they are being told the truth" ("Precarious Truth," 19).

4. UNHCR, "What Is Asylum?"

5. The Convention Relating to the Status of Refugees, or the 1951 Geneva Convention, is limited to the victims of "events occurring before 1 January 1951"; it was only in 1967 that the

is granted at the discretion of an immigration judge. Individuals are only permitted to apply for asylum if they arrive at the US border or are already present in the United States; those outside of the United States must apply for refugee status. To be eligible for asylum, the applicant also must qualify as a refugee under the Immigration and Nationality Act (INA).[6] Drawing on the UN Refugee Convention (1951), the INA defines a refugee as "any person who is outside any country of such person's nationality . . . who is unable or unwilling to return to . . . that country because of persecution or a well-founded fear of persecution on account of race, religion, nationality, membership in a particular social group, or political opinion." Applicants must show that they were persecuted or have a well-founded fear of persecution on account of one or more of the five enumerated grounds. Though there may be mixed motives for the persecution, it must be proven that the central reason is on account of race, religion, nationality, membership in a particular social group, or political opinion.[7] If granted asylum, an individual may be eligible to become a lawful permanent resident, which gives them the right to remain permanently in the US with work authorization and to petition for citizenship after an additional four years.[8]

The refugee status determination (RSD) process involves several stages in the United States. Asylum applicants who are not yet placed in removal proceedings are interviewed by asylum officers of the Department of Homeland Security, and those who receive an affirmative decision acquire refugee status and become eligible for lawful permanent resident status. In the instance of a negative decision, the case is handed over to the immigration court and the applicant must argue her case against the Department of Justice in an adversarial setting. If unsuccessful, applicants are deported unless they file a successful appeal with the Board of Immigration Appeals. If that fails, the

---

Protocol of New York generalized protection to anyone corresponding to the definition of a refugee (Fassin, "Precarious Truth," 6).

6. The United States enacted the Immigration and Nationality Act (INA) in 1980 to bring existing US asylum practices into conformity with the 1967 UN Protocol Relating to the Status of Refugees (October 4, 1967, 606 U.N.T.S. 267), ratified by the United States in November 1968, and the UN Convention Relating to the Status of Refugees, which is incorporated by reference into US law through the protocol.

7. Baker et al., *Expert Witnesses*, 15–16. In practice the asylum regime is constantly evolving, with recent decades witnessing what Fassin describes as an "intimatization of asylum" such that "one is more legitimate claiming to be the victim of cruel treatments on the basis of gender and sexuality than of political engagement, religious belief or ethnic belonging" ("Precarious Truth," 12).

8. Baker et al., *Expert Witnesses*.

last recourse is to apply for judicial review at the Federal Circuit Court of Appeals.[9]

Asylum authorities regularly adjudicate questions involving religious identity, conversion, and persecution. However, although religion is among several protected categories in US federal and international refugee law, the INA employs the term *religion* without providing any statutory or regulatory definition, as does the First Amendment. Most practitioners in the asylum field approach religion as "somewhat self-explanatory for the purposes of asylum law."[10] They look to experts to fill in the details. Karen Musalo explains that factfinders are "encouraged to seek out the assistance of professionals with relevant expertise."[11] Religious organizations also play a part in verifying religious affiliation, as Jaeeun Kim explains:

> For those submitting asylum applications on religious grounds, establishing the religious identity at issue is a necessary, if not a sufficient, condition for successful asylum claims-making. Religious organizations can help asylum-seekers in this regard by issuing certificates of membership and baptism, providing letters or testimonies in court, and teaching proper ways to perform the religious faith at issue. This verification regime devolves part of the state's screening function upon pertinent religious organizations. At the same time, it brings them closely to the position of for-profit migration entrepreneurs, who have long helped identity crafts of aspiring migrants in exchange for fees.[12]

While the sincerity of a claimant's religious belief is central to most proceedings, how belief is ascertained varies. In a typical case from the early 2000s involving a young Chinese woman's claim, described by Musalo, the judge accepted the claimant's testimony that she had practiced Catholicism on a weekly basis with an underground church for five years before fleeing China and had attended church regularly since arriving in the United States. Yet he also found the claimant's "religious claim to be weakened by the fact that she had not been baptized as a Catholic, did not know the name of the

---

9. Kim, "Between Sacred Gift and Profane Exchange," 312.
10. Baker et al., *Expert Witnesses*, 16.
11. Musalo, "Claims for Protection," 205.
12. Kim, "Between Sacred Gift and Profane Exchange," 305. In the cases Kim studied, "the church's assistance for religious asylum-seekers' identity craft can take several forms: the issuance of certificates of membership and baptism included in the application file; the provision of the pastor's affidavit or oral testimony in court; and the teaching of basic knowledge, established practices, and embodied demeanors normally expected of Christians, which asylum officers or immigration judges may look for during the interviews or court proceedings" (314).

current Pope, was never 'formally registered with the Catholic Church,' and had two abortions while in the United States—one of them the result of a pregnancy resulting from repeated rapes at the hands of the smugglers who transported her to the United States." The judge explained:

> The Court is concerned by the fact that the applicant has had two abortions while in the United States. The Court does not dispute the applicant's right under the American legal system to obtain an abortion. However, it is a well-established fact that one of the primary doctrines of the Catholic Church, and probably the most publicly known doctrine of the Catholic Church, is strong opposition to abortion. The Court feels that the fact that the applicant has had two abortions in this country [sic] that detracts from the strength of her claims for religious convictions under Catholicism.[13]

In this case the judge relies on his interpretation of Catholic doctrine to negatively assess the sincerity of the plaintiff's claim to be a practicing Catholic.

Credibility assessments require that judges draw a sharp line demarcating authentic religiosity from "religious impostorhood," or laying claim to a religious identity that one does not truly possess. The process presumes that it is possible for the authorities to differentiate "real" religious identities, reasons, and actions from impostorlike "nonreligious" or political ones. Accusations of religious impostorhood can lead to a negative credibility assessment, as was the case in a 1997 split decision concerning an Iranian practicing Christianity, *United States v. Bastanipour*, in which the Seventh Circuit rejected the applicant's claim on the grounds of insincerity.[14] Although the applicant also had regularly attended church services in the United States, the immigration judge concluded that his conversion was insincere because he did not know the names of the twelve apostles. The Seventh Circuit concurred: "With the Court's understanding that Christianity begins with the life and teaching of Jesus Christ in the New Testament, the 12 apostles have some of the most important, if not the most important, writings of Christianity. . . . The respondent's knowledge about Christianity [was presented] to the Court

---

13. Quoted in Musalo, "Claims for Protection," 221n311, citing a decision of the immigration judge, File #A72 898 126, at 16. At the time Musalo was writing about this case, it was on appeal to the Eighth Circuit, and she did not track it beyond that point. She explained to me that the circuit court may have remanded it back to the Board of Immigration Appeals in an unpublished decision. The board could have either decided it (which they could have done in an unpublished decision) or remanded it back to the immigration judge (email communication with Karen Musalo, March 3, 2019).

14. United States v. Bastanipour, 980 F.2d 1129, 1131 (7th Cir. 1992), cited in Kagan, "Refugee Credibility Assessment," 1220.

in such general terms that any person of any religion can come up with that description of their religion, namely peace, tranquility, and love."[15]

In these cases, the adjudicator's job is to reveal a religious truth or untruth that is understood to exist objectively in the person prior to the process of adjudication. Religion, in this view, is composed of inner convictions and outward manifestations, both of which can be assessed for authenticity by a qualified judge who is trained to "see like a church." Riffing on James Scott's "seeing like a state," Paul Johnson and his coauthors explain that "states might . . . be understood to 'see like a church' when legal courts begin to cast themselves as experts on religious authenticity."[16] The result is a methodical search for what I describe elsewhere as "submerged religion"—religious identity presumed to be unavailable to the naked eye but that may reveal itself to the expert upon interrogation.[17] In these cases, judges and bureaucrats are expected to locate and then verify a claimant's presumably stable yet submerged—but also potentially shifting or disingenuous—religious identity. If the claimant is not verifiably religious, or is religious but found to be insincere, then the grounds for religious asylum are absent.

Unlike in other areas of international law, the United States has adopted much of the international legal infrastructure in this domain, which is largely a colonial artifact, as Lucy Mayblin and Nathalia Justo have ably shown.[18] As a result, religion talk in asylum proceedings is transnational in nature. It echoes back and forth across jurisdictions.[19] This was clear in the 2014–16

---

15. Cited in Kagan, "Refugee Credibility Assessment," 1222. Judges Singleton and Ikuta upheld the denial of asylum but due to the standard of review in administrative law did not engage directly with the analysis that led to the negative credibility assessment. In a preview of the "eye of the persecutor" approach, dissenting Judge Berzon argued that the judge had asked the wrong question: "The question is not what Toufighi believes but what Iran understands him to believe—or, more accurately, not to believe. It is thoroughly plausible that because he attends Christian services and belongs to a Christian church, Toufighi will be taken to have renounced Islam" (cited in Kagan, "Refugee Credibility Assessment," 1221).

16. Johnson, Klassen, and Sullivan, introduction, 7.

17. In such cases the line between religion and nonreligion is understood as significant but hidden from view. It is submerged in the individual subject. Professional tactics and training are required to unearth it. Unlike "countering violent extremism" programs, in which the goal is to police the proper boundary between religion and politics (with the latter understood as extremist politics, psychological disorder, and so on), in asylum cases the object is to surface and verify a submerged and often disputed religious or nonreligious identity. To claim religious asylum in a regime of sincerity and authenticity, religiosity must be named and verified. See Hurd, "Border Religion," 228–45.

18. Mayblin, *Asylum after Empire*; Justo, "Global Politics of Citizenship."

19. On the US and German systems compared see Sonntag, "Testing Religion," 975–1057. On

refugee crisis, when the significance of sincerity, credibility, and authenticity in assessments of religious persecution became apparent, in both the US and the UK. British Conservative politician and House of Lords member Baroness Elizabeth Berridge told the *Guardian* that when it comes to religious asylum, the Home Office is making "incredibly nuanced and difficult decisions to make sure that genuine claims are accepted and non-genuine ones are rejected."[20] According to several members of Parliament, immigration officials interrogated claimants seeking protection on the grounds of conversion to Christianity on the subject of "Bible trivia." Another report confirmed that "interviewers sometimes asked Christians to recite the Ten Commandments or the Lord's Prayer, name the apostles, or explain the meaning of Lent."[21] Former US asylum officer Megan Brewer admitted that "as an officer you can never be informed enough about all the religions and subgroups." But, she continued, there may be ways to determine what religious group a person belongs to, such as their name or choice of clothing, depending on which country they come from. If that doesn't work, "we might ask about behavior or how they practice their religion."[22]

The UNHCR and the European Union (EU) also prioritize sincere and credible belief in assessing refugee claims. The UNHCR states, tautologically, that "credibility is established where the applicant has presented a claim which is . . . on balance, capable of being believed."[23] The guidance stresses the need to ascertain the sincerity of claims to conversion, particularly if they occur after the claimant has departed their home country. Similar assumptions structure the EU regime. Eager to standardize the practice of credibility assessment, judges Uwe Berlit, Harold Doerig, and Hugo Storey describe the forms of religiosity that are required to qualify for a positive assessment in that context. Claimants must evince a sincere, internal understanding of the religion that goes beyond a general or ad hoc knowledge of its tenets and practices: "Merely externally appropriated, general/ad hoc 'intellectual' knowledge of the new religion may well not be enough."[24] Problems arise when applicants

---

the European context see Rose and Öztürk, *Asylum and Conversion to Christianity in Europe*, and Gill and Good, *Asylum Determination in Europe*.

20. Sherwood, "Refugees Seeking Asylum."
21. Blumberg, "Why Trump's Failed Attempt."
22. Blumberg, "Why Trump's Failed Attempt."
23. UNHCR, "Note on Burden and Standard of Proof in Refugee Claims," paragraph 11. These guidelines offer "interpretative legal guidance for governments, legal practitioners, decision-makers and the judiciary, as well as UNHCR staff carrying out refugee status determination in the field" (UNHCR, "Guidelines on International Protection No. 6").
24. Berlit and Doerig are judges at the German Supreme Administrative Court and Storey is

make "non-credible" claims to conversion. The judges find "non-specific and cliché statements" especially suspect: "A serious turn towards the new religion will only be accepted if there is reasonable concern with the content of that faith and a corresponding knowledge of its beliefs/essential features, the religious texts, rituals, traditions, and holidays. . . . Knowledge of the new religion is not to be expected at the level of scientific and theological debate, but completely non-specific and cliché statements may be significant pointers to a non-credible account."[25] In this approach, religion is a stable and knowable entity that exists independent of context and can be verified by the proper (often male) authorities. The truth or falsity of alien conversion must be expertly assessed.[26]

Religious Asylum, Revisited

There are compelling critiques of this regime. Deborah Thebault and Lena Rose have found that European judges favor certain understandings of Christianity over others.[27] Examining asylum decision-makers' presumptions about gender, sexuality, and religion, Elena Fiddian-Qasmiyeh has probed the limits of credibility assessment, observing that LGBTQ+ claimants who persist in self-identifying as Muslim have had their claims dismissed as implausible because decision-makers "believe that it is impossible for LGBT+ refugees to continue self-identifying as Muslim because Islam is constituted through orientalist frameworks as inherently oppressive of sexual minorities."[28] In tracking the political and religious economy of authentic conversion in her study of Korean Chinese asylum seekers in the United States, Kim describes a full-

---

a senior judge at the UK Upper Tribunal and president of the European Chapter of the International Association of Refugee Law Judges (Berlit, Doerig, and Storey, "Credibility Assessment," 658).

25. Berlit, Doerig, and Storey, "Credibility Assessment," 656.

26. Berlit, Doerig, and Storey, "Credibility Assessment," 660. The phrase *true conversion* also appears in a 1997 decision of the US Seventh Circuit, *Najafi v. I.N.S.*, in which the court found that "certainly true conversion does matter in one sense. If one is a believer in a religious faith, one would presumably wish to practice that faith. Religious adherence could take the form of attending services, meeting with others of the same faith, personal prayer, or openly sharing one's belief, to name a few examples. If any activity necessary to a convert could trigger persecution in Iran, such a practice should be brought to the attention of the immigration judge. To evaluate the relevance of this practice to the life of the alien, the immigration judge should be satisfied with the sincerity of the alien's new religious commitment" (*Najafi v. I.N.S*, 104 F.3d).

27. Thebault and Rose, "What Kind of Christianity?," 545. See also Rose and Given-Wilson, "What Is Truth?," 221–35.

28. Fiddian-Qasmiyeh, "Faith-Gender-Asylum Nexus," 217–18.

fledged "migration industry" composed of paralegals, immigration attorneys, and other commercial brokers:

> Paralegals often provide their clients with a thick bundle of papers that pool frequently asked questions about Christianity. Some asylum-seekers would rather study these papers during their free time instead of attending the service and the Bible study group, which disrupt their demanding work schedule. One of my study participants working as a masseur at a Korean spa six and half days a week, including Sunday, proudly recalled how he created 180 index cards out of these papers and studied them day and night while diligently applying pressure to a client on a massage table.[29]

Religious credibility assessment generates a laundry list of unanswerable questions. Does religion learned on flashcards at work count as "real" religion? What is the relevant measure of sincerity or genuineness? Is knowledge of doctrine sufficient? To what extent does knowledge correlate with conviction? Which holidays are mandatory, and which are optional? Do experiential descriptions of religious experience count? Does participation in religious organizations? Is attendance at church or an equivalent sufficient, or must one be an active and dedicated participant? How is that measured? What about dietary practices and religious attire? Ethnicity in relation to religion?[30] Another problem, as Dina Nayeri explains, is that in her experience, "casual converts don't present like church leaders. They're not loud and feverish with devotion, and they live in a mixed-up culture, the Iranian and the Western jumbled all together. They celebrate Christmas with saffron pudding. They make pilgrimages on Easter and Ascension. Out of habit, they mutter to Muslim prophets as they haul their tired bodies off the ground. These are *their* specific, moving contradictions—the natural flaws that bring a story to life."[31]

Critics of the asylum regime include former adjudicators. Michael Kagan has described it as "a special type of adjudication where officials from secular governments and the United Nations conduct formal hearings into religious faith."[32] Tracing the sincerity test to the Supreme Court's 1944 *United States v. Ballard* decision, Kagan describes that test as "a common means of avoiding the problem of defining religion or ruling directly on the truth of religious beliefs."[33] He agrees with Nayeri that it "can work only by making assumptions about how a religious person would talk or act, but ambiguity, ambiva-

---

29. Kim, "Between Sacred Gift and Profane Exchange," 318.
30. Kagan, "Refugee Credibility Assessment," 1186–87.
31. Nayeri, *Ungrateful Refugee*, 240.
32. Kagan, "Refugee Credibility Assessment," 1180.
33. Kagan, "Refugee Credibility Assessment," 1207.

lence, conflicted deeds and words, and apparent incoherency (especially in the perception of outsiders) are all regular parts of religious experience."[34] Kagan recounts an especially trying episode in which the applicant said that she had converted after a friend had preached the Bible to her. The interviewer followed up by asking for a specific Bible reference:

Q: Which part of the Bible did she, I mean your friend, preach to you?
A: The Book of John.
Q: Do you remember which part?
A: I couldn't remember which part, but it was around Chapter 3.
Q: What was the chapter about?
A: You want me to tell you one verse or the whole chapter?
Q: What you know. I don't want you to worry. It's okay if you don't remember.
A: I am very stressed.
Q: Okay, are you willing to continue the interview today or do you want to reschedule?
A: I am not in a good mood now.
Q: I am here for you. You have the choice to reschedule or take another break.
A: I know I make you tired, but maybe we can reschedule.[35]

Exchanges such as this one prompted Kagan and other critics of the sincerity regime to demand a shift in focus in assessments away from credible belief and toward the perceptions of the persecutor. While credibility assessment remains central to the process, this "eye of the persecutor" approach focuses on how the claimant's actions are interpreted by the authorities (and potential persecutors) in the country of origin. Contemporary US jurisprudence, Musalo confirms, requires "proof of the persecutor's intent in order to establish nexus," and "in the U.S. several decisions have ruled that the appropriate test is not whether the adjudicator believes the applicant to be a true believer, but whether the persecuting agents will so perceive him."[36] The rationale, Kagan explains, is that "it matters little why an Eritrean person went to church, whether for belief, for curiosity, for business connections, or to find a spouse. What matters is the impact of Pentecostal church attendance on the actions of the Eritrean government. The interviewer and the adjudicator should seek to determine if the applicant can describe her church attendance in detail and with consistency."[37] Of course, as he concedes, "a smart liar could attend church just to win asylum."[38]

---

34. Kagan, "Refugee Credibility Assessment," 1212.
35. Kagan, "Refugee Credibility Assessment," 1212–13.
36. Musalo, "Claims for Protection," 206, 218–19.
37. Kagan, "Refugee Credibility Assessment," 1224.
38. Kagan, "Refugee Credibility Assessment," 1226.

Their skepticism notwithstanding, proponents of the "eye of the persecutor" approach remain committed to the emancipatory potential of religious asylum as a means of guaranteeing religious liberty. This quixotic guarantee underlies the liturgy of asylum. Kagan reassures skeptics that "refugees who are genuinely at risk will find protection without endangering the integrity of the asylum system or infringing on the religious liberty of asylum seekers."[39] He expresses concern that adjudicators not "deprive asylum seekers of the freedom to experience religion through individual choice."[40] Thebault and Rose seek to improve adjudicators' understandings of the complexity of asylum claims to guarantee the possibility of religious freedom. Tuan Samahon advises US claimants facing adverse credibility determinations to assert claims to violations of the Free Exercise and Establishment Clauses of the First Amendment, noting that the clauses "provide asylum applicants with tools to challenge credibility findings tainted by adjudicator disbelief or adjudicator orthodoxy."[41] Suspicious of the "orthodoxy-establishing character of credibility determinations," Samahon calls for the "creation of a detailed administrative record clearly stating reasons for denied credibility."[42] In short, claimants should avail themselves of the constitutional protections of the First Amendment and bureaucrats should keep better records. If lawmakers and adjudicators would reform the law and get the process right, these critics imply, the proceedings would unfold more justly.

Others are skeptical of the law's capacity to serve as an objective arbiter.[43] In his study of Ahmadi asylum claimants in the German courts, Michael Nijhawan finds that the authorities' verification of the line between authentically religious and nonreligious (or "impostor") subjecthood often determines whether or not an individual receives asylum.[44] Reflecting on the shortcomings of attempts to interpret religion as sincere belief in these proceedings, he suggests that because religiosity "is assessed in the courts as an opaque state, entirely subjective and yet paradoxically in need of certainty for the legal process of granting Ahmadis asylum (based on religious persecution)

---

39. Kagan, "Refugee Credibility Assessment," 1181.
40. Kagan, "Refugee Credibility Assessment," 1219–20.
41. "If the asylum applicant demonstrates that INS adjudicators impermissibly used particular religious practices or beliefs as a standard in evaluating his or her sincerity of conversion (and thus credibility of membership), then the asylum applicant will be able to state an establishment claim from which no compelling state interest could rescue the invalid determination" (Samahon, "Religion Clauses and Political Asylum," 2232, 2225, 2233).
42. Samahon, "Religion Clauses," 2228, 2238.
43. Berger, *Law's Religion*; Schonthal, *Buddhism, Politics and the Limits of Law*.
44. Nijhawan, *Precarious Diasporas*.

to make sense," it "becomes imperative for the courts to determine what counts as normalcy in religious terms and especially so when particular identities bear the mark of either too little or too much of such religion in the current immigration discourse."[45] The pressure to identify what counts as normalcy in religious terms places credibility assessment at "the core of the judicial process."[46] Credibility assessment, or refugee status determination, is, moreover, especially contentious in cases of religious persecution in which "courts engage in RSD to make categorical distinctions between legitimate refugees and so-called religious impostors." As Nijhawan concludes, "when asylum adjudicators set out to decide whether to accept such refugee claims, they can quickly find themselves administering a process akin to a religious trial."[47]

Winnifred Sullivan has persuasively documented the complex and arguably insurmountable obstacles for those seeking to provide or avail themselves of religious expertise in contexts in which religion is legally disestablished, such as in the United States.[48] To provide religious expertise requires that the state, judge, or bureaucrat acting in its name recognize and attend to authorized representatives and representations of "real" religions—a singling out that is certainly tautological and arguably unconstitutional in a regime in which religion is formally disestablished. Who is allowed to speak for which religion? Which doctrines, practices, dress codes, holidays, or hierarchies are considered central to a religion as opposed to merely optional or superfluous? Who decides? In a context of disestablishment, the adjudication of what is religious as opposed to cultural or merely decorative is messy, unpredictable, and arguably impossible.

That these hurdles carry over into the adjudication of religious asylum became clear in the materials consulted for this chapter, including cases and case summaries, secondary literature in the field, and my own experience writing affidavits as a country-of-origin expert on behalf of claimants.[49] Taken together, these cases (approximately forty US federal asylum cases be-

---

45. Nijhawan, *Precarious Diasporas*, 107.

46. Nijhawan, *Precarious Diasporas*, 108.

47. Nijhawan, *Precarious Diasporas*, 108, citing Kagan, "Refugee Credibility Assessment," 1181. See also Oraby, "Law, the State, and Public Order: Regulating Religion in Contemporary Egypt," 574–602, and Marzouki, "Conversion as Statelessness," 69–105.

48. On the logical impossibility of realizing "religious freedom" under a regime of legal disestablishment see Sullivan, *Impossibility of Religious Freedom*, and on the impossibility of 'free exercise" in the same context see Sullivan, *Prison Religion*.

49. Rule 702 of the Federal Rules of Evidence defines an expert as a person with "scientific, technical, or other specialized knowledge" who can "assist the trier of fact."

tween 2008 and 2018 in which asylum was sought on the grounds of religious persecution and, in several cases, at least one other protected status category), suggest that the line between religious "persecution" or "well-founded fear of persecution," on one hand, and "hate crime," "lawlessness," or "harassment," on the other, is often ambiguous if not arbitrary (see, for example, *Pan v. Holder* and *Eric Supangat v. Holder*).[50] Religion and religious persecution tend to mean whatever a particular immigration judge says they mean.[51] There is no rule or pattern. Adjudicators bring their own, often eccentric interpretations of the behavior of the applicants to bear on decision-making processes.[52] Adjudication of credibility involving minor and dissident religions is ad hoc at best.[53] In most cases, the dividing line between religious and political persecution is impossible to locate.[54]

This ambivalence also characterizes academic and advocacy-related work in the asylum field. Like other forms of law talk, religion talk in the asylum domain operates at a certain remove from lived reality. It is oddly desiccated. Scholars and practitioners who are invested in this regime remain deeply reverential nonetheless of the redemptive power of law and human rights, including the right to religious freedom. In the United States and Europe, proceedings often invoke the "freedom to experience religion through individual choice," confirming Lincoln Mullen's argument that "the prevalence of

---

50. *Pan v. Holde*, 132 S. Ct.; *Supangat v. Holder*, 735 F.3d.

51. This aligns with Rose and Given-Wilson's suggestion that in the German context, "much rests on the judges' impression of the claimant and whether they consider the narrative plausible following their own common sense. We observed that this common sense is influenced by the judge's own religious socialization, educational background, or stereotypes that they have developed" ("What Is Truth?," 230). On the German context, see also Schlüter, "Credibility Assessment in Asylum Claims." Fassin's study of the French context concludes that "the last word was rarely that facts were undoubtedly established. Most of the time, the decision relied on personal conviction" ("Precarious Truth," 21). On the Norwegian and Canadian context see also Årsheim, "Sincere and Reflected?," 83–95.

52. "The attitude of a person depends on cultural backgrounds and social habits that the judges usually admitted not to have the means to apprehend. Yet some of them, on the basis of their colonial past, exotic readings or touristic experiences, did not hesitate to offer definitive interpretations, to which few anthropologists would have subscribed" ("Precarious Truth," 22).

53. *Cosa v. Mukasey*, 543 F.3d.

54. "Truth is what institutions decide to be true," although judges "do not create this truth in a political vacuum: they do it in a social environment in which public discourses discredit and stigmatize refugees while officially defending the doctrine of protection and even extending it to new grounds related to gender and sexual questions" (Fassin, "Precarious Truth," 24, 26).

religion as choice instead of religion as inheritance is distinctively (though not uniquely) American."[55]

My earlier work described the effects of US and transnational attempts to construe religion as belief and freedom as choice for the purposes of defining religion and religious freedom globally.[56] The politics of religious asylum involve similar dynamics. Declarations of religious choice, belief, identity, and practice often prove resistant to the task of ascertaining sincerity.[57] Fears of religious impostorhood and politically expedient conversion haunt the process at every turn. The power of state and international law to free the individual remains elusive. Language is slippery. Judges and claimants can be mercurial. At the end of the day, a focus on religious persecution, whether framed in terms of sincere belief, the "eye of the persecutor," the First Amendment, or some other metric, obscures a much broader political-theological field in which these processes unfold. Studying individual cases is helpful only up to a certain point in accessing this field. That requires asking different questions: What conditions sustain the US and, to a lesser degree, transnational regime of religious asylum despite the obvious limitations of the category of religion as deployed in legal contexts? Why do the authorities persist in trying to establish whether a person, action, belief, or practice has been or is at risk of being credibly subject to religious persecution?[58] What is really at stake in these proceedings, and what does it have to do with American borders?

Liturgied into Citizenship

The reliance in US federal and international refugee law and in adjacent literatures on narrow constructs of religion as a protected category obstructs our view of the broader field in which asylum seeking and claiming unfolds.

---

55. Mullen, *Chance of Salvation*, 5. "Americans came to think of religion as an identity that one could and must chose for oneself" (ibid., 10).
56. See Hurd, "Believing in Religious Freedom," 45–56.
57. On how sincerely held religious belief became the legal standard in the United States for determining what counts as authentic religion, see McCrary, *Sincerely Held*.
58. There is an extensive literature on credibility assessment and the asylum bureaucracy; in the European context, see Dahlvik, *Inside Asylum Bureaucracy*; Farrell, *Asylum Narratives and Credibility Assessments*; and Noll, *Proof, Evidentiary Assessment and Credibility in Asylum Procedures*. On inconsistencies in the application of constitutional norms in the analysis of asylum claims in US federal courts, see Ray, "Applying the U.S. Constitution to Foreign Asylum Seekers," 137–83.

CREATING   41

There is more going on than meets the eye. Both the standard treatment of religion in assessments of religious credibility and the "eye of the persecutor" approach rest on the assumption that religion, assigned to its proper place, stands apart from law and politics. The authorities must distinguish between authentic and simulated religion, true conversion and impostorhood, callous lawlessness and genuine religious dissidence—distinctions that are presumed to exist independently of the legal process and performance, but do not. Rarely is there agreement over how to define religion, persecution, conversion, sincerity, or credibility. To make matters worse, there are also repeated attempts to externalize or extinguish the asylum regime altogether by barring claimants from entering sanctuary countries and outsourcing the process to third parties. Such efforts threaten the integrity of the limited protective measures that do exist. For example, in 1992, George H. W. Bush, expanding on a Reagan-era deal with Haitian dictator Jean-Claude Duvalier, ordered the US Coast Guard to intercept Haitian refugees trying to reach the US following the overthrow of Haitian President Jean-Bertrand Aristide. The Supreme Court upheld the order, ruling that US obligations to asylum seekers do not apply outside of US territory. The court drew protest with this decision from those insisting that the order violated a 1967 international protocol signed by the United States that prohibits returning refugees to a state where they will be persecuted.[59] Yet the order stood, and by the mid-1990s, its reach had "expanded to nearly anyone of any nationality caught in the sea, whether out in international waters or a couple of hundred feet from the beach."[60]

The asylum regime does not and never has simply adjudicated the fates of preexisting religious individuals. Instead, it elicits performances of political and religious subjectivity that it claims to have objectively located, thereby contributing to the very indeterminacy that it seeks to overcome.[61] It is a secularist regime in the sense described by Hussein Agrama: a "historical problem-space . . . an ensemble of questions and attached stakes that seem indispensable to the practical intelligibility of political and social life . . . [that] is increasingly fraught with irrevocable indeterminacy."[62] Whether framed in terms of sincerity, credibility,

---

59. See Crisp, "What Is Externalization"; Stack, "Let's Not Pretend."
60. "Pushing migrants and refugees away from the land borders to avoid obligations under law has now become common practice" (Wessler, "Border Where Different Rules Apply").
61. French, "Anthropology of Religion and Law."
62. "Secularism should neither be seen solely in terms of a separation between religion and politics nor in terms of its success or failure in imposing a set of regulatory norms. Rather it is more usefully approached as a historical problem-space, that is, in terms of an ensemble of questions

the "eye of the persecutor," the religion clauses, or some other metric, there is an element of the Inquisition that inheres in these proceedings. They can be cruel. Didier Fassin observes that "the systemic suspicion regarding the asylum seekers transforms the inquiry on truth-telling into a process of lie-detecting, which can sometimes turn into an exercise of public cruelty."[63] Authentication is always insufficient to the task of ascertaining sincerity. Fears of impostorhood, suspicions of political opposition or opportunism masquerading as religious agency, and conjectures about politically expedient conversion or fabricated religious commitment bedevil the process.[64] As a technocratic solution to political problems, the law's capacity is limited. Something more is needed.

The purpose served by these proceedings is larger than the sum of the individual cases admitted for legal scrutiny. They form an essential component of the collective liturgy of the American nation-state. The liturgy of asylum invokes the promise of freedom, salvation, and redemption not through conversion to a particular world religion but to the American project itself. Claimants are, as explained in the following paragraphs, "liturgied into citizenship." Asylum seeking is a form of theological or religious politics, then, but not if one is confined to a strict understanding of political theology as the importation of theological forms into secular political theory and practice.[65] Asylum seeking is religious in the sense of being grounded in an overarching faith in the realization of freedom, grace, and redemption through conversion to Americanness. The liturgy of asylum conjures a (proto-)American subject of free will and unencumbered religious and political choice. It positions Americans as offering a magnanimous gesture or gift that protects the religious freedom of the persecuted and precarious subject by saving them from suffering inflicted in foreign, and often fanatical, home countries.[66] The success of this regime and the bargain that it upholds hinges on the collective affirmation of a religious and political difference between Americans and others. The liturgy of asylum creates a border in the minds of Americans, asylees, and others. It transports the successful asylee across that border via performance, repetition, and embodied rituals. As Nayeri observed of her mother's testimony, it was her performance that mattered. Performing the

---

and attached stakes that seem indispensable to the practical intelligibility of political and social life.... [I]t is an expression of the state's sovereign power and ... it is increasingly fraught with irrevocable indeterminacy." Agrama, *Questioning Secularism*, 71–72.

63. Fassin, "Precarious Truth," 18–19.
64. For extended examples see Nayeri, *Ungrateful Refugee*.
65. See Bain, *Political Theology of International Order*.
66. On the history of religious fanaticism in the US at home and abroad, see Wheatley, *American Fanatics*.

liturgy of asylum matters. In modernity, as Peter Van der Veer notes, the nation-state is the dominant form of political and religious practice.⁶⁷

The liturgy of asylum is political-theological in another sense. It positions the American state and society as capable of offering redemption by conjuring something larger than itself. That is the point. Redemption does not issue directly from the American people but from something deeper than state or society, something that grounds and secures its conditions of possibility. The process depends on (and conjures) a truth and goodness that transcends the polity to the extent that despite the brokenness of the overwhelmed actual US asylum courts, the spirit of American sovereignty shines through as a guarantor of religious and political freedom. The liturgy affirms Americans' self-understanding as part of a potentially universalizable project that defines itself as offering an unmatched opportunity for anyone anywhere to experience true freedom and true religion. These are inseparable. The repeated bipartisan invocation of an ideal free US subject and its tacit juxtaposition with an anonymous unfree foreign other helps define the borders of Americanness in contrast with the unfreedom that lies beyond. To be clear, some unfree others may be physically located within the territorial boundaries of the United States. Some may even be American citizens. This is not about national identity in the sense of holding or not holding a US passport; it is about gesturing toward and genuflecting to a form of religious and political freedom that is guaranteed through but also transcends the polity. To traverse the US border successfully, and permanently, requires claimants to attest to the universality of *this* American political religion. The asylum inquiry disciplines and subjectifies by demanding confession. It baptizes seekers as American.

A brief etymology of the term *liturgy* is useful here. The etymology given in the *Oxford English Dictionary* (*OED*) describes its dual ecclesiastical and Greek roots:

> Post-classical Latin *liturgia* < ancient Greek λειτουργία public service, service of the gods, public worship, < λειτουργός (also ληιτ-, Hesych.) public servant, minister, < *λεῖτος (believed to be a variant of *λήιτος, public, recorded in the substantive uses λήιτον public hall, λήιτη, λήτη priestess; apparently a derivative of λεώς, λαός people) + -εργος that works. Compare French *liturgie* (16th cent.).⁶⁸

The *OED* defines liturgy as "a form of public worship, especially in the Christian Church; a collection of formularies for the conduct of divine service. Also, public worship conducted in accordance with a prescribed form," as in

---

67. Van der Veer, *Value of Comparison*, 148.

68. All definitions in this section are from the *Oxford English Dictionary* (© 2023 Oxford University Press).

the liturgy of the Church of England.[69] The term also was adapted and used as a verb, in the sense of the following example from a derivative definition excerpted from Myles Davies's *Athenæ Britannicæ, 1716–1719*: "All the Presbyterians ... unanimously agree to go to the Church-Service, to be Liturgy'd into Wedlock and into the Grave."

A second *OED* definition, from the ancient Greek, refers to "a public office or duty which the richer citizens discharged at their own expense." Examples of the latter include a December 25, 1880, edition of the *Saturday Review of Politics, Literature, Science and the Arts*, referring to "a species of liturgy—a voluntary contribution to a great public object." Another cites George Grote's *A History of Greece* (first edition, 1846–56), which refers to "the Liturgies of the State, as they were called, unpaid functions such as the trierarchy, choregy, gymnasiarchy, which entailed expence and trouble upon the holder of them." The trierarchy referred to "the position or office of a trierarch; the equipment and maintenance of a trireme or other vessel, as a public service or 'liturgy'; *the system by which a fleet was thus maintained*" (emphasis added); choregy refers to the provision of choirs in ancient Athens; and gymnasiarchy refers to the "office or function of gymnasiarch" charged with "providing for the expence of the torch race."

The liturgy of asylum as it is performed today is a voluntary unpaid function that contributes to a "great public object:" the (re)production of a popular sovereign American citizenry through the creation of a border between Americans and others. It is a performative act through which state sovereignty is invested in the people. It could be seen as an element of the people's "second body" in action. The liturgy of asylum is among the "guises and modalities" through which political theologies of popular sovereignty are expressed. As Santner explains, "The further shift from the political theology of royal sovereignty to ostensibly de-theologized, fully secularized political theories of popular sovereignty (and the forms of life framed by them) brings such complexities and ambiguities ever more to the fore, though in new guises and modalities."[70] Adapting the quote from Myles Davies's *Athenæ Britannicæ, 1716–1719*, one could say that the asylum seeker goes to the judge to be "Liturgy'd into Citizenship." Asylum is one of several "Liturgies of the State" that entails "expence and trouble upon the holders of them." Beyond its legal implications and expectations, this liturgy works to instantiate a border between Americans and others while simultaneously affirming the boundlessness and emancipatory potential of the US American project. These proceedings evince, affirm, and enact a faith in the realization of freedom and grace

---

69. The *OED* also notes that *the* liturgy refers to the Book of Common Prayer.
70. Santner, *Royal Remains*, xii.

through conversion to Americanness. The process is sacred and worldly. The gap that it affirms between Americans and others performs the exceptionalist promise of the US national project. It makes it real. Its audience goes beyond those involved in the asylum process; it is for all Americans and would-be Americans. It is for everyone. The liturgy of asylum does important social, political, and religious work.

Robert Yelle's discussion of the antinomian sacred as a political category is helpful in grasping how the liturgy works. *Antinomian* means "against or without law." The *antinomian sacred* refers to a space of exception comparable to Schmitt's notion of the "sovereign exception" or Weber's notion of "charisma." As noted earlier, Yelle proposes that "what we call 'religion' or the 'sacred' encompasses the dynamic interplay between a normative order and the drive to go beyond this order, either to escape or to legitimate it."[71] The liturgy of asylum is an expression of the dynamic interplay between the normative (b)order and the drive to go beyond it. It captures the fleeting and paradoxical expression of "bordered borderless-ness" that can be appreciated if one concedes that "human beings aim at something more than reason and legality alone." Religion, as Paul Johnson interprets Yelle's argument, appears "as exit sign, as a kind of transcendence, not of the world itself but of transactional modes of occupying the world." It is "a series of states of exception that may equally take the form of radical violence and radical pardon, from sacrificial massacre to the democratic benevolence of the Roman and then biblical Jubilee." Yelle, he continues, makes religion interesting by situating it in "the blasts of radical excess, a transcendence of the usual economies."[72]

The liturgy of asylum transcends the usual economies. It enacts the Jubilee. It celebrates redemption and salvation. It enacts radical violence (in its denial) and radical pardon (in its granting). Like other aspects of US border making, maintenance, transcendence, and subversion—including the subversions of the Rio Grande as we see later—this process outruns the rationalistic, mechanistic, and legalistic vocabularies that strive to channel and contain it. It speaks in a different register. It reaches toward and is guided by an idealized subject of freedom, free will, and unencumbered choice, a subject that is in this mythology only capable of being fully realized in the United States, or perhaps, though with great ambivalence, in the so-called West. (This equivocation accounts for the relatively effortless transnationalization of the asylum regime.) Webb Keane has observed that an important feature of modernity is the production of religious and political subjects that understand themselves to be free

---

71. Yelle, *Sovereignty and the Sacred*, 8.
72. P. C. Johnson, "Book Review: Sovereignty and the Sacred," 241–42.

because they exercise particular kinds of individual agency. "What is at stake," he writes, "is not just the transmission of correct doctrine but also the production of human subjects who are (relatively) free because they fully grasp the agency that is rightly theirs."[73] In the context of asylum seeking, this includes an obligation, as Mullen would remind us, to freely choose one's religion. The juridical invocation, legal validation, and extralegal summoning of an ideal subject completely free to choose their religious and political preferences illustrates "the play of the ideal in the real" in this American political theology.[74]

The liturgy of asylum fits hand in glove with a naturalized and secularized form of Christianity described by J. Kameron Carter. This form of (universal, secular) Christianity "conceives of itself as that religion that can be beyond religion, that is, that can be 'secular,' it can serve as a mediator and pedagogue for the rest of the world. Put simply, it can be 'the way, the truth, and the life' (cf. John 14:6)."[75] It is a form of religion that goes beyond religion. The asylum adjudicator comes to stand in for the state, civilization, humanity, and, at times, God herself. "To be saved," then, "is to be made 'religious' in the proper way within a properly ordered secular space; those who cannot or who refuse to enter this 'order of things' must be annihilated for the sake of the Kingdom."[76] To be saved, one must be "liturgied into citizenship."

Conclusion: A Will to Redemption

The liturgical performance of asylum is predicated on the world religions model. That model is an influential framework for understanding religions as distinct and separate. It regards "conversion" from Islam to Christianity by an asylum seeker as suspect and in need of interrogation precisely because it holds that the two religions are mutually exclusive, such that a conversion from one to another implies forsaking one to make room for the other. Like

---

73. Keane, *Christian Moderns*, 76.
74. I am grateful to Constance Furey for this phrase.
75. Carter, "Unlikely Convergence," 179.
76. "In turning first to Barth and then to Du Bois, I want to demonstrate that this process was also a theo-political one built on a specific religious anthropology. It was (and, to a large extent, remains) one in which the constitution of the White Masculine as Imperial Man was tied to his assuming a messianic and mediatory role in the world, as he accumulated divinity for himself. As Imperial Savior, he functioned by 'divine right' to establish a Utopian kingdom—a kingdom of whiteness, we might say—as the Kingdom of God. Those who enter this Kingdom can be saved. Yet to be saved is to be made 'religious' in the proper way within a properly ordered secular space; those who cannot or who refuse to enter this 'order of things' must be annihilated for the sake of the Kingdom" (Carter, "Unlikely Convergence," 189).

its conceptual partner, secularism, the world religions model takes religion as a self-evident category that is assumed to be autonomous from its legal and political surroundings. Religion is presumed to influence its surroundings without being influenced by them. There is an appealing simplicity in treating religion in this way. The conviction that world religions are equidistant from their political and legal contexts reinforces deep-seated institutional interests. It legitimizes the discipline of religious studies as a stand-alone enterprise and, separately, the discipline of political science—and law. It is a comforting myth that tells us more about the history of these academic disciplines than it does about the world they describe. What we call "religion" continually upsets these disciplinary boundaries, blurring into secular institutions, histories, and practices.

The liturgy of asylum is hard to apprehend from within a secularist epistemology in which religion is conceived as segregated from politics and law. It demands that we reconsider the assumption that there is or ever has been a clean line dividing religions and politics, sacred and secular. The US is a very religious country, and not only in the sense of being saturated with (while also shaping particular forms of) evangelical Protestantism, though it is and does that too.[77] The asylum liturgy enacts a collective will to be redeemed through membership in the American people, who are defined by their unique capacity to choose to be free, both religiously and politically. This is what asylum seekers are seeking. Their search for freedom, salvation, and redemption reaffirms the capacity of the American state and society to provide access to these goods while at the same time confirming their scarcity or absence in other countries and contexts. The search for asylum depends on and conjures a truth and goodness that transcends the American state and society. Despite the brokenness of the system, the spirit of American sovereignty is redeemed. It rises above.

The liturgy of asylum confirms that Americans have something that others do not. Americans have freedom and others have establishment. Americans have choice and others have compulsion. Americans have disestablishment and others have state religion. The performance of the liturgy affirms an unbridgeable religious and political difference between Americans and others while affording the opportunity to be saved to a select few.

---

77. See the classic account by Mead, *Lively Experiment*.

INTERLUDE I

Border/less

> Established for the practice of Mexican law, we examine and obtain for persons or companies Mining Titles, Land Titles, Water Rights, Surface Rights, Patent Rights, Trade Marks, Railroad, Banking and Industrial Concessions, Registration and Organization of Companies, Corporation and Commercial Concessions, etc.
>
> ADVERTISEMENT FOR LAW OFFICE OF GREGG & VIESCA, DOUGLAS, ARIZONA, 1904[1]

> The Tohono O'odham have resided in what is now southern and central Arizona and northern Mexico since time immemorial.
>
> TOHONO O'ODHAM NATION, 2024[2]

Bordered

On a sunny winter morning, a friend and I set out to visit the Tohono O'odham Nation Cultural Center and Museum, or Himdag Ki:, located eight miles south of Sells, Arizona and roughly twenty miles as the crow flies from the US-Mexico border. Himdag Ki:, which opened in 2007, was built to house the numerous O'odham sacred objects that were to be repatriated after the passage of the 1990 Native American Graves Protection Act (NAGPRA).[3] At just over an hour's drive southwest of Tucson, the center sits at the intersection of Federal Indian Route 19 and Fresnal Canyon Road in Topawa.[4] An

---

1. St. John, *Line in the Sand*, 83, citing the *Douglas Daily Dispatch*, March 30, 1904. A report by the Cochise County Historical Society notes that "the International Law Office of Gregg and Viesca, which specialized in Mexican land law, mining law and water rights, had offices in the Pirtle-Douglas building" and that "a regular newspaper column reported on business investments in Sonoran natural resources" (Hadley, "Border Boomtown," 30).

2. Tohono O'odham Nation website. "No Wall."

3. The center's full name in O'odham is Himdag Ki: Hekĭhu, Hemu, Im B I-Ha'ap ("House of Culture: The Past, Present, and into the Future") (Mack, "A:cim O'odham," 12). On NAGPRA, see US Department of the Interior, Bureau of Land Management, "Native American Graves Protection and Repatriation Act," https://www.blm.gov/NAGPRA; on its implementation, see Johnson, *Sacred Claims*.

4. "The mission of Himdag Ki: Hekĭhu, Hemu, Im B I-Ha'ap, Tohono O'odham Nation Cultural Center & Museum is to instill pride by creating a permanent Tribal institution to protect and preserve O'odham jewed c himdag. Working with elders, the Cultural Center & Museum will promote understanding and respect for O'odham himdag through educational programs and public outreach" (Tohono O'odham Nation Cultural Center & Museum, "About").

officer at a Border Patrol checkpoint stopped us along the way. "US citizens?" the agent asked, lackadaisically waving us through after a quick glance into the back seat of our rental car. Border Patrol maintains two vehicle checkpoints on major routes to and from the Tohono O'odham reservation, on Federal Route 15 and Arizona Highway 86.[5]

Driving to the Cultural Center, I was struck by the beauty of the Sonoran desertscape and its slow-growing saguaro cacti. The saguaros (Ha:sañ in O'odham) can grow forty to sixty feet high and live up to two hundred years. They have provided food and shelter for Sonoran Desert animals and humans for generations, and the Tohono O'odham (whose name means "desert people") revere them as beings with personhood.[6] I had heard that construction crews working on the border wall were using explosives to blast a path for the wall in Organ Pipe Cactus National Park, uprooting cacti as they went. Though Border Patrol claims to transplant saguaros when displacing them for the wall, they can weigh up to two tons when hydrated and are not easily moved.[7] One journalist observed, "Along the border today, the transplanted specimens stand a few feet beyond the cleared roadway, marked by small wooden posts. They often stand in perfect rows, like tiny, lonely gardens tucked against the long slashing line of steel bars. Scientists predict that over the next decade many of these cacti will wither and die."[8] Another noted, "Saguaros rely on a carrot-shaped tap root that runs several feet deep and a complex network of shallow roots that can extend nearly 20 feet and are difficult to reestablish, especially if they're moved to a different type of soil."[9]

Upon our arrival, I was saddened to see the landscape around the Cultural Center pocked with metallic towers scattered about the gardens and grounds, their piercing blue lights signaling to disoriented or ill migrants that they had the option of surrendering to Border Patrol at the press of a button. We walked inside to visit the center's exhibitions. It was hard to reconcile the towers, the buzzing of Border Patrol helicopters overhead, the watchtowers, the stories of saguaro corpses, and the checkpoints with the insistence on O'odham sovereignty that we encountered in the exhibition. A panel titled "International Leadership and Sovereignty" explained, "As one of few Native

---

5. On checkpoints, see Tracey, "Checkpoint Dreams."

6. See Upholt, "Saguaro, Free of the Earth." Upholt recounts that the cacti were given their scientific name, *Carnegiea gigantea*, in the early twentieth century by scientists in Tucson hoping to flatter Andrew Carnegie into making a donation for research on aridity.

7. Hennessy-Fiske, "It's Illegal to Destroy Saguaro Cactuses."

8. Upholt, "Saguaro, Free of the Earth."

9. Hennessy-Fiske, "It's Illegal to Destroy Saguaro Cactuses."

American tribes whose land holdings are intersected by an International boundary, the Tohono O'odham Nation has become a major stakeholder in border policy as it affects our culture, connection to the land, and sovereignty.... As a sovereign Nation, we must have a voice in all conversations that affect our land and citizens. This means ensuring that our Nation's members are able to access services and ceremonies on both sides of the border."

The intensification of US control of the O'odham homelands took hold gradually in the 1800s, culminating in today's tightly restricted border zone. The O'odham experience of progressively heavy-handed US control over the border in the 1800s contrasts sharply with the experience of borderlessness afforded to wealthy US investors and ranchers looking to buy land in the area during the same period. This interlude explores this disjuncture.

The Tohono O'odham tribe has thirty-four thousand members, including more than two thousand residing in Mexico.[10] Today, in the United States, O'odham bands are divided into four federally recognized tribes: the Tohono O'odham Nation, the Gila River Indian Community, the Ak-Chin Indian Community, and the Salt River (Pima Maricopa) Indian Community, as well as one unrecognized tribe, the Hia-C'ed O'odham of southwestern Arizona. All speak various dialects of the O'odham language, which is derived from the Uto-Aztecan language group.[11] The O'odham's predecessors are the Hohokam, desert dwellers who created sophisticated canal systems to irrigate crops of cotton, tobacco, corn, beans, and squash. The Tohono O'odham Cultural Center, located in Baboquivari district, is named after the most sacred peak in O'odham Himdag, or culture, Waw Giwulk (Baboquivari Peak).

The United States is a recent presence in these O'odham homelands. US control and eventual militarization of the borderlands began with the Treaty of Guadalupe Hidalgo (1848) and the Gadsden Purchase/Treaty of La Mesilla (1853), which divided traditional O'odham lands between the United States and Mexico. At the time, neither US nor Mexican authorities consulted any of the tribes in the area. Most tribes were unaware that a border had been drawn and remained so for decades. Tribal members continued to travel normally around their homeland despite the presence of the border, passing back and forth across what had overnight, and somewhat unremarkably, become an international boundary.

Between 1874 and 1955, the US sought to strengthen its control of the region. A series of executive orders and acts of Congress established various areas of noncontiguous land as the nation's reservations. The tightening of

---

10. Tohono O'odham Nation website, "No Wall."
11. Tohono O'odham Nation website, "History and Culture."

US control began with President Ulysses S. Grant's executive order of July 1, 1874, which set aside roughly 71,000 acres for the Papago Indian Reserve, as the Tohono O'odham were known until 1986 when they adopted their current name, "for the use of the Papago and such other Indians as it may be desirable to place therein."[12] Over the next few decades, another 2,775,000 acres of noncontiguous lands were added to the reservation, though the value of that land has been threatened by diminishing access to water due to overuse by non-Indigenous populations. The era of US expansion was also an era of Indigenous land loss. As Rachel St. John explains, although "some Tohono O'odham took jobs as cowboys with Mexican and American ranching outfits and became integrated as wage earners into the lower rungs of the transborder economy, the broad picture was one of land loss."[13] Diminished to one-tenth of its original size, today the Tohono O'odham reservation spans 2.7 million acres—roughly the size of the state of Connecticut—making it the second-largest reservation in the United States.[14]

The US Customs Service arrived in O'odham lands in 1924. Former Texas Ranger Jefferson Davis Milton (1861–1947), son of the Confederate Florida governor John Milton, was sent to establish a US customs and immigration station. Milton had joined the Customs Service in 1887, serving in the Bureau of Immigration in 1904 as a mounted inspector charged with enforcement of the Chinese Exclusion Act, and, according to Custom and Border Protection's (CBP) history, becoming, at age sixty-two, "the first officer appointed to the U.S. Immigration Service Border Patrol," where "for the next 8 years he pursue[d] border patrol work with unbridled enthusiasm."[15] During his stint with Border Patrol, Milton worked under Sheriff John Slaughter, whom we will meet momentarily. US control over the borderlands intensified as the twentieth century progressed. In 1916, President Woodrow Wilson "established a permanent reservation for the O'odham and erected the first US-Mexico border fence."[16] In 1937, President Franklin Roosevelt established the Organ Pipe Cactus National Monument. In 1976, the United Nations Educational, Scientific and Cultural Organization (UNESCO) designated Organ Pipe as a biosphere reserve. A 1974 congressional mandate established the Shadow

---

12. US Department of the Interior, "Entitlements to Water," citing Kappler, ed., *Indian Affairs*.
13. St. John, *Line in the Sand*, 75.
14. Schaeffer, *Unsettled Borders*, 63.
15. US Customs and Border Protection, "Jefferson Davis Milton."
16. Schaeffer, *Unsettled Borders*, 63.

Wolves, an all-Native Border Patrol who work with US Border Patrol.[17] Since their establishment, the Shadow Wolves have been assigned to the Homeland Security Investigations tactical patrol unit operating in the Tohono O'odham Nation, and the unit has trained border guards, customs officials, and police in a range of far-flung, border-challenged locales, including Latvia, Lithuania, Estonia, Kazakhstan, and Uzbekistan.[18] The O'odham Nation also has supported the construction and operation of two CBP forward operating bases on the nation's lands in addition to an on-reservation Immigration and Customs Enforcement office, an anti-drug-smuggling task force, and CBP checkpoints on reservation highways.[19]

Despite these cooperative measures, over the years tribal members have encountered more and more barriers to crossing the US-Mexico border, making it "difficult to collect and transport traditional foods and materials, and to visit family members and sacred sites."[20] Like other tribes, the O'odham have limited legal recourse in this situation because, with the exception of the Kickapoo Tribe in southern Texas, neither the United States nor Mexico acknowledged tribal border-crossing rights in the mid-nineteenth-century agreements or in subsequent federal laws.[21] Since the passage of the Homeland Security Act of 2002 and the Department of Homeland Security Western Hemisphere Travel Initiative (WHTI), crossing the border has become onerous and at times impossible for tribal members.

The WHTI is part of the Intelligence Reform and Terrorism Prevention Act of 2004. It requires US citizens to have a passport or other acceptable document to reenter the United States from Canada or Mexico. WHTI, which went into effect in 2007 for air travel and 2009 for land and sea, created what the National Council of American Indians describes as an "unfunded mandate" for tribes to develop their own federal Enhanced Tribal ID Cards to meet federal compliance standards.[22] In April 2008, the WHTI determined that enhanced identification documents of federally recognized Indian tribes, such

---

17. Schaeffer, *Unsettled Borders*, 66.
18. Wheeler, "Shadow Wolves."
19. The nation "leads a multi-agency anti-drug smuggling task force staffed by Tohono O'odham Police Department detectives, ICE Homeland Security Investigations special agents, Border Patrol agents, and the Federal Bureau of Investigation through the Native American Targeted Investigations of Violent Enterprises task force, the only tribe-led High Intensity Drug Trafficking Area ('HIDTA') task force in the United States" (Tohono O'odham Legislative Council, "Border Security and Immigration Enforcement").
20. Marchbanks, "Borderline."
21. Marchbanks, "Borderline."
22. National Council of American Indians, "Tribal Governance."

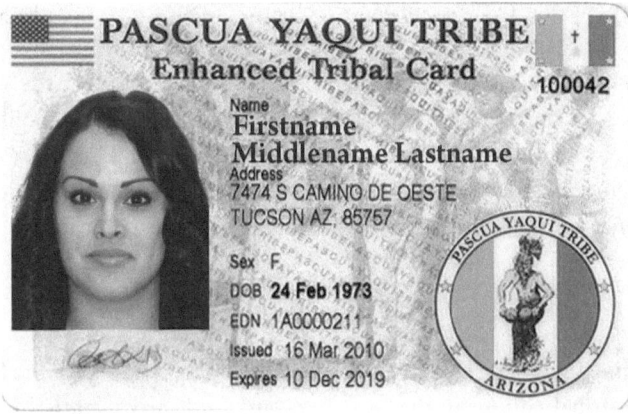

FIGURE 5. Pascua Yaqui tribal ID.
Source: Reproduced in Joseph Flaherty, "Arizona Tribe Expands High-Tech IDs to Ease Border Crossing," *Phoenix New Times*, July 11, 2017, https://www.phoenixnewtimes.com/news/yaqui-tribe-expands-high-tech-ids-9477002.

as the O'odham, would only be acceptable alternatives to a passport *if* they meet requirements similar to those of states developing WHTI-compliant identification.[23] Although the Pascua Yaqui tribe announced the creation of a WHTI-compliant Enhanced Tribal ID card in 2011,[24] the first of its kind (figure 5), Mexico still insists that all US citizens traveling in Mexico possess a US passport, including tribal members whose homelands border Mexico.

Increasingly strenuous border surveillance and enforcement in urban centers, such as San Diego and El Paso, since 9/11 has led to an intensification of US control over the O'odham homelands, as human and narcotics smugglers are funneled away from urban centers and into more remote areas to cross the border. This trend has exhausted the limited resources of tribal medical facilities, police, and trash-removal systems.[25] In 2002, the US federal government responded with a new policy ordering national park rangers to double as border patrol agents, rendering the line between conservation and border security increasingly ambiguous.[26] A 2012 National Park Service (NPS) report confirmed that the NPS supports "national security initiatives in and around Organ Pipe Cactus National Monument, including: joint border enforcement operations; the construction of a vehicle barrier and pedestrian fence, and the

23. Allen, "Don't Leave Home without It," 38–39.
24. Reproduced in Flaherty, "Arizona Tribe Expands High-Tech IDs."
25. Marchbanks, "Borderline."
26. Schaeffer, *Unsettled Borders*, 145.

establishment of a network of high-tech surveillance towers."[27] In response, Indigenous organizations such as the Tohono O'odham Legislative Council, Indigenous Alliance without Borders, O'odham Voice against the Wall, and Indivisible Tohono have protested the environmental, cultural, political, and spiritual costs of border surveillance and enforcement. They have opposed the border wall and, as suggested by the exhibit at Himdag Ki:, continue to demand recognition of Indigenous autonomy and sovereignty.[28]

Borderless

At the same time as the US-Mexico border was materializing for the O'odham and other tribal nations in the late nineteenth and early twentieth centuries, the same border was proactively and successfully circumvented by wealthy US capitalists seeking to invest in the Mexican side of an emergent borderlands capitalist economy. A Mexican federal law of 1856 had explicitly barred US citizen investors from purchasing land in Mexico by prohibiting foreign land ownership within twenty leagues (about sixty miles) of Mexico's borders. However, with the assistance of law firms such as Gregg & Viesca, whose advertisement is cited in the epigraph to this interlude, US investors managed to circumvent the Mexican law and effectively erase the border, economically and legally speaking. They did so by invoking the construct of corporate nationality, which permitted them "to access all the economic advantages of Mexican citizenship without giving up their identity and status as individual U.S. citizens."[29] As St. John explains, "under Mexican law, any company incorporated under the laws of Mexico carried all the rights of citizenship, save voting. By forming a Mexican corporation, or *sociedad anónima*, American capitalists legally transcended the limitations of their U.S. citizenship."[30] They overrode US sovereignty, even as they also enacted a parodical form of miniature sovereignty over their own land. When it came to business interests across the line, as far as these investors were concerned, the US was borderless. Corporate entities owned by Americans and incorporated under Mexican law were Mexican corporate nationals. In this case, the legal fiction of corporate personhood allows for the transcendence of borders. The impulse of American expansionism and the license of transnational capitalism combined to override and overwrite assertions of territorial sovereignty

---

27. Sturm, "Wild Matters," cited in Schaeffer, *Unsettled Borders*, 145.
28. Leza, "What Is the U.S.-Mexico Border?"
29. St. John, *Line in the Sand*, 81.
30. St. John, *Line in the Sand*, 81.

by the Mexican state. This capitalist circumvention of borders recurs in different guises throughout this book and is among the paradoxes it raises for consideration.

Among the wealthy investors taking full advantage of the loophole offered by Mexican corporate nationality was John H. Slaughter (1841–1922), a Texas cattleman and "wild west" sheriff who arrived in Arizona in the late 1870s.[31] Slaughter served two terms as sheriff of Cochise County, during which he allegedly helped track the legendary warrior Geronimo, a prominent leader of the Bedonkohe band of the Ndendahe Apache people and a notorious opponent of the US and Mexican militaries' conquest of what would become the US American Southwest.[32] In 1884, John Slaughter acquired the San Bernardino Ranch, a sixty-five-thousand-acre property spanning the Arizona-Sonora boundary line in the San Bernardino Valley.[33] Now a National Historic Landmark, the ranch sits about fifteen miles east of Douglas, Arizona, near the US-Mexico border. The 1853 Gadsden Treaty had drawn the international boundary line straight through the ranch, leaving one-third in Arizona and the remainder in Sonora. Slaughter established his headquarters right on the boundary line: "Not only did his cattle graze back and forth across the boundary line within the boundaries of the San Bernardino Land Grant, but the ranch also became a way station through which cattle passed as Slaughter bought them from Sonoran ranchers and then sold them to both local and far-off American consumers." Slaughter and other wealthy ranchers integrated land on both sides of the border "into a landscape of private property and a market in real estate." The scale of their ranches was impressive:

> By the end of the nineteenth century, the animals that moved through Slaughter's ranch joined hundreds of thousands of cattle that grazed on both sides of the border. Ranchers then loaded them onto Southern Pacific and AT&SF railroad cars and sent them to markets throughout the United States. In 1887, just one ranch, the San Rafael operated by brothers Colin and Brewster Cameron just east of Nogales, ran a herd of more than 17,000 cattle. Raised on

---

31. This section draws on St. John, *Line in the Sand*, chap. 3. The characterization of Slaughter as a "wild west" sheriff comes from the National Park Service, "San Bernardino Ranch."

32. For an interesting, and heartbreaking, discussion of Geronimo's life, see Graber, *Gods of Indian Country*.

33. National Park Service, "San Bernardino Ranch." The title to the ranch stemmed from an 1822 land grant "made by the short-lived Mexican Empire to First Lieutenant Ignacio Pérez, a member of the extended Elías family, in exchange for his military service" (St. John, *Line in the Sand*, 74).

borderlands grasses, these cattle were sent to markets as far away as California, Colorado, Kansas, Missouri, and Montana.[34]

Both the US and Mexican governments were committed to privatizing public lands and worked to facilitate the transition to private landownership by wealthy settlers. In a sense, both states actively contributed to an "outsourcing" of sovereignty to the ranchers. As St. John explains, "the United States dispatched government surveyors and passed the 1862 Homestead Act and 1877 Desert Land Act to facilitate the distribution of public land. The Mexican government contracted private surveying companies, which received large tracts of land in exchange for their surveys."[35] This led to "the appropriation of millions of acres of land that were inhabited, used, or claimed by Indians and other borderlands people." Native peoples in the region were hit especially hard:

> As surveyors marched into the Yaqui River Valley in southern Sonora, they contributed their efforts to the Sonoran government's long war to remove the Yaquis from their land and helped to push many Yaquis to relocate across the border in Arizona. The Tohono O'odham, or, as they were known by contemporary Americans and Mexicans, the Papago, also saw their claims to lands they had inhabited for years erased in the governments' push to create private property. Despite the Tohono O'odhams' history of cooperation in fighting the Apaches, the U.S. government did not even acknowledge them in adjudicating competing claims to Arizona's Upper Santa Cruz Valley where they had lived for generations. Without title to the most desirable parts of their homeland, the Tohono O'odham continued to live in Tucson and the more isolated stretches of the desert on both sides of the Arizona-Sonora border. By the twentieth century, many Americans seemed unaware that the Tohono O'odham had even been dispossessed.[36]

The history of transnational dispossession of the O'odham and selective border enforcement in favor of wealthy US settlers extended well beyond Slaughter's San Bernardino Ranch. As St. John explains, "operated in conjunction with U.S. corporations of different names, but identical objectives and personnel, American-owned Mexican corporations became the linchpins in the transborder economy. By the beginning of the Mexican Revolution in 1910, these corporations dominated mining, ranching, irrigation, and real estate speculation along the boundary line."[37] By the early twentieth

---

34. St. John, *Line in the Sand*, 74.
35. St. John, *Line in the Sand*, 75.
36. St. John, *Line in the Sand*, 75.
37. St. John, *Line in the Sand*, 81.

century, Americans owned most of the land on both sides of the US-Mexico border. A half century later, in 1964, Slaughter was inducted into the Hall of Great Westerners of the National Cowboy & Western Heritage Museum in Oklahoma City, which describes itself as "America's premier institution of Western history, art and culture."[38] In recent decades, there has been a shift away from a political economy of US territorial and economic expropriation in the borderlands and toward a politics of conservation and securitization, with the NPS and the Border Patrol working hand in hand, as previously mentioned. In 1982, the Johnson Historical Museum of the Southwest purchased the San Bernardino Ranch. It is now known as the Slaughter Ranch Museum. According to NPS, the museum, located in Cochise County in far southeastern Arizona:

> keeps the adobe ranch house decorated and furnished as it could have been during the Slaughter era. The museum provides visitors with a chance to learn about American ranch life in the southwest inside the ranch house as well as with an outdoor recreational area by the pond, where there are trees for shade, picnic tables, and charcoal grills. Near the historic Slaughter ranch district, over 2,300 acres of the original Mexican land grant are now part of the San Bernardino National Wildlife Refuge, a unit of the U.S. Fish and Wildlife Service, that offers seasonal hunting, hiking, and bird-watching.[39]

The US Historical Marker Database's Statement of Significance for the San Bernadino Ranch offers a similar history:

> The center of a cattle ranching empire that straddled the U.S.-Mexico border, this ranch illustrates the continuity of Spanish and American cattle ranching in the Southwest. Until late in the 19th century, the San Bernardino Valley, a well-watered area occupying southern Arizona and northern Mexico, was not successfully occupied by Europeans due to the threat of Apache attack; in 1884, however, John H. Slaughter, a Texas cattle rancher, leased a portion of the Mexican land grant and began the development of a ranch that would span up to 100,000 acres, supplying beef, fruits, and vegetables to the surrounding settlements and military posts.[40]

The frontiersman Slaughter provisioned surrounding settlements, continuing the noble tradition of Spanish ranching in what was to become the American Southwest and dispatching Apache attackers in the process. The only mention of the existence of tribal nations by the Park Service and on the Historical

---

38. National Cowboy & Western Heritage Museum website.
39. National Park Service, "San Bernardino Ranch."
40. Historical Marker Database, "San Bernardino Ranch."

Marker Database is in reference to the threat posed by "Apache raids," an astonishingly durable trope in US accounts of the history of the southwestern borderlands, as any visitor to the Alamo before its recent renovation can attest. In the NPS's version of history, "Apache Indian raids throughout the region prevented the Spanish from building a garrison there in the 1770s and forced a Mexican rancher to abandon his land in the 1830s, but in the 1880s, an American rancher and 'wild west' sheriff—John H. Slaughter—settled San Bernardino with his family and founded a successful cattle ranch." Meanwhile, during the same era, the Tohono O'odham were encountering a newly established and emboldened Border Patrol, led by none other than "Texas John" Slaughter's former Cochise County Sheriff's Office employee, Jim Milton. In accordance with official US government policy, Milton refused to acknowledge tribal rights to cross the border. His former boss, however, was permitted to not only cross the border but also own it.

CHAPTER 2

Enforcing National Security

> Sovereignty itself is, of course, not subject to law, for it is the author and source of law; but in our system, while sovereign powers are delegated to the agencies of government, sovereignty itself remains with the people, by whom and for whom all government exists and acts.
> JUSTICE THOMAS STANLEY MATTHEWS, majority opinion in *Yick Wo v. Hopkins*

> Putting the People in place of the King cannot ultimately be done. The forms of the social outrun their various incarnations.
> T. J. CLARK, *Farewell to an Idea: Episodes from a History of Modernism*

On January 3, 2020, the US government assassinated Major General Qasim Soleimani, the leader of Iran's elite paramilitary Quds Force, while he was riding in a convoy near Baghdad International Airport. Shortly thereafter, a memo leaked from the Customs and Border Protection (CBP) Seattle field office that ordered US border agents to interrogate and detain individuals of Iranian heritage, regardless of citizenship status.[1] The US government feared domestic reprisals from the Quds Force and its allies after the targeted killing of the Iranian general. The leaked memo instructed agents to be wary of those who might claim to follow a different religion to mask their intentions: "Even if they are not of SHIA faith, anyone can state they are Baha'i, please question further to determine this is the case. When in doubt send for high side checks. What NTC is looking for is membership in a specialized unit-QUDS forces; however, this group is so elite and well trained to evade. Anyone can state they are from a different faith to mask their intentions."[2]

Press reports indicated that during this episode US border agents held more than sixty Americans of Iranian descent, as well as many lawful permanent residents, in secondary inspection at the Peace Arch US-Canada border

---

1. Grubb, "Source Provides Directive."
2. US Customs and Border Protection, "Iranian Supreme Leaders," reproduced in Grubb, "Source Provides Directive."

crossing in Blaine, Washington. Most were questioned at length, some for up to ten hours, and others were denied entry into the United States.[3] The questioning of Iranians and Iranian Americans was not limited to Washington State. John Ghazvinian, an Iranian American historian at the University of Pennsylvania and a US citizen, was subject to additional questioning upon landing at New York's JFK airport. "Well, just landed at JFK and—no surprise—got taken to the special side room and got asked (among other things) how I feel about the situation with Iran," he tweeted, "I wanted to be like: my book comes out in September, preorder now on Amazon."[4]

Violations of civil rights in response to fear of subversive and anti-American forms of religion and politics emanating from the Middle East are a mainstay of US immigration and national security practice. A leaked memo confirming anti-Muslim and anti-Iranian discrimination at US borders is no surprise. When civil rights violations become public, advocates accuse government officials of anti-Muslim and anti–Middle Eastern racism and demand more robust protections for freedom of religion and respect for ethnic and religious diversity. The two camps settle in for a well-worn debate pitting civil liberties against national security. Should Middle Easterners and Muslims be considered a threat to US national security, or do they deserve even-handed treatment by law enforcement? Does Islam qualify as a religion that merits full First Amendment protection, or is it a special case?[5] Religion—with Islam considered as the "most religious" of religions—is rendered as either a divisive source of sectarianism and violence or as a unifying catalyst of intercommunal understanding and human flourishing. This narrative about religion and social order has repeated itself to the point of banalization.[6] In the meantime, it is national security that does the real religious and political work. Who lives and who dies?[7] Who stays and who goes? Who is banned, detained, and harassed, and who is permitted entry into the US without even

---

3. Kanno-Youngs, Baker, and Padilla, "U.S. Stops Dozens of Iranian-Americans Returning from Canada."

4. Gardner, Lippman, and Blatchford, "Border Stops for People of Iranian Descent Spark Outrage." John H. Ghazvinian is the author of *America and Iran: A History, 1720 to the Present* (New York: Knopf, 2021).

5. Ingram, *How Islam Became a Religion*.

6. Hurd, *Beyond Religious Freedom*.

7. "Exceptionalism . . . rests, beyond the rule of law, on the sovereignty of the people, which, before being legal, is first and always existential, a sovereignty that decides who lives and who must die for the sake of life itself, or the preservation of the people" (Carter, "Politics of the Atonement").

getting a passport out of their pocket? In the United States, it is national security, and not only religion, that is vested with the authority to enforce, circumvent, or transcend the law in the name of order, control, and social harmony. And in the words of CBP, "border security is national security."[8]

This chapter explores the religious work of national security at US borders. National security has always had lofty, even otherworldly, aspirations. According to historian Andrew Preston, "the concept was invented by fusing long-standing, traditional concerns about U.S. territorial sovereignty with a newer, thoroughly revolutionary desire to protect and promote America's core values on a global scale."[9] Many analysts are wary of the concept. Theologians admonish apologists for national security for their collective worship of the nation-state and the violence it sanctions.[10] Legal and foreign policy experts warn that few constraints, whether constitutional or statutory, hinder the executive if its actions can be justified as pursuant to national security or the national interest. The assassination of Soleimani barely set off even a faint ripple of protest in the United States despite its condemnation as illegal under international law by the United Nations special rapporteur on extrajudicial executions.[11] Even as experts debate the finer points of international legal constraints on state behavior,[12] however, the extralegal aspects of the exercise of sovereign authority—the processes through which that authority comes to occupy a space that is felt to be beyond the reach of the law—go missing from the discussion.

This chapter addresses this imbalance. I explore the religious work performed by the figure of national security in the debate surrounding the 2017 "Muslim ban." Here I approach the idea of religion, and of national security as religious, in Kathryn Lofton's sense of "enshrining certain commitments stronger than almost any other acts of social participation."[13] What can it mean, Lofton asks, "to divide the tourist from the pilgrim, or the celebrity from the god, or the corporation from the sect"?[14] Or, one could add, the

---

8. US Customs and Border Protection, *2022–2026 U.S. Border Patrol Strategy*, 5.
9. Preston, "Monsters Everywhere," 479.
10. For Christian theological critiques of the idolization of the US, see Cavanaugh, *Migrations of the Holy*; Hauerwas, *War and the American Difference*; and R. Hughes, *Christian America*.
11. The rapporteur, Agnes Callamard, found that "the targeting of General Soleimani, and the deaths of those accompanying him, constitute an arbitrary killing for which, under international human rights law, the US is responsible" (Mekay, "UN Report").
12. Coates, *Legalist Empire*; I. Hurd, *How to Do Things with International Law*.
13. Lofton, *Consuming Religion*, 6.
14. Lofton, *Consuming Religion*, 6.

CBP officer from the Inquisitor?[15] Perched precariously at the threshold between legality and extralegality, neither fish nor fowl, national security evokes a rich political-theological history of raison d'etat. It is often insulated from the reach of law. It enshrines commitments that are stronger than almost any other acts of social participation. It rides on a tidal wave of enthusiastic bipartisan appeal. Among government officials, political scientists, constitutional law experts, the media, the entertainment industry, law enforcement, the military and defense establishment, and the American public in general, to proselytize in the name of national security is not only admired but expected.

National security straddles the sacred and the secular. It does religious and political work. A decade ago, legal philosopher Paul Kahn noted that the state "is not the secular arrangement that it purports to be."[16] Today, scholars of political theory, religious studies, and political theology are experimenting with new vocabularies—less Eurocentric, less Christian-centric, and perhaps less patriarchal than their predecessors—to describe with more specificity the religious and spiritual, visceral and embodied, dimensions of modern statecraft.[17] In *Soldiers of God in a Secular World*, Sarah Shortall criticizes political theology for taking its cue from Carl Schmitt and replicating his "focus on the pre-modern theological origins of modern political concepts, treating theology as something that existed in the past but whose formal features have now been taken over by the political." Shortall challenges us to rethink "where the boundaries of the political lie."[18] Political theorist Jason Frank invokes the notion of the "democratic sublime" to refer to forms of collective political enchantment elicited by the emergence of popular sovereignty and democratic politics.[19] To describe the people as sublime, he explains, "decenters the subject in the face of vast powers that exceed it. The sublime elevates the subject beyond itself, to transcend itself."[20] National security decenters the subject in the face of vast powers that exceed it. It is a form of collective political enchantment that outruns the political-religious divide. It is more than a political domain that religious actors confront from the outside. It is religious and political from the inside out.

---

15. The comparison only appears far-fetched until one considers the extraordinary cruelty of the Trump administration's family separation policy. See Jordan, "U.S. Born Children."
16. Kahn, *Political Theology*, 18.
17. Manrique, "Foucault's Political Theologies," 77.
18. Shortall, *Soldiers of God in a Secular World*, 76. Shortall draws on the history of the 1930s and 1940s French *nouvelle théologie* "to rethink what constitutes a political act and where the boundaries of the political lie" (76).
19. Frank, *Democratic Sublime*.
20. Frank, "Democratic Sublime," lecture.

Banned at the Border

In September 2017, Presidential Proclamation 9645, known popularly as the "Muslim ban," closed US borders for four years to foreign nationals hailing from a set of primarily majority-Muslim countries. Legal challenges to the ban wound their way up to the Supreme Court, where the majority and both dissents agreed that President Trump's public statements in the lead-up to the ban exhibited anti-Muslim animus. That was not the legal question. Indeed, the majority subordinated anti-Muslim animus to national security and deferred to a tradition of extraordinary executive authority, known as plenary power, over US borders and immigration policy to uphold the ban by a 5–4 margin.[21] Elevating national security beyond its own powers and purview in deference to the plenary power of the executive, the court enshrined the ban with a sense of untouchability despite its discriminatory motivations and consequences.

Few doubted that the orders primarily targeted Muslims.[22] Within a week of his inauguration in January 2017, Donald Trump issued Executive Order 13769, "Protecting the Nation from Foreign Terrorist Entry into the United States" (EO-1),[23] suspending entry to the US for citizens of Iran, Iraq, Libya, Somalia, Sudan, Syria, and Yemen.[24] The order was immediately enjoined in the federal district courts.[25] On March 6, 2017, Trump rescinded EO-1 and

---

21. *Trump v. Hawaii.*
22. This is clear in the first ban's reference to "honor killings" as part of its justification, which locates the ban as part of a long history of relying on the defense of gender equality and women's rights to uphold imperial feminism in majority-Muslim contexts (Abu-Lughod, *Do Muslim Women Need Saving?*).
23. White House, "Protecting the Nation from Foreign Terrorist Entry into the United States."
24. "EO-1 discriminated against Muslims on its face. It contained express preferences for 'religious minorities' in the seven Muslim-majority countries targeted by the ban, establishing special benefits only available to individuals who were not Muslim. Section 5(b) authorized the Secretary of State 'to prioritize refugee claims made by individuals on the basis of religious-based persecution, provided that the religion of the individual is a minority religion in the individual's country of nationality.' Because the countries that were the subject of the ban were overwhelmingly Muslim, these religious minorities were non-Muslim people. Section 5(e) contained a similar explicit preference for individuals who were not Muslim from the seven banned countries" (*Zakzok v. Trump*, 9).
25. *Washington v. Trump*, No. C17–0141-JLR (enjoining sections 3(c), 5(a)-(c), and 5(e) of EO-1); *Darweesh v. Trump*, No. 17 CV 480 (prohibiting Government from removing individuals pursuant to EO-1); *Aziz v. Trump*, No. 1:17 CV 116 (granting preliminary injunction of portions of EO-1 on establishment clause grounds).

signed a new executive order (EO-2) bearing the same title and imposing nearly identical bans. EO-2 temporarily banned entry of immigrant and nonimmigrant nationals of six of the seven predominantly Muslim countries identified in EO-1: Iran, Libya, Somalia, Sudan, Syria, and Yemen. It too was enjoined before taking effect.[26] He then issued a third iteration, Proclamation 9645, "Enhancing Vetting Capabilities and Processes for Detecting Attempted Entry into the United States by Terrorists or Other Public-Safety Threats"[27] on September 24, 2017, and by October, a federal district court in Hawaii had granted a nationwide injunction barring its enforcement. On its face, Proclamation 9645 blocked citizens of banned countries from obtaining certain US immigrant and nonimmigrant visas by placing entry restrictions on the nationals of eight states who had information sharing systems that the president had deemed inadequate. In January 2020, the Trump administration extended the order to include Eritrea, Kyrgyzstan, Myanmar, Nigeria, Sudan, and Tanzania. Until its revocation by President Joseph Biden Jr. immediately following his inauguration in January 2021,[28] the ban restricted entry to the United States of citizens from Iran, Libya, Somalia, Syria, and Yemen[29] as well as Venezuela and North Korea; Chad was delisted in April 2018.[30]

The human costs faced by those subjected to the ban were significant, and continue to impact individuals from banned countries seeking entry to the United States despite the ban's formal revocation.[31] The ban reshaped US

---

26. *Int'l Refugee Assistance Project v. Trump*, 241 F. Supp. 3d 539; *Hawaii v. Trump*, 241 F. Supp. 3d 1119. The US Supreme Court granted certiorari and partially stayed the injunction. *Trump v. Int'l Refugee Assistance Project*, 137 S. Ct. EO-2's travel and refugee bans subsequently expired and the US Supreme Court dismissed the case as moot (*Trump v. Int'l Refuge Assistance Project*, 138 S. Ct.; *Zakzok v. Trump*, No. 17-cv-02969-TDC, 11–12).

27. White House, "Enhancing Vetting Capabilities and Processes for Detecting Attempted Entry into the United States by Terrorists or Other Public-Safety Threats."

28. Biden, "Proclamation on Ending Discriminatory Bans on Entry to the United States."

29. On the devastating effects of the ban on Yemeni and Yemeni American families, see Center for Constitutional Rights and Rule of Law Clinic at Yale Law School, "Window Dressing the Muslim Ban."

30. The third iteration of the ban set up a waiver process whose official criteria involved a three-part test assessing whether denying entry to an applicant would cause "undue hardship," if entry of the person would not pose a threat to the United States, and if it would be in the national interest to grant the waiver. The US granted waivers to only 6 percent of visa applicants subject to the ban during its first eleven months between December 8, 2017, and October 31, 2018, and data from December 2017 through April 2018 showed that waivers were issued in only 2 percent of visa applications filed by people subject to the ban. There is no application for the waiver; according to the State Department it considers applicants for it "automatically" (Torbati, "Exclusive").

31. According to the State Department, since December 2017 more than 79,700 visas had

vetting procedures and the refugee resettlement process.[32] It was not the first measure of its kind. In fact, Proclamation 9645 expanded the Obama administration's Visa Waiver Program Improvement and Terrorist Travel Prevention Act of 2015. That act disqualified the visa waiver for applicants from forty countries if they had made any trips to Iraq, Syria, Iran, Sudan, Libya, Somalia, or Yemen on a government assignment or military order. Every one of the seven countries targeted by the 2017 ban had been restricted in earlier changes to the visa waiver program under Obama.[33] That policy was particularly onerous for Shia Muslims, whose pilgrimages, *ziyarah*, or "visits," take them to Iran and Iraq.[34]

Rewritten to pass legal scrutiny by addressing the shortcomings of its predecessors, Proclamation 9645 enacted what lead counsel for the plaintiffs, Neal Katyal, described as "a ban on foreign nationals' entry to the country using a facially neutral policy that predominantly impacts Muslim-majority nations."[35] The AP described the ban's third iteration more colloquially as "a watered-down version intended to withstand legal scrutiny."[36] In June 2017, the Ninth Circuit Appeals Court upheld the Hawaii district court's decision to grant a preliminary injunction on statutory grounds, noting that the proclamation likely contravened two provisions of the Immigration and Nationality Act, 1182(f) and 1152(a)(1)(A).[37] Provision 1182(f) authorizes the president to "suspend the entry of all aliens or any class of aliens" (only if) he "finds" that their entry "would be detrimental to the interests of the United States"; 1152(a)(1)(A) provides that "no person shall . . . be discriminated against in the issuance of an immigrant visa because of the person's race, sex, nationality, place of birth, or place of residence." The Ninth Circuit did not reach the establishment clause claim in its deliberations. The lawsuit reached the Supreme Court in 2018 as *Trump v. Hawaii*, with the State of Hawaii, three individuals with foreign relatives affected by the entry suspension, and the Muslim Association of Hawaii as plaintiffs. They alleged that the primary purpose of the ban was religious animus, and that the president's stated concern about

---

been subject to the ban (as of 2020) (Kanno-Youngs, "Trump Administration Adds Six More Countries to Travel Ban").

32. Chishti and Bolter, "Travel Ban at Two."
33. Nixon, "U.S. Expands Restrictions on Visa-Waiver Program for Visitors."
34. Asma-Sadeque, "Shia Muslim Scholars Denied Entry into US Suspect Religious Bias."
35. Katyal, "*Trump v. Hawaii*."
36. LeMire, Mascaro, and Colvin, "White House Considering Dramatic Expansion of Travel Ban."
37. US Congress, United States Code: Immigration and Nationality.

vetting protocols and national security were mere pretexts for discriminating against Muslims. The ban, they argued, was unconstitutional.

The plaintiffs lost. On June 26, 2018, the Supreme Court reversed and remanded to the Ninth Circuit with instructions to dismiss the case as moot, ruling 5–4 in favor of the government. The majority set aside the question of anti-Muslim animus in deference to national security, citing the plenary power's granting of exceptional powers to the president in the domains of foreign and immigration policy. Plenary power is especially potent at the border. The two dissenting opinions, authored by Justices Stephen Breyer and Sonia Sotomayor, respectively, countered that the ban was motivated by anti-Muslim animus and was therefore unconstitutional. All the justices, however, treated national security as untouchable. Even the dissenters did not question the majority's recourse to the plenary power; instead, they contested the majority's argument that the ban was based on national security concerns rather than anti-Muslim animus. Both majority and dissenting arguments were grounded in the erroneous assumption that in the United States the practice of national security and anti-Muslim animus are separate and unrelated.

The Court's decision to uphold the ban sparked a vigorous backlash. Protestors rushed to local airports, signs in hand, eager to offer solidarity to those delayed or detained as they arrived, unsuspecting, at US borders. Immigration attorneys and translators mobilized on a pro bono basis to support those caught in the crosshairs. Protestors decried the rampant anti-Muslim rhetoric at the highest levels of the administration, citing as evidence Trump's notorious and oft-quoted 2015 campaign statement calling for a "total and complete shutdown of Muslims entering the United States until our country's representatives can figure out what is going on."[38] The Court stood accused of racism, xenophobia, Islamophobia, and of effectively reinstating (while also formally overturning) the infamous 1944 *Korematsu* decision.[39] *Korematsu* was a controversial Supreme Court decision sanctioning the internment of Japanese Americans during World War II and upholding an exclusion order based on what dissenting Justice Robert Jackson described as a "mere declaration" that it was "reasonably necessary from a military viewpoint."[40]

---

38. Johnson, "Trump Calls for 'Total and Complete Shutdown of Muslims Entering the United States.'"

39. Katyal, "*Trump v. Hawaii*." Sotomayor explains, "By blindly accepting the Government's misguided invitation to sanction a discriminatory policy motivated by animosity toward a disfavored group, all in the name of a superficial claim of national security, the Court redeploys the same dangerous logic underlying *Korematsu* and merely replaces one 'gravely wrong' decision with another" (*Trump v. Hawaii*, 754).

40. *Korematsu v. United States*, 245.

Even as the protestors focused their ire on the injustice of anti-Muslim discrimination, it was national security that did the legal heavy lifting in *Trump v. Hawaii*. The majority largely *agreed* with the ban's opponents that anti-Muslim animus was very likely a motivating factor in Proclamation 9645. That was not at issue. It was rather the Court's extreme deference to the president's interpretation of national, and specifically border, security that ultimately rendered dissenters' concerns about religious and racial discrimination impotent. By privileging national and border security and effectively setting it beyond the reach of the law, the majority ceded a form of sovereign immunity to the executive. With this grant of immunity, in the name of plenary power, the Court managed to avoid confronting the contentious history of racial and religious animus embedded in the lived practice of US national security since the founding of the country. The ban took its place in a long bipartisan history of sovereign immunity granted in the name of national security. It was, in an important sense, sacralized.

The Religious Work of National Security: Plenary Power and the Royal Remains

The plenary power as evoked in the context of immigration is a set of legal conventions positing that rules for entry and exit to the United States and the determination of the status of aliens are federal powers that are largely insulated from judicial review. Neal Katyal, attorney for the plaintiffs in *Trump v. Hawaii*, describes it as a "very-near-blind deference to the executive branch."[41] The plenary power doctrine was determinative in *Trump v. Hawaii*; for legal scholar Aziz Huq, the ruling "entrenches a basic division in the constitutional law of discrimination: Those challenging public order policies—in the [domains of] policing, immigration, and national security—will obtain no relief from the Courts."[42] Even if anti-Muslim animus had been a motivating factor in the ban, the majority interpreted the plenary power as requiring that assessing motivation for the orders fell outside the purview of the court's authority. In other words, the expression of religious animus does

---

41. Katyal, "*Trump v. Hawaii.*" Erin Delaney suggests that it is "rooted in the stark racism of the late-nineteenth century" ("Immigration in the Age of Trump"). See also Litman, "Unchecked Power Is Still Dangerous No Matter What the Court Says"; Heer, "Don't Just Impeach Trump. End the Imperial Presidency"; and Emmons, "Commander in Chief Trump Will Have Terrifying Powers. Thanks, Obama."

42. Huq, "Future of Constitutional Discrimination Law After *Hawai'i v. Trump.*"

not override the president's unchecked sovereign authority to regulate the border in defense of national security. Where does that authority come from?

The political theology of sovereignty is discussed at length by historians Ernst Kantorowicz and Eric Santner. Though focusing on different time periods, medieval and modern, both authors are interested in the "immortal aspect" of the king's second body—that is, the immutable and eternal body politic which outlives the king's natural body. In the wake of the transition from divinely sanctioned to popular sovereignty, Santner explains, this "second body" has sought but never found a settled resting place in modern democracies. How can "the people" incarnate the excarnated principle of sovereignty?[43] How to put forth a body that would incarnate the now empty place of the king?[44] In the rocky and incomplete transition to popular sovereignty, suggests Santner, "the bodies of the citizens of modern nation-states take on a surplus element, one that actually challenges the entire ideology of disenchantment and secularization and that introduces into immanence an excess that it cannot fully close in upon."[45] This surplus of immanence, this excess, both blesses and plagues the citizens of modern democratic nation-states: "The charms, the stuff of enchantment, not only have never disappeared from the modern world but . . . insinuate themselves even more powerfully into the fabric of everyday life." Now that the king has lost his head, this argument goes, the substance of what had been his responsibility—the "real stuff" of fantasy, the flesh—circulates in the social space under new names. It is a rocky transition. As T. J. Clark puts it and as cited in the epigraph to this chapter, "putting the People in place of the King cannot ultimately be done. The forms of the social outrun their various incarnations."[46]

Santner's notion of "the flesh" attempts to capture one of these forms of the social. The flesh evokes a visceral, embodied aspect of the remainder of the king's second body conceived as "that 'thing' in the king that cannot be contained in his natural life and body but only—and indeed *only barely*—in a second one."[47] While persuasively tracking what he describes as the "vicissitudes of the flesh" in literature, philosophy, painting, and political thought, Santner is less attentive to political practice. If, as he claims, we can "grasp crucial features of modernity" by "following the transformation of the complex tensions belonging to the political theology of royal sovereignty into the

---

43. Santner, *Royal Remains*, 92.
44. Santner, *Royal Remains*, 92.
45. Santner, *Royal Remains*, 98.
46. Clark, *Farewell to an Idea*, 47, cited in Santner, *Royal Remains*, 92.
47. Santner, *Royal Remains*, 12.

biopolitical pressures of popular sovereignty," then we also need to consider how such pressures are managed, contained, or elided in contemporary practices of sovereignty. In the legal response to the Muslim ban, plenary power offers itself as a vessel to cope with and contain the unbearable excess of responsibility that is vested in the people as the ultimate bearers of popular sovereignty. It is tasked with bearing the residual "too-muchness" of this investment. It is an outlet for biopolitical pressures. It can thus be considered part of the inheritance, or haunting, of the migratory "royal remains" lingering in the experience of popular sovereignty. The plenary power doctrine does religious work, then, not only by elevating presidential authority above the reach of the law but also by providing an outlet for the material excess that the ideology of disenchantment and secularization "cannot fully close in upon." This is the terrain that Santner describes as the material or carnal dimensions of sovereignty.

Extending Kantorowicz's account of the king's two bodies in medieval and early modern Europe, Santner emphasizes that the dynamics of sovereignty associated with those earlier contexts "do not simply disappear from the space of politics once the body of the king is no longer available as the primary incarnation of principle and functions of sovereignty; rather, these structures and dynamics . . . 'migrate' into a new location that thereby assumes a turbulent and disorienting semiotic density."[48] Among these structures and dynamics is Kantorowicz's notion of *arcana imperii*, or "secrets of state." This concept has migrated variously into national security, including security clearances, the absolute power of border agents, and the immigration plenary power doctrine, among other locations. Plenary power can be considered amid these and other extreme modes of deference to national security as contemporary expressions of the political theology of sovereignty.

In his essay "Mysteries of State: An Absolutist Concept and Its Late Medieval Origins," Kantorowicz anticipated aspects of his magnum opus, *The King's Two Bodies*.[49] As Miguel Vatter explains, "Mysteries of State" specifically explores the transference of the notion of *arcana ecclesiae*, or "the mysteries of the church," from church to state. This transfer gave rise to the notion of *arcana imperii*, which became a privileged marker of state sovereignty, as Vatter explains: "The origins of "reason of state" are to be located within a providential scheme in that the state becomes itself providential, "l'Etat providence." It is not that Hegel's Rechtsstaat "secularizes" a theological providential scheme as Löwith believes, as if the state carries out God's providence,

48. Santner, *Royal Remains*, 33.
49. Vatter, *Divine Democracy*.

but rather the state internalizes providence, so that it becomes governmental or administrative for the sake of the People."[50] The plenary power doctrine inherited aspects of the *arcana imperii*. Santner alludes to this in a discussion of Hannah Arendt's account of the contradictions inscribed into the constitution of the modern nation-state: "The very entity that was to guarantee the rule of law thus occupied a domain above or beyond the law; the seemingly *given* or naturally *particular*—the nation or the People—was in some sense 'higher' than or above the universal—the law as constituted."[51] This unwieldy element in the political theology of popular sovereignty, above and also within the law, circulates through practices of national security, including in the plenary power.[52]

Although Congress attempted to check the recourse to plenary power following the Watergate scandal, the framework that was put in place during the 1970s to constrain presidential conduct has eroded, and the invocation of plenary power has since run rampant.[53] Since 9/11, both political parties have supported virtually unlimited presidential powers in the name of national security; Peter Shane describes our era as one of "aggressive presidentialism."[54] In *Trump v. Hawaii*, the majority reinforced this pattern of extreme deference to the executive by effectively removing the Court from the equation in deference to the demands of raison d'etat. In the words of Chief Justice Roberts, "by its terms, §1182(f) exudes deference to the President in every clause." The scope and depth of executive authority in immigration and national security overshadowed the administration's vitriolic anti-Muslim rhetoric and action. Roberts declared, "At the heart of their case is a series of statements by the President and his advisers both during the campaign and since the President assumed office. The issue, however, is not whether to denounce the President's statements, but the significance of those statements in reviewing a Presidential directive, neutral on its face, addressing a matter within the core of executive responsibility. In doing so, the Court must consider not only the statements of a particular President, but also the authority of the Presidency itself."[55]

---

50. Vatter, *Divine Democracy*, 148, 172.

51. Santner, *Royal Remains*, 51–52.

52. On earlier vestiges of a monarchical past in early nineteenth-century American history, and specifically how white Protestants reenacted the authority of a seemingly rejected king through sovereign rituals, see Logan, *Awkward Rituals*.

53. Rudalevige, *New Imperial Presidency*.

54. Shane, *Madison's Nightmare*.

55. *Trump v. Hawaii*, 670.

National security and plenary power also rode roughshod over the constitutional protection of the right to religious freedom. In a seething indictment of the majority, Justice Sonia Sotomayor, joined by Justice Ruth Bader Ginsburg, admonished the majority for abandoning the United States' exceptional constitutional commitment to religious liberty. Sotomayor accused the majority of brushing aside the fact that the Proclamation clearly "runs afoul of the Establishment Clause's guarantee of religious neutrality," noting that "a reasonable observer would conclude that the Proclamation was motivated by anti-Muslim animus."[56] Like other critics of the ban, however, Sotomayor reinforced the mutual exclusivity of national security and religious animus, observing that "the Proclamation was driven primarily by anti-Muslim animus, rather than by the Government's asserted national-security justifications."[57] She concludes, almost wistfully, that the First Amendment "stands as a bulwark against official religious prejudice and embodies our Nation's deep commitment to religious plurality and tolerance."[58]

The majority decision confirmed that the First Amendment does not and never has stood as a bulwark against religious and racial prejudice. US legal and religious historians have documented the patchy and selective privileging of majoritarian understandings of religion by the court.[59] Legal construals of national security have always been shot through with cultural assumptions about what it means to be moderately religious, properly American, and truly free. The law, in the US and in other jurisdictions, conscripts and institutionalizes particular understandings of religion, freedom, and moderation via mechanisms ostensibly aimed at preserving and promoting national security.[60] As suggested in chapter 1's discussion of religious asylum, legal and public constructs of religion shift and modulate over time to accommodate certain practices and sanction others, depending on the social and political exigencies of the moment. For the FBI in the 1950s, for instance, religion among Black people was required to be politically quiescent to count as religion. "Once a group began to articulate a position that ran counter to the dominant politics of the Bureau," explains Edward Curtis, "it stopped being religion proper."[61] In the 1970s, the group MOVE, a Philadelphia-based community

56. *Trump v. Hawaii*, Sotomayor, 729, 728.
57. *Trump v. Hawaii*, Sotomayor, 737.
58. *Trump v. Hawaii*, Sotomayor, 751.
59. Lloyd, *Land Is Kin*; McCrary, *Sincerely Held*; Sullivan, *Church State Corporation*; Weiner and Dubler, *Religion, Law, USA*; Sullivan, *Impossibility of Religious Freedom*.
60. Hussin, "New Global Politics of Religion," 94.
61. Curtis, "Black Muslim Scare," 92. See also Johnson and Weitzman, *FBI and Religion*, and the 2021 biographical crime drama *Judas and the Black Messiah*.

that followed the teachings of John Africa, was denied First Amendment protection in a free exercise case involving Frank Africa's request for a special diet while in prison. The court ruled that MOVE lacked the proper qualities to define the community as a religion deserving of First Amendment protection. As Winnifred Sullivan wrote, "the Court put up a mirror to Africa in which only white religion could be seen."[62] In the early 2000s, in a precursor to Proclamation 9645, George W. Bush's Special Registration program created what Moustafa Bayoumi describes as a "legal geography of suspicion" that drew "a burdensome zone around Muslim-majority countries."[63] Special Registration "reinscribed, through a legal mechanism, the cultural assumption that a terrorist is foreign-born, an alien in the United States, and a Muslim, and that all Muslim men who fit this profile are potential terrorists."[64] The same presumptions underlie the leaked CBP memo discussed at the beginning of this chapter.

That Trump's anti-Muslim animus motivated Proclamation 9645 was as clear as it was legal.[65] The law is poorly equipped to remedy these situations because it is, as we have seen, in part responsible for creating them.[66] US national security policy and practice incorporate and, at times, formalize discriminatory racial and religious hierarchies in the name of order, freedom, security, and public health. Bordering practices amplify them. Documenting the creation of what she calls "borders of belonging" in the long nineteenth century, Barbara Young Welke challenges progressivist narratives of a gradual expansion of rights: "From the outset, personhood, citizenship, and nation were imagined in abled, racialized, and gendered terms: able white men alone were fully embodied legal persons, they were America's 'first citizens,' they were the nation. Able white male legal authority . . . created law's borders; it defined belonging."[67]

Pressures of Popular Sovereignty

While extreme deference to the executive served as *legal* justification for the Supreme Court's decision to uphold the ban, plenary power was rarely, if

---

62. Sullivan, *Church State Corporation*, 151. On MOVE's theology see Evans, *MOVE*.
63. Bayoumi, "Racing Religion," 277.
64. Bayoumi, "Racing Religion," 275.
65. Manuel, "Executive Authority to Exclude Aliens: In Brief."
66. Ngai, *Impossible Subjects*; see also Welke, *Law and the Borders of Belonging*, and Zolberg, *Nation by Design*.
67. Welke, *Law and the Borders of Belonging*, 2.

ever, invoked in public debates either in defense of or in opposition to the ban. For the ban's proponents, the pressures of popular sovereignty instead coalesced around an argument in favor of legal exceptionalism in the name of self-preservation. The biopolitical pressures of popular sovereignty circulated for these populations in the form of a visceral fear of a racial and religious other. Supporters of the ban drew on popular fears of Muslims as an existential threat to Americans and the United States. In their eyes, national security demanded both anti-Muslim animus *and* the suspension of the law in the name of protecting innocent Americans. This was not discrimination, they reasoned, but self-preservation. Though recourse to plenary power rendered discrimination legal in the eyes of the court's majority, the designation of Muslims as a threat to national security galvanized affective support for the ban and mobilized its political constituency. The ban resonated with a white population that identified itself as the "real" American nation. Legal national security exceptionalism thus worked in tandem with a racialized image of popular sovereignty to uphold state-sponsored discrimination.

The stage had been set for the representation of Muslims and majority-Muslim countries as existential threats to Americans long before the Trump administration rose to power. Nadia Marzouki's *Islam: An American Religion*, which appeared in English in 2017, the same year as the first iteration of the ban, identified a movement in US politics in the early 2010s among Tea Party partisans and affiliates that she described as "far from the liberal approach to constitutional democracy, which affirms equal rights for all and extends legal protections to religious minorities to shelter them from the chance winds of popular will."[68] In this movement, which came to full political fruition after 2016, the sovereign people, "united and already constituted, may at any moment decide to suspend the guaranteed constitutional protections when faced with a threatening minority that is not part of 'the people' "[69]—precisely what occurred in the case of the ban. The administration and its supporters tapped into fear of a threatening minority to defend draconian border policies that would allegedly protect Americans against a minority that was, they claimed, not legitimately part of "the people." Contrary to the arguments of the ban's opponents, then, including dissenters on and off the court who insisted that the order was *not* about national security but rather anti-Muslim animus,[70] for

---

68. Marzouki, *Islam*, 110.

69. Marzouki, *Islam*, 110. On the intersections of politicized Christianities and populist movements in Germany, France, and the US, see Viefhues-Bailey, *No Separation*.

70. "The Proclamation repeatedly asserts a national security rationale. Yet the Proclamation does not further national security interests" (*Zakzok v. Trump*, 15). And, "The Proclamation, like

proponents the ban *was* about national security. It was national security that demanded collective action at the border against a "threatening minority that is not part of 'the people.'"[71] National security would define and defend a visceral sense of popular sovereignty in which an endangered majority had no choice but to fight for itself using any means at hand. This image of popular sovereignty was then sutured to the exercise of unchecked sovereign authority via the plenary power. Liberal opposition to the ban cast in the language of rights appeared anemic when faced with a population that, perhaps evoking the "undifferentiated flesh" of the nation contemplated by Santner, self-identified *as* the American nation. The liberal focus on rights and proceduralism struggled to stand up to the visceral nationalism and drive for (border) exceptionalism embodied in the defense of the "will of the people."[72] As Hannah Strømmen has argued in reference to far-right Bible use in Europe, and which also applies to the travel ban, it is crucial to study these dynamics "not as an aberration from the norm but as part of norms that become unquestioned."[73]

The racial and religious animus of the ban's proponents contributed to a draconian practice of national security that was shielded from legal and political accountability through the court's elevation of institutionalized discrimination above the reach of the law in the name of plenary power. This allowed for the targeting of Muslims and those perceived to be Muslim as a threatening minority while shielding the policy from (formal) accusations of religious animus. This double move was crucial to the ban's (temporary) success. The justices proclaimed repeatedly that the proclamation was motivated either by religious animus, in which case it was likely illegal, *or* by national security, in which case it was likely permissible. Chief Justice Roberts put it baldly: the order is "expressly premised on legitimate purposes . . . The text says nothing about religion."[74] The dissent countered that the ban is motivated not by national security but religious animus, thus rendering it unconstitutional. Yet

---

EO-1 and EO-2, is driven by religious animus and not reasonably related to legitimate national security considerations" (14).

71. The FBI identifies "nine persistent extremist movements" in the United States: "white supremacy, black identities, militia, sovereign citizens, anarchists, abortion, animal rights, environmental rights, and Puerto Rican Nationalism" (Winter and Weinberger, "FBI's New U.S. Terrorist Threat").

72. This also explains the limited resonance of liberal opposition to the targeting of suspect populations in governmental programs to "counter violent extremism" (Mauleón, "It's Time to Put CVE to Bed") and surveil "Black identity extremists" (Beydoun and Hansford, "F.B.I.'s Dangerous Crackdown").

73. Strømmen, *Bibles of the Far Right*, 3.

74. *Trump v. Hawaii*, Roberts, 34.

the majority, Justice Kennedy's concurrence, and Justice Breyer's dissent all concurred that the ban rests (legitimately) on either a national security justification or (illegitimately) on anti-Muslim bias. While critics argued that national security was irrelevant to the ban,[75] for proponents the ban was anything but irrelevant to national security. It was in the name of national security that anti-Muslim animus received political cover and legal validation. The ban vindicated the views of Americans for whom national security and anti-Muslim animus are indissociable while inoculating national security as construed by the executive from legal scrutiny, if not from political criticism.

The airport protestors were not easily silenced. Their insistence however that government-sponsored discrimination at the border is un-American was for the most part aspirational. As was their claim that religious freedom protections would save the day. American border history is replete with examples of institutionalized legal discrimination enshrining racial, religious, gender, and other forms of favoritism in the name of public health, safety, and security. I mentioned the *Korematsu* decision earlier. The Indian Removal Act of 1830, signed by President Andrew Jackson and considered an early example of state-sponsored ethnic cleansing, provided "for an exchange of lands with the Native Americans residing in any of the states or territories, and for their removal west of the river Mississippi."[76] It cleared the way for the gradual dispossession of the Tohono O'odham Nation, discussed in the first interlude, as a result of President Grant's executive order of July 1, 1874, creating the Papago Indian Reserve. The Chinese Exclusion Act of 1882 suspended Chinese immigration for ten years and declared the Chinese ineligible for naturalization. The Johnson-Reed Act of 1924 limited the number of immigrants permitted to enter the United States through a national origins quota that provided immigration visas to 2 percent of the total number of people of each nationality in the United States as of the 1890 national census, excluding immigrants from Asia altogether.[77] In a series of rulings between 1901 and 1922, known as the Insular Cases, the Supreme Court limited the extension

---

75. Critics of the ban reinforced the false binary between religious animus and national security. Faiza Patel of the Brennan Center's Liberty and National Security Program stated, "The Muslim ban has been in effect for over a year, upheld by the Supreme Court despite overwhelming evidence that it was motivated by religious animus not national security" ("Fight against Trump's Muslim Ban Isn't Over"). Another opponent declared its irrelevance to national security "obvious" because since 2001 not a single fatal attack had been carried out by immigrants from the countries that it targeted (Singh, "Expanded Travel Ban.").

76. Indian Removal Act (1830).

77. US National Archives and Records Administration, Chinese Exclusion Act (1882); US Department of State, Immigration Act of 1924.

of constitutional rights to individuals in several recently acquired US territories. These decisions, which addressed the status of the inhabitants of the US territories of the Philippines, Puerto Rico, and Guam, all acquired during the Spanish-American War, found that full constitutional protection of rights does not automatically extend (ex proprio vigore) to all territories under US control. The Insular Cases formalized what Michael Graziano describes as a legal gradient of US citizenship,[78] across what Daniel Immerwahr refers to as "the greater United States."[79] The cases upended the illusion of a clean domestic/foreign distinction, divided governed populations on civilizational terms, and hardened racial and religious hierarchies that were mapped onto degrees of perceived Americanness. Far from an exception, Proclamation 9645 is part of a long history of legal discrimination in border enforcement.

78. The reimagining of US citizenship by those opposed to the Fourteenth Amendment resulted in the classification "citizen" being applied to African Americans without imbuing them with the same legal or theological protections afforded their white counterparts (Graziano, "Race, the Law, and Religion in America," 9–11).

79. Immerwahr, "Greater United States."

INTERLUDE II

Unbordered
Land without Law

> Limbo (noun): a borrowing from Latin; ablative singular of *limbus* (used *technically* in lit. sense of "border" or "edge";): A region supposed to exist on the border of Hell as the abode of the just who died before Christ's coming, and of unbaptized infants; used *gen.* for: Hell, Hades. *Obsolete*; Prison, confinement, durance; Any unfavourable place or condition, likened to Limbo; *esp.* a condition of neglect or oblivion to which persons or things are consigned when regarded as outworn, useless, or absurd; a type of anti-submarine mortar.
>
> OXFORD ENGLISH DICTIONARY[1]

In 2015, a colleague and I organized a public reading of *Guantánamo Diary*, Mohamedou Ould Slahi's autobiographical account of his fourteen-year imprisonment by the US military at Guantánamo Bay.[2] Members of the Northwestern community signed up for fifteen-minute time slots to read a few pages of the book aloud. We started at 8:00 a.m. on a Saturday morning. It wasn't easy. The Defense Department had heavily redacted the only version of the book that was available at the time, and censored lines appeared with a thick black line through them.[3] When readers encountered redacted lines, they would ring a tabletop service bell, one ring for each line censored. The bell rang at regular intervals, and at times, it continued to ring repeatedly for several minutes, denoting redacted sentences, paragraphs, or several consecutive pages. It took nine hours to get through the book. As a reader, I found it hard to resist imagining what was behind those black lines: torture techniques, names or other identifying markers of the torturers, information

---

1. Other meanings of *limbo* when used as a noun include "a dance originating in Trinidad and Tobago in which the dancer bends backwards to pass under a horizontal bar" and "a South African name for a kind of coarse calico."

2. Slahi, *Guantánamo Diary*. There are other autobiographical accounts by detainees; see, for example, Adayfi, *Don't Forget Us Here*.

3. In 2017, Back Bay Books released a restored edition of *Guantánamo Diary* that includes previously censored material. In 2021, a restored media tie-in edition, *The Mauritanian*, was published to coincide with the release of a film based on Slahi's memoir. *The Mauritanian* is directed by Kevin MacDonald and stars Tahar Rahim, Jodie Foster, Shailene Woodley, and Benedict Cumberbatch.

about clandestine US detention centers, or "black sites." A handful of people were present for most of the day, coming in and out, listening quietly, scattered about the room in small groups. Some were visibly upset; a few were crying. People comforted one another. My turn to read came over the lunch hour, and at one point, I found myself alone for several minutes, ringing the service bell and reading Slahi's words aloud to a large empty room with high ceilings and an ornate balcony.

The US held Mohamedou Ould Slahi without charge from 2002 to 2016. Was he inside or outside the United States during his detention? Is there a US border surrounding Naval Station Guantánamo Bay, or is the naval station part of the State of Cuba? Where *is* Naval Station Guantánamo Bay?

Naval Station Guantánamo Bay (NSGB, or GTMO, as the military refers to it)[4] is a forty-five-square-mile American base located on the coast of Guantánamo Bay in southeastern Cuba. GTMO is the oldest overseas American Navy base in the world and the only base located in a country with which the US does not maintain diplomatic relations. With its rugged terrain and "dry, sun-blasted hills, where cactus and scrub clung to outcroppings of barren rock," historian Paul Kramer explains, the Spanish left this corner of the Caribbean largely alone for centuries, and it sat suspended in the colonial margins.[5] Kramer describes it as "no state's domain, a haven for pirates and slaves escaping both Cuba and Haiti, only a hundred miles across the Windward Passage at its nearest point. For them, Guantánamo had meant something like freedom."[6]

In the early summer of 1898, US warships sailed into Guantánamo Bay under the command of Bowman H. McCalla to fight alongside Cuban rebels against the Spanish fleet in a nine-day battle of the Spanish-American War.[7] The war ended with the signing of the Treaty of Paris in December 1898. As a result, Spain lost control of what remained of its overseas empire and the US inherited most of Spain's possessions. Congress had no intention of relinquishing control of Cuban affairs. When the Cuban Constitutional Convention began deliberations in July 1900, it was notified that the US

---

4. "Sailors boasting of their access to Cuban women jested that it was not called 'git' mo' for nothing" (Kramer, "Useful Corner").

5. Kramer, "Useful Corner."

6. Kramer, "Useful Corner." On the history of Guantánamo Bay and its role in the imperial designs of British sailor Lawrence Washington, half brother of future US president George Washington, see Hansen, *Guantánamo: An American History*.

7. Tensions had been mounting for some time, culminating in the sinking of the USS *Maine* in Havana Harbor on February 15, 1898. The US declared war against Spain on April 25 and the Spaniards surrendered on July 16, 1898.

Congress intended to attach an amendment to the Cuban Constitution.[8] In 1901, US Secretary of War Elihu Root drafted a set of articles as guidelines for future US-Cuba relations that became known as the Platt Amendment, after its sponsor, Senator Orville Platt of Connecticut. The Cubans reluctantly included the Platt Amendment in the constitution, and Cuba became a virtual US protectorate. In 1903, the amendment was incorporated into a permanent treaty between the two countries (figure 6) that according to the National Archives, and in an interesting turn of phrase given the argument of this book, "permitted extensive U.S. involvement in Cuban international and domestic affairs for the enforcement of Cuban independence."

The relevant articles from the treaty are articles 3 and 7:

> III. That the government of Cuba consents that the United States may exercise the right to intervene for the preservation of Cuban independence, the maintenance of a government adequate for the protection of life, property, and individual liberty, and for discharging the obligations with respect to Cuba imposed by the treaty of Paris on the United States, now to be assumed and undertaken by the government of Cuba.

> VII. That to enable the United States to maintain the independence of Cuba, and to protect the people thereof, as well as for its own defense, the government of Cuba will sell or lease to the United States lands necessary for coaling or naval stations at certain specified points to be agreed upon with the President of the United States.

The US conditioned Cuban independence on constitutional provisions that would allow the US Navy to occupy the area "for the time required." Kramer describes the American taking of Guantánamo as "gunboat tenancy." The Cubans themselves "opposed the Platt Amendment in speech, pamphlet, and mass protest; Juan Gualberto Gómez, a delegate and a former general, charged that it would transform Cubans into a 'vassal people.'"[9] Nevertheless, under pressure, a divided convention adopted it.

---

8. This paragraph draws on the document as found at US National Archives and Records Administration, Platt Amendment (1903).

9. The terms reflect US strong-arm tactics at the time of Cuban independence: "While Cuba's constitutional convention gathered in late 1900 and early 1901, Secretary of War Elihu Root listed provisions that 'the people of Cuba should desire' for their constitution; these included granting the United States the right to intervene freely in Cuban affairs and access to land for naval bases. These demands went into the Platt Amendment, passed by the U.S. Senate on March 1, 1901, and submitted to the convention for adoption; the United States would withdraw its forces from the island only after the delegates incorporated it into their constitution" (Kramer, "Useful Corner").

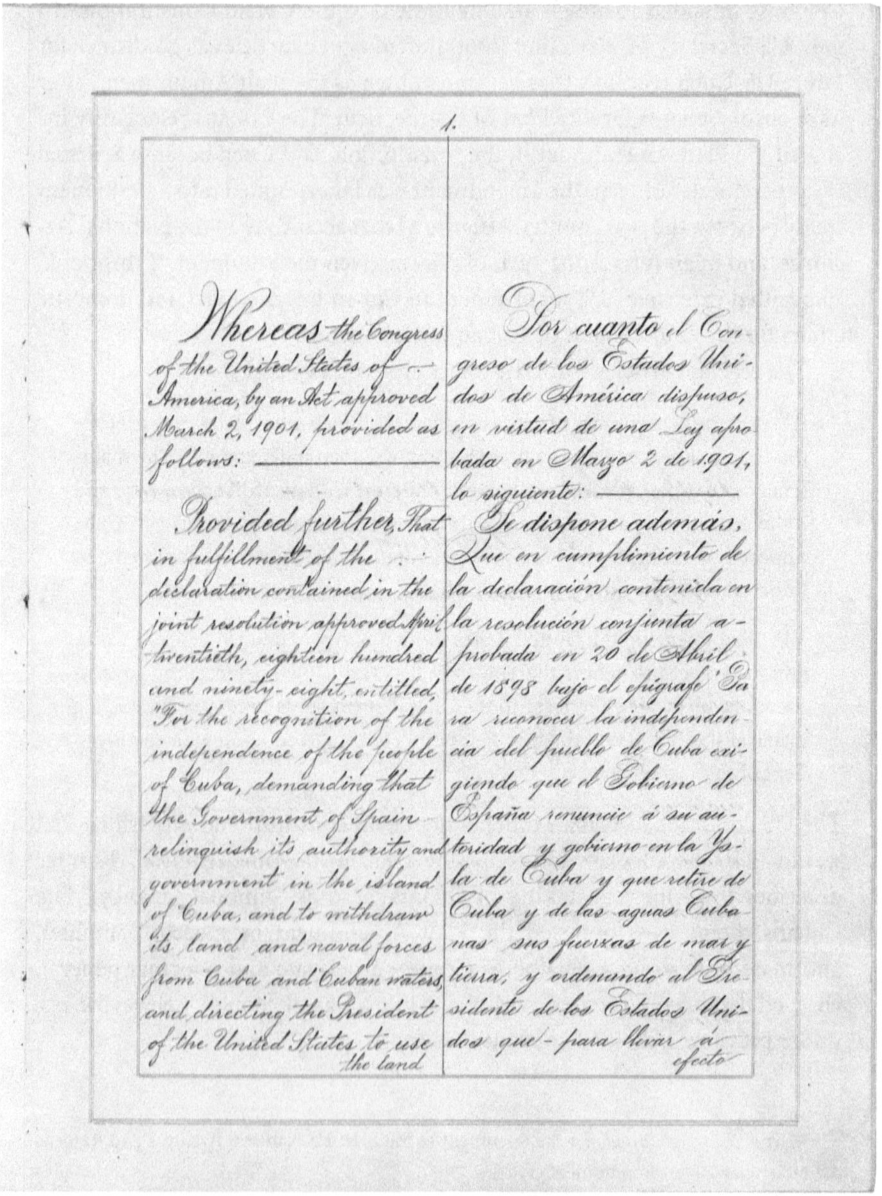

1.

Whereas the Congress of the United States of America, by an Act approved March 2, 1901, provided as follows:

Provided further, That in fulfillment of the declaration contained in the joint resolution approved April twentieth, eighteen hundred and ninety-eight, entitled, "For the recognition of the independence of the people of Cuba, demanding that the Government of Spain relinquish its authority and government in the island of Cuba, and to withdraw its land and naval forces from Cuba and Cuban waters, and directing the President of the United States to use the land

Por cuanto el Congreso de los Estados Unidos de América dispuso, en virtud de una Ley aprobada en Mayo 2 de 1901, lo siguiente:

Se dispone además, Que en cumplimiento de la declaración contenida en la resolución conjunta aprobada en 20 de Abril de 1898 bajo el epígrafe "Para reconocer la independencia del pueblo de Cuba exigiendo que el Gobierno de España renuncie á su autoridad y gobierno en la Ysla de Cuba y que retire de Cuba y de las aguas Cubanas sus fuerzas de mar y tierra; y ordenando al Presidente de los Estados Unidos que — para llevar á efecto

FIGURE 6. Platt Amendment. Treaty between the United States and the Republic of Cuba Embodying the Provisions Defining Their Future Relations as Contained in the Act of Congress. Approved March 2, 1901; May 22, 1903; Perfected Treaties, 1778–1945; General Records of the United States.
Source: https://www.archives.gov/milestone-documents/platt-amendment.

Article VII of the Platt Amendment authorized the United States to lease or buy lands for the purpose of establishing naval bases and coaling stations in Cuba. Rent on the US lease of Guantánamo as a coaling station and naval base was set at $2,000 per year beginning in 1903, paid in gold. In 1934, Cuba extended the lease and doubled the rent, with payment set at $4,085 to match the value in gold in dollars, an amount that remains unchanged to this day. The Platt Amendment was used repeatedly to legitimize US interventions in Cuban affairs in 1906, 1912, 1917, and 1920. By 1934, however, widespread public criticism led to its repeal as part of Franklin D. Roosevelt's Good Neighbor policy. The US retained its lease on Guantánamo Bay, however, and continues to pay rent to Cuba via the Swiss embassy, which represents US interests in Cuba. After coming to power in 1959, Fidel Castro famously refused to cash the US checks because he saw the base as an illegitimate tool of the counterrevolution. Yet under the terms of the lease, the United States retained "complete jurisdiction and control" over the southern portion of the bay, even as Cuba retained "ultimate sovereignty."[10] The only way to end this arrangement would be through US withdrawal or bilateral agreement; the Cubans are not permitted to withdraw unilaterally from the lease.

The base at Guantánamo has proven useful to the US military over the years. US invasions and occupations of Haiti in 1915 and the Dominican Republic in 1916 were launched from Guantánamo. In World War II, the base became a major US strategic asset, and by the mid-1940s Guantánamo was the second-busiest port in the Western Hemisphere, after New York, and was used by the navy to repel Nazi U-boats.[11] According to the navy's official history, "the base's activities have at times included fleet training, ship repair, refueling and resupply, migrant operations, regional humanitarian relief and disaster assistance, search and rescue support, and detention operations. Today it remains the forward, ready, and irreplaceable US sea power platform in the Caribbean, giving decision makers unique options across the range of military and interagency operations."[12]

Although the United States does not claim sovereignty over Guantánamo, it does maintain "complete jurisdiction and total control" over GTMO.[13]

10. Miroff, "Why the U.S. Base at Cuba's Guantanamo Bay Is Probably Doomed."
11. There is a rich literature on the history of the base. For a military history, see Schwab, *Guantánamo, USA*; on the lives of ordinary people working on the base, see Lipman, *Guantanamo*.
12. US Navy, "History."
13. The lease reads as follows: "While on the one hand the United States recognizes the continuance of the ultimate sovereignty of the Republic of Cuba over the above described areas of land and water, on the other hand the Republic of Cuba consents that during the period of the occupation by the United States of said areas under the terms of this agreement the United States

Whether there is or is not a border between the US and Cuba on the island is difficult to say. Kramer describes the boundaries of the base as "indefinite." GTMO is, in many ways, beyond borders. The Cubans have nonetheless remained adamantly opposed to the US presence at Guantánamo since the Revolution of 1959. In 1958, wary of infiltrators, the navy put up a perimeter fence enclosing the base that still stands today. By late 1960, as relations between the US and Cuba deteriorated, a minefield containing over fifty thousand mines and spread over seven hundred acres divided the two parts of the island; at the time, it was the largest minefield in the world.[14] Following the 1961 Bay of Pigs debacle—a failed military attack organized by Cuban exiles working with the CIA to oust Fidel Castro—the Cubans added a barrier of uncrossable Maya cacti that became known as the "Cactus Curtain." In 1964, Cuban foreign minister Raúl Roa shut off water and electricity to the base after the US Coast Guard intercepted four Cuban fishing boats in American waters in the Florida Keys and imprisoned the thirty-six crewmen in a Florida jail. The water supply was never restored, and since then, GTMO has had its own supply. Land mines, concertina wire, and thickets of cacti continue to mark a divide between the base and the remainder of the island. There is no access to the base from within Cuba.

And yet, there were nineteen Cubans living on the base as of 2021. They are known as special category residents (SCRs) and are considered US citizens.[15] Most are elderly. In 2021, Ellie Kaufman profiled one of them: Noel West, then eighty-nine, a retired clerk living on the base across the street from the Cuban Community Center. West and the other SCRs receive home health care and other support from the base. West began working on the base in 1955 as a clerk ordering fuel for planes and vehicles, commuting daily to his home in the small Cuban town of Guaro. An avid baseball fan and umpire, in February 1964 he chose to stay late for a game and spent the night at the Cuban barracks on the base. The next day, his next-door neighbor from Guaro called to warn him that Cuban soldiers had been searching for him, possibly

---

shall exercise complete jurisdiction and control over and within said areas with the right to acquire (under conditions to be hereafter agreed upon by the two Governments) for the public purposes of the United States any land or other property therein by purchase or by exercise of eminent domain with full compensation to the owners thereof" (Yale Law School, "Agreement between the United States and Cuba").

14. Kramer, "Useful Corner." US officials claim to have removed thousands of these land mines and replaced them with lights and motion sensors (Kaufman, "Cubans Still Reside on Guantánamo Bay Base").

15. Kaufman, "Cubans Still Reside on Guantánamo Bay Base."

because he had mentioned to a friend that he was not a fan of the Castro regime. He never returned to Cuba, staying on the base even after retiring in 2011 after fifty-five years of service.

Beginning in 1991, and for the next decade, GTMO served as a detention camp and processing center for Haitian refugees fleeing the aftermath of the 1991 coup against Jean-Bertrand Aristide. By July 1991, nearly 37,000 people were confined on the base in tent cities surrounded by barbed wire. The US authorities determined that 26,000 of these refugees failed to qualify for political asylum (they were not "screened in"). Another 267 Haitian refugees did receive asylum but were denied entry under a 1987 law blocking immigrants who were HIV positive.[16] The HIV travel ban remained in place for twenty-two years, closing the US border to anyone testing positive for the virus. At GTMO, the Haitians testing HIV positive who had been "screened in" were held in a separate detention area, Camp Bulkeley, where detainees burned tents, hurled rocks at their captors, and engaged in a hunger strike to protest their mistreatment.[17]

In 1993, in sympathy with the protestors, a team of students and professors from Yale Law School filed suit on behalf of the detainees on the grounds that they should enjoy constitutional protections because the base is legally under the "complete jurisdiction and control of the United States."[18] The government responded that the base was "a military base in a foreign country" and "not United States territory." Detainees being held at the base, the government

---

16. The ban added HIV to a list of excludable conditions, prohibiting all infected persons from obtaining US tourist visas or permanent residence status unless they obtained a special waiver. One of Andrew Sullivan's readers explains: "The Reagan White House pressured the Public Health Service to include HIV on the list of excludable conditions in 1987. They did. There were protests about that, as the vast majority of public health experts believed that only active tuberculosis belonged on the list. In response, and in order to make sure the PHS' decision was protected, Sen. Jesse Helms (R-NC) authored an amendment in the Senate to put HIV on the list statutorily. The Senate adopted it on a voice vote, with Democrats thinking that because HIV was already on the list, the amendment was redundant" (Daily Dish, "HIV Travel Ban").

17. Kramer, "Useful Corner." Winston and Beckwith explain that "regulations restricting entrance to the United States based on medical diagnoses were first combined into one formal body of law in the INA in 1952. The medical reasons barring entrance to the United States included mental health disorders, substance abuse, epilepsy, tuberculosis, leprosy, or 'any dangerous contagious disease'" (US Congress, Immigration and Nationality Act of 1952, Sec. 212[a]; Winston and Beckwith, "Impact of Removing the Immigration Ban," 709–11).

18. *Sale v. Haitian Ctrs. Council, Inc.* This episode served as the basis of Brandt Goldstein's book *Storming the Court*, featuring Harold Hongju Koh's role as the professor at the helm of the student civil case. Koh later became a leading human rights lawyer and legal adviser to the US State Department as well as dean of Yale Law School.

argued, were "outside the United States and therefore they have no judicially cognizable rights in United States courts." Judge Sterling Johnson Jr. responded: "You're saying, if I hear you correctly, that assuming that they [government officials] are arbitrary and capricious and even cruel, that the courts would have no jurisdiction because the conduct did not occur on U.S. soil? That's what you're saying?" The government's lawyers concurred.

In June 1993, the US lost the case, shut down the camp, and transferred the remaining detainees to the United States. Judge Johnson ruled that due process guarantees under the Constitution extended to the base, including the right to a lawyer, to proper medical care, and to not be held indefinitely without charge. Aside from those protections, however, according to Kramer, Johnson also told an INS attorney that the state possessed unchecked authority "to take, kidnap, or abscond, whatever you want to call it, take a group and put them into a compound, whether you call it a humanitarian camp or a prison, keep them there indefinitely while there has been no charge leveled against them and there is no light at the end of the tunnel."[19] In any event, Johnson's ruling granting even limited rights to the detainees made the Clinton administration uneasy. "The Clinton Justice Department . . . pursued a deal with the Haitians' legal team: the Administration would comply with Johnson's orders and drop an appeal; in return, Johnson's decision would be vacated from the record. The advocates agreed, fearing that an appeal would prolong their clients' detention and might, ultimately, succeed. According to one official, the Clinton Administration wanted to preserve 'maximum flexibility.'"[20]

The camps were back up a year later, and by 1994, they were sheltering 16,800 Haitians and 22,000 Cubans in tent cities on the runway. When the Cuban American Bar Association, Cuban refugee associations, and the Haitian Refugee Center sued on behalf of the refugees, they were initially granted injunctive relief by the US District Court for the Southern District of Florida. On appeal, the Eleventh Circuit Court of Appeals overturned that decision and, using another nickname for the base, "firmly situated Gitmo outside the United States and constitutional limits on state power."[21] The appeals court rejected the argument that leased military bases abroad "which continue under the sovereignty of foreign nations" were functionally equivalent to land borders or ports of entry, noting that laws mandating asylum hearings "bind the government only when the refugees are at or within the borders of the

19. Cited in Kramer, "Useful Corner."
20. Kramer, "Useful Corner."
21. *Cuban American Bar Ass'n, Inc. v. Christopher.*

United States."[22] As Kramer concludes, "apparently, Gitmo was not at or within these borders." The Cubans were released into the United States the next year, and the Haitians were involuntarily returned to Haiti. The base stood.

In 2002, GTMO opened its doors to its latest ignominious chapter as a US prison camp for unlawful combatants who, according to then secretary of defense Donald Rumsfeld, "do not have any rights under the Geneva Conventions."[23] In December 2001, Justice Department deputy assistant attorney general John Yoo prepared the legal ground for indefinite detentions at GTMO with a memo to Pentagon general counsel William Haynes by making the case that Guantánamo is "foreign territory, not subject to U.S. sovereignty,"[24] as part of an effort to make it less likely that US courts would grant GTMO detainees habeas corpus rights.[25] On January 11, 2002, the first twenty captives arrived. As of August 2024, thirty detainees remain imprisoned at the base.[26] A total of 779 men have been detained there since 2002.[27] The youngest prisoner was thirteen years old and the oldest was eighty-nine. A total of twenty-one children have been imprisoned at GTMO. The youngest death by apparent suicide was Yasser Talal Al Zahrani, who was captured at age sixteen and died at age twenty-one. 86 percent of detainees were reportedly turned over to Coalition Forces in response to a bounty offer. US taxpayers spend $13 million annually on each detainee, for a total of over

---

22. Wessler elaborates: "People intercepted at sea, even in U.S. waters, have fewer rights than those who come by land. 'Asylum does not apply at sea,' a Coast Guard spokesman told me. Even people who are fleeing violence, rape and death, who on land would be likely to pass an initial asylum screening, are routinely sent back to the countries they've fled. To try to get through, people held on Coast Guard ships have occasionally taken to harming themselves—swallowing sharp objects, stabbing themselves with smuggled knives—in the hope that they'll be rushed to emergency rooms on land where they can try to claim asylum" (Wessler, "Border Where Different Rules Apply").

23. Cited in Whitlock, "Legal Limbo."

24. Philbin, memorandum for Haynes, 5.

25. Yoo contrasts Guantánamo with the Philippines cases arising out of World War II, describing the latter as an "insular possession" until 1946 "and not a mere U.S. leasehold interest" (Philbin, memorandum for Haynes, 5).

26. *New York Times*, "Guantánamo Docket." For more information on detainees held as of this writing and represented by the Center for Constitutional Rights's (CCR) "GITMO bar," see the CCR website's page on Guantánamo. CCR describes the base as "a prison of aging men in rapidly deteriorating physical and mental health for whom continued detention could be a death sentence."

27. The information in this paragraph is taken from an ACLU interactive graphic, "Guantánamo by the Numbers."

$540 million per year. GTMO is the most expensive detention program in the world.[28]

GTMO's most well-known detainee, Mohamedou Ould Slahi, wrote *Guantánamo Diary* in 2005. A heavily redacted version was published a decade later. Though a judge ordered his release in 2010, noting that the US government had not proven that Slahi was a member of Al Qaeda at the time of capture, he was held for six more years at GTMO. Slahi was released from the prison camp on October 17, 2016, returning to his native Mauritania. The US never filed charges. *Guantánamo Diary* offers a firsthand account of Slahi's detention and torture at Guantánamo and other US government sites, including Bagram Air Force Base in Afghanistan and a Jordanian black site. He recounts the harsh interrogations and torture at the hands of the Americans, including being force-fed seawater, sexually molested, subjected to a mock execution and repeatedly beaten, kicked and smashed across the face.[29] Slahi was subjected to "extended interrogation techniques" including a mock rendition orchestrated by the notorious former Chicago Police Department homicide detective Richard Zuley, known for obtaining confessions from suspects through torture.[30] Zuley, posing as "Captain Collins," used torture techniques honed in Chicago on the city's poor and nonwhite citizens.[31] In his account, Slahi expresses compassion for his guards while calmly conveying the extraordinary efforts required to survive daily life in the camp.[32]

Though often seen as an exception among US prisons, GTMO is closer to the norm when it comes to US carceral practices in sovereign gray zones. In fact, according to Darryl Li, a legal anthropologist and expert on these zones, GTMO stands in for a vast array of long-standing US practices involving the use of client states and partners to carry out the US government's dirty work.

28. Rosenberg, "Cost of Running Guantánamo Bay: $13 Million Per Prisoner."

29. Slahi, *Guantánamo Diary*, 250-263. See also the book's website at http://guantanamodiary.com.

30. For details on the mock rendition as recounted by Slahi's captors and Slahi himself, including the recruitment of Arabic-speaking American linguists on the base who were told to play Jordanian and Egyptian secret police and to scare Slahi, see Koenig and Chivvis, *Serial*, season 4: Guantánamo, episode 2, "The Special Project."

31. "Dick Zuley's history as a military interrogator at Guantánamo and a police interrogator in Chicago . . . suggests a continuum between police abuses in urban America and the wartime detention scandals that continue to do persistent damage to the international reputation of the United States" (Ackerman, "Bad Lieutenant").

32. For the results of the US government's self-study of the torture of detainees at GTMO and elsewhere during this period, see the US Senate, *Senate Intelligence Committee Report on Torture*, known as the *Torture Report*.

Li describes the base as "one node in a global network of carceral circulation" and clarifies that although new transfers had slowed by 2003 (and stopped entirely by 2008), "it was the older pattern of arms-length detention through local clients that has endured and continued to sustain GWOT [global war on terror]."[33] Sites run in and by the United Arab Emirates and by Kurds in eastern Syria have "enabled the US to warehouse, interrogate, and dispose of thousands of more people with far greater flexibility and far less scrutiny than at GTMO."[34] Jothie Rajah describes these US actions not as an absence of law but rather as an instance of a "necropolitical law" unconstrained by state borders: "the apparent zero point generated by war-on-terror exceptionalism has scripted a law invested in the discounting of some lives so that others may live, that is, necropolitical law."[35]

State borders around GTMO and other black sites are not unwittingly or intentionally unbordered. They are purposefully ambiguous. Like the asylum claimants described in chapter 1, detainees are intentionally held in limbo. As described in the epigraph, the term *limbo* refers not only to prison or confinement but to "any unfavourable place or condition, likened to Limbo; *esp.* a condition of neglect or oblivion to which persons or things are consigned when regarded as outworn, useless, or absurd."

There have been attempts to extract the island's detainees from limbo. One strategy is to legally normalize them by effectively instating a border and bringing them US constitutional protections. An example is the case of Lakhdar Boumediene, an Algerian-born citizen of Bosnia and Herzegovina who was the subject of a 2008 Supreme Court decision, *Boumediene v. Bush*, that ruled that detainees were *not* barred from seeking habeas corpus or invoking the suspension clause merely because they had been designated as enemy combatants or held at Guantánamo.[36] Boumediene's detention began in 2002, when he and five other Algerians were seized by Bosnian police because US intelligence officers suspected their involvement in a plot to attack the US embassy in Bosnia.[37] The US government classified the men as enemy combatants in the war on terror and imprisoned them at GTMO. Boumediene filed a petition for a writ of habeas corpus (lit: "that you have a body," a

---

33. Li, *Universal Enemy*, 198–99.
34. Li, *Universal Enemy*, 200.
35. Rajah conjoins Achille Mbembe's notion of necropolitics to a capacious understanding of law as "that which orders society by expressing norms, legitimacy, and authority, both through state law and through ostensibly nonlegal texts, images, and events" (*Discounting Life*, 8–9).
36. *Boumediene v. Bush*. See also Boumediene, "My Guantánamo Nightmare."
37. This account of the case is from *Boumediene v. Bush*.

form of legal recourse against unlawful detention), alleging violations of the Constitution's due process clause, various statutes and treaties, the common law, and international law. The district court granted the government's motion to have his claims dismissed on the ground that Boumediene, as an alien detained at an overseas military base, had no right to a habeas petition. The US Court of Appeals for the DC Circuit affirmed the dismissal. The Supreme Court then reversed this decision in *Rasul v. Bush*,[38] holding that the habeas statute extends to noncitizen detainees at Guantánamo. The Court ruled that foreign nationals held at GTMO could petition federal courts for writs of habeas corpus to review the legality of their detention.

In 2006, two years after the ruling in *Rasul v. Bush*, Congress passed the Military Commissions Act of 2006 (MCA), which eliminated federal courts' jurisdiction to hear habeas applications from detainees who had been designated as enemy combatants according to procedures established in the Detainee Treatment Act of 2005. When Boumediene's case was appealed to the DC Circuit for the second time, he and the other detainees argued that the MCA did not apply to their petitions and that even if it did, it was unconstitutional under the suspension clause. The suspension clause reads, "The Privilege of the Writ of Habeas Corpus shall not be suspended, unless when in Cases of Rebellion or Invasion the public Safety may require it." The DC Circuit ruled in favor of the government on both points, citing language in the MCA applying the law to "all cases, without exception" that pertain to aspects of detention. One of the purposes of the MCA, according to this court's interpretation, was to overrule the Supreme Court's opinion in *Hamdan v. Rumsfeld*, which had allowed petitions like Boumediene's to go forward. The circuit court thus held that the suspension clause only protects the writ of habeas corpus as it existed in 1789 and that the writ would not have been understood in 1789 to apply to an overseas military base leased from a foreign government. The court held further that constitutional rights do not apply to aliens outside of the United States and *that the leased military base in Cuba does not qualify as inside the geographic borders of the United States.*

The Supreme Court took the case and ruled that if the 2006 MCA were considered valid, its legislative history would require that the detainees' cases be dismissed. However, they also found that because the procedures laid out in the Detainee Treatment Act are not adequate substitutes for the habeas writ, the MCA operates as an unconstitutional suspension of that writ. The detainees therefore were *not* barred from seeking habeas or from invoking

---

38. *Rasul v. Bush.* The Court's 6–3 ruling reversed a DC circuit court decision that held that the judiciary has no jurisdiction to hear any petitions from foreign nationals held in Guantánamo.

the suspension clause merely because they had been designated as enemy combatants or were being held at Guantánamo. With the Court's reversal of the DC Circuit's ruling, the border starts to come into focus. It appears as a faint dotted line that provisionally and tentatively encircles the detainees at Guantánamo and perhaps other "enemy combatants" at other sites as well.

Some years ago, J. Kameron Carter asked, "What might a politico-theological examination of the political look like if it were carried out from the vantage of those constructed as 'enemy,' or . . . from the vantage of those deemed 'abject,' " understood as "that which is neither wholly a part of the body nor wholly apart from it"?[39] Though he was not writing about Guantánamo, he could have been. The "abject," Carter explained, "is neither friend (subject) nor enemy (object). The abject exists in the zone between life (full citizenship) and death (the enemy as one who must be killed)." The category of *abject*, or *homo sacer* (sacred man, in Roman law), includes detainees at Guantánamo and others in border limbo. It includes Jews in mid-twentieth-century Europe and the figure of the slave, "modernity's abject par excellence,"[40] all of whom have been forced outside the bounds of humanity. It includes Palestinians in Gaza. It includes those banned by Proclamation 9645 and many unsuccessful asylum applicants. Giorgio Agamben described the figure of the homo sacer as a person who could be killed with impunity. The homo sacer is excluded from recognition or protection. His existence consists of "bare life," stripped of dignity or rights.[41]

Borders are brokers of abjection. They are at these times purposefully hard to see. The abject exists in a border zone between life and death. Neither in nor out. Neither domestic nor foreign. Neither wholly part of the body nor wholly apart from it. He is in limbo, alongside other liminal subjects cast into the margins and peripheries of the modern state system. Borders participate in the state of exception, conceived by Agamben as "the legal form of what cannot have legal form." In *Downes v. Bidwell*, one of the Insular

---

39. Carter, "Politics of the Atonement." Examples of abject substances are tears, saliva, feces, and urine.

40. "Such abject sites are those of the slave ship, the transatlantic slave routes, the slave plantation, the black body itself, or what Fanon called 'the lived experience of the black' (Carter, "Politics of the Atonement").

41. Agamben, *Homo Sacer*. On the application to the Patriot Act of 2001 and GTMO, see Franks, "Guantanamo Forever," 264–65. "What is new about the USA Patriot Act is that it radically erased any legal status of the individual, thus producing a legally unnamable and unclassifiable being" (Agamben, "State of Emergency as a Paradigm of Government"). Agamben defines the state of exception as "the original structure in which law encompasses living beings by means of its own suspension."

Cases discussed in chapter 2, Justice Melville Weston Fuller concluded, "If an organized and settled province of another sovereignty is acquired by the United States," Congress would retain the power "to keep it, like a disembodied shade."[42] The Court famously ruled that "Porto Rico belongs to the United States, but . . . is not a part of the United States."[43]

GTMO too belongs to the United States but is not part of it. So do other unbordered, partially bordered, or shadow US possessions, such as Native American reservations. Beyond the lower forty-eight, the US claims Puerto Rico and the US Virgin Islands and, in the Pacific, Guam, the Commonwealth of the Northern Mariana Islands, American Samoa, the Federated States of Micronesia, the Republic of the Marshall Islands, and the Republic of Palau. These liminal jurisdictions are kept by the United States, in the words of Justice Fuller, "like a disembodied shade, in an intermediate state of ambiguous existence for an indefinite period."[44] They are the America that Americans forget.[45] They are "places that are home, but not."[46]

In August 2022, the navy unveiled a $3 million modern postal facility to serve a community at Guantánamo "that has sent and received mail out of a converted horse stable since 1952" (figure 7). Mail service, the announcement read, "is vital to this unique island community, where military transport a few times a week is the only means of travel to the United States."[47] So GTMO is not the United States. Or is it?

---

42. *Downes v. Bidwell*, the leading case in a series of early twentieth-century Supreme Court decisions known as the Insular Cases, was brought to recover moneys exacted by the collector of customs at the port of New York as import duties on two shipments of fruit from ports in Puerto Rico to the port of New York in November 1900. The majority found that "Porto Rico belongs to the United States, but nevertheless, and notwithstanding the act of Congress, is not a part of the United States subject to the provisions of the Constitution in respect of the levy of taxes, duties, imposts, and excises."

43. For a subtle retelling of the colonial lives of property in the transition from Spanish to American establishment in Puerto Rico through an analysis of property disputes between the Catholic Church and the new government that "re-created the juridical personality of the Catholic Church in Puerto Rico while it streamlined the concordats between Spain and the Vatican into American corporate law," see Maldonado Rivera, "Perfect, Irrevocable Gift," 38.

44. Justice Fuller, dissenting in *Downes v. Bidwell* on the status of Puerto Rico.

45. Topol, "America That Americans Forget."

46. Whitt, "Empire, Religion, and the United States Military," 120.

47. Steele, "Where Mail Is the Lifeblood." The navy boasts of "an exceptional quality of life for our residents" while admitting that "living and working at NSGB is not, however, for everyone. There is no access to the rest of Cuba" (US Navy, "Installation Guide").

FIGURE 7. US Post Office, NSGB, 2022.
Photo by Jeannette Steele. *Source*: Office of Corporate Communications, NAVSUP FLC Jacksonville, August 23, 2022, https://cnrse.cnic.navy.mil/News/News-Detail/Article/3136670/where-mail-is-the-life blood-naval-station-guantanamo-bay-to-open-new-post-office/.

CHAPTER 3

Suspending AmericaIsrael

> The flag of Israel, with a Star of David between two horizontal stripes all in a dark sky-blue on a white background, is the perfect standard to display at your home or church to show your love and support for the land and its people.
> HOLY LAND EXPERIENCE THEME PARK ONLINE STORE, Orlando

> The sacred can exceed its designated space.
> MATEO TAUSSIG-RUBBO, "Sacred Property: Searching for Value in the Rubble of 9/11"

Our American Israel

In an attempt to capture the sensibility of the Left Behind series, historian Amy Kaplan wrote that "Israel is to other nations what believers are to unbelievers."[1] Left Behind was a smash hit multimedia apocalyptic fiction series in which heroic white Americans and converted conservative Israelis "unite as natural allies" in futuristic action-thrillers "about the seven years of Tribulation between the Rapture and the Second Coming," forming "a mighty guerrilla group bent on saving souls for Christ and thwarting the tyranny of the Antichrist on the road to Armageddon."[2]

Discussions of the religious foundations of the US alliance with the State of Israel often invoke premillennial dispensationalist theology, the driving force behind the Left Behind series.[3] Many scholars have written of the

---

1. Kaplan, *Our American Israel*, 227. She continues, "When demonic locusts swarm over the earth gnawing at human flesh, they miraculously pass over anyone who has become a believer, just as when rivers turn to blood all over the world, water runs clear in the Holy Land" (227).

2. Kaplan, *Our American Israel*, 225–26. The Left Behind book series was published between 1995 and 2007.

3. Premillennial dispensationalism gained popularity in the late nineteenth and early twentieth centuries, initially among biblical literalists. Hillary Kaell describes it as follows: "The Jewish covenant is still intact and human history is divided into a series of seven covenants, called 'dispensations.' When the Jews rejected Christ, their dispensation ended and they were put aside until God deals with them again. At this point, the 'End Times' will (or have begun to) unfold in a series of steps: Christians will be raptured (lifted bodily) into heaven, the Antichrist will

contributions of Christian Zionism—a global movement in which Christians' support for the return of Jews to Israel is seen as aligning with biblical prophecy and as necessary for Jesus to return to earth—to the rise of a muscular white evangelicalism in the United States and to US support for Israel.[4] Dispensationalist theology, Christian and Jewish Zionisms, and Jewish American support for a Jewish state in the Middle East are all seen as essential to the "special relationship." Commentators attribute US political support for the State of Israel to the influence of a powerful global military-industrial complex, the horrors of the Nazi Holocaust, historical affinities between the two nations' political institutions, a joint preoccupation with the threat posed by Iran and its regional proxies, and the political economy of oil.[5]

All these factors are important. The affective intensity of many Americans' commitment to the State of Israel, however, including many US politicians and pundits, suggests a relationship that is more complex, capacious, and conflicted than can be accounted for by conventional religious and political explanations. This chapter explores the long-range cultural and affective foundations of the US commitment to Israel and its embeddedness in the religious politics of American borders and borderlessness.[6] It is the compulsory *suspension* of the US border, rather than its enforcement, that takes precedence in this case. At certain moments, in a quixotic expression of universal sovereignty and boundless collective self-realization, the US-Israel border fades and becomes nearly imperceptible. It is as if it were soluble. I refer to this supra-national figure as "AmericaIsrael." At the height of its expression, the idea of Israel and the idea of America operate in concert as transcendent, interwoven expressions of redemption.[7] Both countries are imagined as Holy Lands. Both are home to chosen peoples.[8] Tapping into shared fantasies of

---

appear, and the seven-year battle between good and evil will commence. Once the godly forces win, Jesus will rule for a millennium of peace until the Antichrist returns and is defeated once more, culminating in the resurrection of the dead, followed by the final judgment. Modern Jews, whom dispensationalists understood to be the direct descendants of biblical Israelites, still have a role to play in ushering in the return of Christ, since a significant number of the 'remnant' must fulfill prophecy by returning to the land God promised them (e.g. Isaiah 10:20–23)" (*Walking Where Jesus Walked*, 38–39). See also Boyer, *When Time Shall Be No More*.

4. See, for example, Kobes de Mez, *Jesus and John Wayne*. On Christian Zionism see Hummel, *Covenant Brothers*.

5. On the latter, see Vitalis, *Oilcraft*.

6. Related dynamics apply in other contexts; on the Australian-Israeli relationship, see, for example, Burla and Lawrence, *Australia & Israel*.

7. Thanks to Geoff Levey.

8. Contrasting public and political understandings of "chosenness" in the US and Canada, Benjamin Berger describes the boundless ethical horizon of US chosenness in terms that resonate

unmatched military prowess, Holy Land fascination on both sides of the Atlantic, and myths of civilizational advancement defined by a capacity to fend off retrogressive and shadowy threats on all sides, AmericaIsrael celebrates the frontier mentalities of both nations.[9] It evokes the Promised Land and the Golden Land. It elides US military debacles from Wounded Knee to Vietnam to Afghanistan.[10] It turns a blind eye to the Sabra and Shatila massacre, the brutalities of Israeli occupation, and the violence and death in Gaza. It evokes a miracle in the desert reflecting not only Zionist religious and political ideals but a broad spectrum of American nationalist fantasies, many of which predate the foundation of the State of Israel. It is a masculinist and patriarchal figure.[11] Though AmericaIsrael has played a crucial role in US electoral, racial, and religious politics for the past seventy-five years, the American impetus to transcend borders is much older. A redemptive vision of US borderlessness predates the State of Israel. Resonating with American exceptionalists and nationalists of all stripes, AmericaIsrael has deep roots in US history, as shown by Amy Kaplan, Melani McAlister, Burke Long and other historians.[12]

If AmericaIsrael invokes an easy, heroic overcoming of borders, a gesture that recurs throughout this book, it also evokes another recurring theme: an inability or unwillingness to incorporate an inassimilable racial and religious other. AmericaIsrael is, paradoxically, also a story of anti-Jewish racism. It invokes a complex combination of attraction, repulsion, fascination, hierarchy, and dominance. It is about borders that ban and pin people into categories and territories. It partakes in what Carter, citing W. E. B. DuBois and Sylvia Wynter, describes as the "religion of Whiteness," referring not primarily to skin color but to a privileged inscription in the history of power and a form of presence in the world.[13] AmericaIsrael conjures an impossible attempt to assimilate an unassimilable sacred-abject-Jew within a majority Christian

---

with this chapter. He suggests that it gives Americans the confidence to "traverse other particularities" ("Two Theologies of Chosenness").

9. For an example see Kirk, "Christian Zionist Cowboys."

10. See chapter 4, "The Good Fight: Israel after Vietnam, 1972–1980," in McAlister, *Epic Encounters*. On the frontier, see Grandin, *End of the Myth*.

11. Shapira for example finds that for the Minutemen, "their presence on the border serves as a moral bulwark against the pollution and contamination of the body politics—the nation is a family, and the Minutemen are the patriarchs" (*Waiting for José*, 118).

12. McAlister, *Epic Encounters*; Kaplan, *Our American Israel*; Long, *Imagining the Holy Land*.

13. Carter elaborates on this notion of Whiteness as "the will to rule the earth . . . a planetary structure of governance driven by Christian liberal humanism with western man at its apex." He asks, "How does imagination of the Jews relate to this Western civilizing humanism that organizes the planet?" ("Jews and the Religion of Whiteness").

nation. This narrative surfaces frequently in American politics; white power protestors in Charlottesville chanted "Jews will not replace us." Numerous Republicans, according to an exposé in the *New York Times*, "echo antisemitic tropes despite declaring support for Israel."[14] AmericaIsrael quietly reproduces a subterranean strain of anti-Semitism that conceives of Jewish lives as bare (un-Christian) lives. This is part of its affective intensity and its danger.

The sway of AmericaIsrael as a religio-political consensus marginalizes dissenting formations of Jewish politics. Some travel under the headings of non-, post-, or anti-Zionisms. The latter often oppose not only certain Zionist interpretations of Judaism but also US foreign policy toward Israel, insofar as the latter collapses the distinction between Judaism and the Jewish state. These dissenting expressions are not part of the "official religion" promoted jointly by the US and Israeli governments. They do not map onto the liberal-conservative political spectrum and, at times, they elude a simple opposition between Jewish and non-Jewish. As such, they harbor a potential to generate new possibilities for thought and action. My turn toward these nonstatist and dissenting perspectives in US politics toward the end of the chapter emphasizes the heterogeneous, polyvalent, and essentially disputed character of the religious in relation to US-Israel relations, and in foreign policy more broadly.

Visualizing AmericaIsrael

At times, AmericaIsrael speaks loudly. Former New York governor Andrew Cuomo announced, "If you boycott Israel, New York will boycott you."[15] Texas governor Greg Abbott proclaimed that "anti-Israel policies are anti-Texas policies."[16] Julia Bacha, director of the 2021 documentary film *Boycott*, noted that "in America today, if you want to keep your public contract, you need to sign a pledge promising that you're not going to boycott Israel."[17] AmericaIsrael is also expressed visually. The hybrid AmericanIsraeli flag reproduced in figure 8, described by the vendor as an "American Jewish flag," is an expression of this hybrid sovereignty.

---

14. Yourish et al., "How Republicans Echo Antisemitic Tropes."

15. In 2023, disgraced former governor Cuomo announced plans to establish a new pro-Israel organization, "Progressives for Israel," targeting Democrats following his resignation from the governorship in 2021 after a report from New York attorney general Letitia James found that he had sexually harassed at least eleven women while in office.

16. Abbott, "Anti-Israel Policies are Anti-Texas Policies."

17. Cited in Mansour, "Laws Preventing Boycotts of Israel."

FIGURE 8. "American Jewish Flag."
Source: https://www.flagwix.com/products/american-jewish-flag-trl1163f/.

The flag suggests that Israel is lodged behind and within the United States. They are inseparable. If you mess with the US, Israel has its back and vice versa. Another flag for sale on the same website presented the US and Israeli flags as sewn together by doves, suggesting that peace ensues when the two nations act as one.[18] These flags are visual representations of AmericaIsrael. They contribute to normalizing the US recognition of Jerusalem as the capital of Israel, the relocation of the US embassy from Tel Aviv to Jerusalem, Israeli sovereignty over the Golan Heights, and the joint US/Israeli assassination of Iranian general Qassim Soleimani.[19] They make US and Israeli cooperation in military, antiterrorism, and border enforcement seem natural.[20] The Minutemen, for example, describe their fence on the border in southern Arizona

---

18. A third flag that became available after October 7, 2023, shows a US flag bleeding into an Israeli flag, with large block letters superimposed on the joint flag, reading, "Sanctuary Home for Jews Fleeing Democrats" (Flagwix.com, accessed March 13, 2024).

19. As Trump told Israeli journalist Barak Ravid in 2021, former Israeli prime minister Netanyahu was "willing to fight Iran to the last American soldier" (Ravid, "Ex-Israeli Intel Chief").

20. On the pooling of border security and enforcement technologies among US and Israeli security specialists, see Miller, *Empire of Borders*, part two, "The Global Pacification Industry on the Palestine-Mexican Border," 57–88. On US attempts to imitate the IDF after 9/11, see Kaplan, *Our American Israel*, chap. 7, "Homeland Insecurities." On the globalization of the Israeli security complex, see Grassiani, "Commercialised Occupation Skills."

as "Israeli style."²¹ In 2021, the US House of Representatives voted 420–9 to fund Israel's Iron Dome missile defense system at a price of $1 billion. On the same day, the House approved a $740 billion annual defense bill, adding roughly $24 billion more to the Pentagon's budget than had been requested by the Biden administration.²² In 2023, Biden requested an additional $14 billion from Congress in security assistance to Israel to fund the war in Gaza, beyond the $3.8 billion that the US provides annually.

The flags do more than symbolize a close alliance between states. The flag pictured in figure 8 is called an American *Jewish* flag rather than an American Israeli flag. It conflates Judaism and the Israeli State. It implies that the State of Israel represents Jewish communities in general rather than only Israeli citizens. It posits the Israeli State as the proper and natural repository of Judaism and Jewishness. This erases non-Jewish Israelis. It erases Palestinians and Jewish anti-Zionists. What it entails for Jewish Americans and other diasporic Jews is left unsaid: Do they *really* belong in the US? Or are they crypto-Israelis? The flag subtly establishes a certain distance between an (implicitly non-Jewish, Christian) America and a (Jewish, Israeli) non-America. America's role in maintaining this equation is to defend Judaism, Jews, Jewish democracy, and Israel, albeit from a certain distance, even as Americans also draw inspiration from Israel's strength and perseverance.²³ Sociologist Harel Shapira, camped out with the Minutemen in southern Arizona, encountered the force of this narrative in a revealing interaction with a Minuteman named Earl, who was initially suspicious of Shapira and his origins:

"Anyway, what kind of a name is Harel? I mean that doesn't sound too good either."

I realized I should start thinking about a different research topic. I explained to Earl, grudgingly, that I was born in Israel and moved to America as a child.

Earl removed his gun from his holster. My heart dropped. Laying the gun across the palm of his hand, he told me he uses a Glock-17, "just like they do in Israel."

I listened warily. He told me his holster was made in Israel. "I figured if it's from Israel you know it's gonna be quality . . . You know there is no group of people I have more respect for than the Israelis." Incapacitated by this bizarre turn of events, I could only nod when Earl asked me if the pants I was wearing were from the "IDF" (Israeli Defense Forces). He recognized the stitching

21. Shapira, *Waiting for José*, 104.
22. Edmondson, "House Approves $1 Billion."
23. Thanks to Melani McAlister.

from those he saw in the military supply catalogues. "Us military people know these things," he proudly noted, "we study these things." Regaining my composure, I explained that the pants belonged to my father. Before I could continue, while pointing to the empty desert that lay ahead of us, Earl announced: "This is our Gaza."[24]

AmericaIsrael and the Ambivalence of Borders

The ambivalence of borders is by now familiar to readers of this book. Long before the creation of the State of Israel, the United States had refused to contain itself within the limits of the sovereign state system. The American project is defined by a willingness to challenge, if not to outright defy, domestic and international political (b)orders in the name of something greater. In these moments of expansive grandeur, such as during the settlement of the American West in the name of manifest destiny,[25] in the construction of the Panama Canal, at the height of what historians refer to as the Pax Americana in the post–World War II era, and in grandiose aspirations to bring democracy to the Middle East and elsewhere, the United States anoints itself as the indispensable nation.[26] It considers itself the author of international rules, but not their subject.[27] US borders follow suit. In the case of AmericaIsrael, border ambivalence or selective solubility is an ordinary aspect of US politics and (foreign) policy. The boundary between "domestic" and "foreign" is perennially difficult to distinguish.[28] Border ambivalence with Israel is part of a larger collective national drama in which the American people work to realize something greater than themselves.

Unlike in the case of the flags, however, AmericaIsrael is so deeply embedded in the US experience that it can be hard to see.[29] It blends into the background. Neither fully secular nor fully religious, it distinguishes itself from the specificities of religion.[30] If, as Robert Yelle suggests, religion involves a dynamic interplay between a normative order and a drive to transcend it,[31]

---

24. Shapira, *Waiting for José*, 12.
25. See Stephanson, *Manifest Destiny*.
26. Coined in 1996 by journalist Sidney Blumenthal and historian James Chace, the phrase is associated with former secretary of state Madeleine Albright. For another example, see Lieber, *Indispensable Nation*.
27. I. Hurd, *How to Do Things with International Law*.
28. See the essays in Hurd and Sullivan, *At Home and Abroad*.
29. Bender, "America Is Hard to See."
30. The phrase is Bender's, "America Is Hard to See."
31. Yelle, *Sovereignty and the Sacred*, 8.

SUSPENDING 99

the normative order is the sovereign state system and the drive to transcend it the gravitational pull of American sovereign exceptionalism. AmericaIsrael pulls the US toward the latter. It embodies the productive interplay between sovereign territoriality and an American aspiration to collective transcendence of the international order. Performing AmericaIsrael is an exercise in refiguring sovereignty and aspirational borderlessness. This can be seen in the 1985 US-Israel Free Trade Agreement (FTA), the first free trade agreement of its kind.[32] World Trade Organization rules allow FTAs only if they are regional; therefore, the US and Israel have maintained since 1985 that they are a legal "region" together.[33] No party has challenged this claim in WTO courts, and so it stands.

AmericaIsrael is part of a larger mission to realize an American—and would-be universal—political morality. It is not the only example; America-Ukraine is another.[34] Overwriting sovereign norms of territoriality, and enacting an exception that is also the rule, AmericaIsrael is an example of what Giorgio Agamben describes as "the legal form of what cannot have legal form."[35] It is an American political theology, in the sense described by Vincent Lloyd, as "a shorthand for religion and politics more generally, or where they overlap, that part of the Venn diagram where religion and politics are connected and that could be approached in a lot of different ways."[36]

32. Office of the United States Trade Representative, "Israel Free Trade Agreement."
33. Strong economic ties have joined the two countries since 1985. US exports to Israel totaled $12.8 billion in 2021, a 25.8 percent ($2.6 billion) increase from 2020; US imports from Israel totaled $18.7 billion, a 22.3 percent ($3.4 billion) increase; and the trade deficit was $5.8 billion, a 15.2 percent ($770.9 million) increase. US Department of Commerce, "U.S. Trade with Israel."
34. A few weeks after the Russian invasion of Ukraine, on March 3, 2022, Biden's Homeland Security Secretary Alejandro Mayorkas announced the grant of temporary protected status for eighteen months for certain Ukrainians already present in the United States. On April 21, 2022, the administration announced plans to welcome up to 100,000 Ukrainians through various entry pathways. The US temporarily lifted the border and allowed a reported 20,000 Ukrainians who arrived at the US-Mexico border without authorization to enter, ending the practice in late April. On April 21, the US announced "Uniting for Ukraine," a special immigration pathway for Ukrainian citizens and their immediate family members who are outside the US to come to the US and stay temporarily in a two-year period of parole. On November 11, 2022, the Biden administration announced that Ukrainians granted parole are automatically eligible for work authorization as part of their parole status (Rodriguez and Batalova, "Ukrainian Immigrants in the United States"; US Citizenship and Immigration Services, "Uniting for Ukraine"). On US security assistance to Ukraine since the Russian invasion, see US Department of State, "U.S. Security Cooperation with Ukraine: Fact Sheet."
35. Agamben, "State of Emergency."
36. Lloyd continues, "The people who use the term political theology in this really expansive sense tend to be from the humanities, they tend to be thinking about ideas and practices,

One does not have to be religious to participate in this collective endeavor. It is not a world religion in the sense that Americans conceive of the term. One can stand behind AmericaIsrael as a patriotic American, a supporter of border security, a committed believer in freedom, or even just a fan of the Wild West. One can be a Jewish Zionist, a Christian Zionist, or an atheist. Or none of the above. AmericaIsrael offers itself up as an irenic source of redemption, much like the US asylum regime discussed in chapter 2. Part of this redemptive gesture involves the collapse of Judaism into the State of Israel. They become coterminous. Judaism is collapsed into Israel, Israel into America, and America into universal freedom. It is conciliatory and comforting in its simplicity.

In presenting support for Israel as support for freedom, democracy, and religious diversity, the US also sets this relationship apart, placing it outside the bounds of legitimate critique. Much like religious freedom in the United States, AmericaIsrael stands as an ideal that reaches toward what Bender describes as an "American national sublime":

> By retaining the designation of "religion" for the various groups that are understood to flourish and expand in number in America . . . the American "sublime"—the religiousness of civil religion—becomes available as a postreligious project or orientation or experience. Distinguished from the specificities of "religion," civil religion and national sublime offer ways to summon the sacred nation without (it appears) summoning religion.[37]

AmericaIsrael summons a sacred nation without, on the surface, summoning "religion." While some Americans do not experience the US relationship with Israel as a religious object, others do. AmericaIsrael leverages this ambivalence by brokering and, to an extent, outrunning the secular-religious divide, permitting the United States and Israel to appear as interdependent Holy Lands by tapping into a history of American fascination and identification with the "original" Holy Land in the Levant. AmericaIsrael plays with the lines between religious and secular even as it also replicates familiar distinctions between good (secular, civilized, modern) religions and backward (theocratic, dangerous, antimodern) ones. It is "'religious,' and at the same time an experience of becoming America."[38] Operating beyond the reach of

---

approaching through texts, approaching through anthropological methods or literary methods or political theory, the history of political ideas, but looking for those sites at which religion and politics overlap" (Cavanaugh and Lloyd, "Why Does Political Theology Matter?").

37. Bender, "America Is Hard to See," 102.

38. Referring to the technological sublime, Bender explains that "anyone can experience this, and it is through this experience that Americans (or humans) shuck off their 'divisions

law and diplomacy, it attests to Yelle's observation that "human beings aim at something more than reason and legality alone."[39] It is about sovereignty and the sacred.

In a discussion of sovereignty and sacrality in the aftermath of the 9/11 attacks, legal anthropologist Mateo Taussig-Rubbo examines the sacralization of the material detritus of the attacks, including dust, bones, I-beams, snow globes, dirt, and office detritus. He distinguishes between two alignments of sacred property and sovereignty. In the first alignment, sacred property is subsumed under the sovereign as just another form of property. Examples are church property or the sacred property of Indigenous groups that is fully under the control of those who govern them. In these cases, the sacred is contained or banished, in that "property (and the legal order more generally) contains the sacred, typically having stripped the relevant community of sovereign powers."[40] Such modernist efforts to contain the sacred do not always work, however. The sacred can exceed the legal order. In the second alignment between sacred property and sovereignty, the sacred "encompasses and overwhelms the property designation . . . the sacred seems aligned with sovereignty, and it transcends and grounds property." This is what occurred after 9/11, argues Taussig-Rubbo. The sacralization of the 9/11 detritus belies modernist narratives of disenchantment in which "the political sphere is no longer permeated by the divine." "The 'religious,'" he concludes, "is not the only place we find the sacred."[41]

The sacred exceeds its designated spaces in US relations with Israel. It works outside formal diplomatic and political relations. It aligns with sovereignty and transcends property. This aspect of the US-Israel relationship eludes conventional analyses of religion and US foreign policy, focused as they are on organized religious politics, the power and pocketbooks of the Israel lobby,[42] the influence of Christian Zionism, and historic and institutional ties between the two countries. These accounts miss something important about this alliance. The US-Israel partnership enjoys the support of constituencies that extend beyond certain evangelical Christians, premillennial dispensationalists, and Jewish American communities. The mix of affective, religious,

---

among elements of the community.' It is 'religious,' and at the same time an experience of becoming America" ("America Is Hard to See," 101).

39. Yelle, *Sovereignty and the Sacred*, 184.
40. Taussig-Rubbo, "Sacred Property," 324.
41. Taussig-Rubbo, "Sacred Property," 325.
42. Mearsheimer and Walt, *Israel Lobby and U.S. Foreign Policy*.

political, nationalist, and theological commitment that sustains it implicates a broader swathe of the US population, cutting across entrenched political and religious divides and galvanizing support in far-flung places. The next section examines the cultural materials from which this consensus is built.

Holy Lands: Cultural Politics of AmericaIsrael

AmericaIsrael finds its cultural antecedents in the American fascination with the Holy Land, which predates the founding of the State of Israel. A sense of commingled religious histories and destinies with Holy Land places and peoples has always been central to the story Americans tell about themselves. These affinities animate countless Holy Land monuments and parks dotting the United States, from the "Holy Land USA" park in Waterbury, Connecticut,[43] down the road from where I went to college at Wesleyan, to the Holy Land Experience (HLE), a once popular, now bankrupt, family theme park in Orlando, Florida.

Opening to the public in 2001, HLE was a Christian Disneyland and family vacation destination that combined popular Christianity, commerce, entertainment, pilgrimage, and politics.[44] Founded by Russian Jewish convert and ordained Baptist minister Marvin Rosenthal, a self-described Christian Hebrew who purchased the property in 1989, the park offered a romanticized and commercialized replica of the "real thing" in the Middle East: a fifteen-acre historical simulation re-creating the ancient city of Jerusalem in first-century Judea. An actor playing Jesus wandered the grounds. Live animals populated the manger. In 2007, Trinity Broadcasting Network purchased the park from Rosenthal and added a miniature golf course called "Trin-i-tee," featuring Bible-story dioramas. As Chelsea Taylor writes, the park delivered

---

43. The mission of Holy Land USA, which opened in 1958 and boasts a fifty-six-foot color-changing LED cross visible from all over Waterbury, is "to protect in perpetuity for Christian purposes the 18-acre site atop Waterbury's Pine Hill known as Holy Land USA. In keeping with Attorney John Greco's original mission of presenting 'a pictorial story of the life of Christ,' Holy Land USA will continue by means of Masses, Christian prayer services, concerts and other mountaintop events to rebuild and restore this special place of prayer where the God of the Bible can be found" (Holy Land USA website).

44. The fourteen-acre theme park was open for twenty years; it went bankrupt in 2021 and was sold to a Seventh-day Adventist health care company for $32 million in 2021 (Silliman, "Holy Land Experience"). On the transformation of biblical sites into experiential environments, see Bielo, *Materializing the Bible*, and Rose, "Nazareth Village and the Creation of the Holy Land in Israel-Palestine," 335–55.

"a clean, safe, conflict-free version of the biblical holy land which includes American comfort food and memorabilia for purchase."[45]

Before going bankrupt in 2021, the park also incorporated a collective reverence for the State of Israel into its American Holy Land fantasy. Its online store had a section called "Judaica." Among other items for sale, the store offered an Israeli flag in three sizes; the largest, sixty by ninety inches, was available for purchase for forty dollars. The description of the flag, cited in the epigraph, read: "The flag of Israel, with a Star of David between two horizontal stripes all in a dark sky-blue on a white background, is the perfect standard to display at your home or church to show your love and support for the land and its people." Other product categories in the "Judaica" section included "Olive Wood," "Menorahs," "Mezuzahs," "Tallits," and "Instruments." This commingling of Israeli flags and Jewish communities and their ritual objects subtly communicated that Jews belong in Israel/the Holy Land, rather than in other parts of the Middle East and North Africa.[46] The HLE online store presented Judaism and the State of Israel as coterminous, with the Israeli flag as part of the category of Judaica. HLE collapsed Judaism/Judaica into Israel. It laundered American affective and cultural investments in the (actual) Holy Land into a commercial interest in Judaica and into broader political and religious support for the state of Israel and Zionism.

The history of American identification with the Holy Land is the subject of Burke Long's book *Imagining the Holy Land*. Among other episodes, Long describes American efforts to re-create Jerusalem in St. Louis as part of the World's Fair of 1904. The alignment of a vision of America as a chosen nation alongside the fantasy of a (fictional) Jerusalem in Missouri is evocative. As Long explains, "the elaborate fantasy of Jerusalem as Holy Land thus lent

---

45. Taylor, "American Christians and the Holy Land," 3–4. See also Stevenson, *Sensational Devotion*, and Long, *Imagining the Holy Land*.

46. A challenge to the mainstream narrative about the place of Jews in the Middle East and North Africa region is emerging in the "Reimagining Jewish Life in the Modern Middle East, 1800–Present: Culture, Society, and History" project, co-led by Lior Sternfeld, who explains that "most history books just want to show that Zionism [a movement for the reestablishment and the development and protection of a Jewish nation in what is now Israel] was the only alternative for Jews living in the Middle East. To say that Jews were subject to restrictions that would not allow them to prosper and live in the Middle East is just nonsense. Jews were part of the society from Morocco to Afghanistan, and from central Asia to Yemen. We are going to look at Jews not as a group of people waiting for redemption by Zionism but as people who live and prosper and work and suffer and cry and laugh in the Middle East as part of Middle Eastern societies" (Burlingame, "NEH Grant Will Help Scholars Challenge Current Views of Jews in the Middle East").

moral and religious authority to the exclusions, celebrations, and paradoxical aspirations to universality that were embedded in a particular vision of America and her limitless future."[47] Documenting the organizers' efforts to normalize an understanding of the US as a "chosen nation," Long quotes an editor from the *St. Louis Mirror* who assures readers that the exhibit would "vitalize for everyone the story that has wrought the world into what it is today . . . [and] recall to all the actuality of the history upon which Christianity has been [sic] builded to its present mighty influence."[48] The exhibit's organizers encouraged fairgoers and investors to visit the "Jews' Wailing Place," which Long reads as evidence of a persistent Christian theology of displacement rather than an homage to Jewish spirituality. "The sight of 'pale, deformed, and sad Jews,' investors were assured in the Exhibit's Prospectus, would be 'reproduced in all its picturesqueness.' "[49] The organizers also portrayed Muslims as "ornamental" and "alive religiously only in Christian imagination." In another orientalist flourish, the president of the Jerusalem Exhibit Advisory Board, Dr. Palmore, celebrated "the weird and thrilling call of the muezzin from the mosque of Omar."[50] Meanwhile, the director of exhibits and displays, a certain Madame Mountford, captured the "flavor of Holy Land infatuation and Christian, America-first mercantile nationalism" with a flamboyant pronouncement to fairgoers: "You cannot go to Jerusalem, so Jerusalem comes to you. To American energy all things are possible."[51]

AmericaIsrael picks up where the World's Fair of 1904 and the Holy Land Experience leave off, affirming, as scholars of religion have shown, that in the United States there has never been a clean line demarcating religion from politics, entertainment, tourism, or consumption.[52] Americans' historical, religious, eschatological, and commercial fascination with the Holy Land, rather than necessarily or even primarily connections to or respect for Judaism or Zionism, helps generate and sustain an intense affective commitment to (America)Israel. Few Americans would distinguish cleanly between religious attachments to the Holy Land and political support for the State of Israel.

Hillary Kaell's ethnography of contemporary North American pilgrims to the Holy Land documents these attachments to the Holy Land/Israel. The

---

47. Long, *Imagining the Holy Land*, 49.
48. Long, *Imagining the Holy Land*, 52, citing *Prospectus of the Jerusalem Exhibit Company*, 27.
49. Long, *Imagining the Holy Land*, 56, citing *Prospectus of the Jerusalem Exhibit Company*, 6–10.
50. Long, *Imagining the Holy Land*, 62–63.
51. Long, *Imagining the Holy Land*, 61–62.
52. Vaca, *Evangelicals Incorporated*; Sullivan, *Church State Corporation*; Kaell, *Walking Where Jesus Walked*; Bielo, *Ark Encounter*.

pilgrims with whom she traveled "frame[d] individual consumption of souvenirs, and the trip itself, as contributing to another moral national project: Americans' responsibility to support Israel."[53] Numerous American Christian organizations dedicate themselves to the Israeli cause, including, and perhaps most prominently, Christians United for Israel (CUFI),[54] for whom, as Amy Fallas explains, "support for the modern state of Israel is a scriptural obligation with ramifications for the end of times."[55] For CUFI, Israel is "ultimately invincible, in accordance with God's plan to end history."[56] When Jews are restored to Zion, according to prophecy, the countdown to Armageddon begins.[57] Amy Kaplan describes the reciprocal nature of the US-Israel alliance during the Cold War, citing a widely held belief among Americans that "Christians had an obligation to arm Israel in its battle for survival, while Israel in turn played a crucial role in saving America as it struggled for survival against secularists at home and communists abroad."[58]

While American fascination with the Holy Land as the "headquarters of Christianity" dates to the earliest days of the republic, the emergence of a robust political consensus in the US in support of the State of Israel is more recent. For the anti-Zionist American Council for Judaism, or ACJ, for example, founded in 1942, "the idea of the Jews as a nation—rather than a religion—was an anathema that would only provoke anti-Semitism and charges of dual loyalty." At an emergency conference of American Zionists in 1942 at the Biltmore in New York, at which Albert Einstein spoke in opposition to the idea of a Jewish state, the president of the ACJ, Lessing Rosenwald, criticized the overwhelming support for a Jewish state among attendees. Rosenwald rejected what he described as "the Hitlerian concept of a Jewish state" and warned of the dangers of "Jewish nationalism." His minority view raised hackles at the hearing, with one delegate sensing what Kaplan describes as "mental daggers in the audience behind him." Yet the American cochair, Judge Joseph C. Hutcheson Jr., "agreed with Rosenwald that a Jewish lineage no more determined nationality than did his own Scottish heritage."[59]

---

53. Kaell, *Walking Where Jesus Walked*, 126.

54. Durbin, *Righteous Gentiles*. Founded in 2006, CUFI advocates for continued US military aid to Israel, the expansion of Israeli settlements, and, at times, war between Israel and Iran (Zonszein, "Christian Zionist Philo-Semitism").

55. Fallas, "Pueblo de Israel." Fallas tracks the influence of Christian Zionism in Latin America in the work of groups like Philos Latino, funded by pro-Israel philanthropist Paul Singer.

56. Kaplan, *Our American Israel*, 213.

57. McAlister, *Epic Encounters*, 3.

58. Kaplan, *Our American Israel*, 221.

59. Kaplan, *Our American Israel*, 18–19.

Spaces for this kind of disagreement became increasingly constricted in the United States after the 1967 war as organized political expressions of Christian Zionism began to hew more closely to a muscular and militarized US political backing for the State of Israel. The Israeli government encouraged this development. When Israel gained control of the major Christian holy sites in 1967, it created its own Department for Encouragement of Pilgrimage.[60] Many American evangelicals not only became strong supporters of the State of Israel as a political entity during this era but also looked to Israel as "the setting for the Second Coming of Jesus Christ, and as the primary actor in hastening that event."[61] As Fallas notes, "evangelical figures such as Hal Lindsay, John Hagee, and Pat Robertson preached that a rapture of believers and a reckoning with God's chosen people will unfold in the state of Israel, the Promised Land."[62] Support for Israel commingling theological and political justifications courses through Christian and Jewish advocacy groups such as CUFI and the American Israel Public Affairs Committee (AIPAC).[63]

Responding to these developments, certain liberals and progressives have been keen to justify and excuse US support for Israel as part of the price of (other people's) irrational religious commitments. Yet as shown in this chapter it would be a mistake to attribute religious motivations for US support for Israel exclusively to Christian and Jewish Zionisms. This is a convenient shortcut for those seeking to explain away unflappable US support for Israel as the natural outcome of old-world religiosities, but the history and breadth of American commitment to the Holy Land/Israel suggests a different story. These attachments are more complex and capacious than is captured by liberal disdain for religion or religionists. To segregate evangelical Protestant and Jewish American support for Israel from that of other Americans underestimates the role of liberal secularists and others in keeping the consensus afloat. AmericaIsrael is not only an evangelical-Zionist-Israeli government project; it attracts pro-Israel Catholics, mainline Protestants, and an increasing number of Americans who elude conventional religious categories of identification altogether.[64] This fragile accord, however, may not last. While it

60. Kaell, *Walking Where Jesus Walked*, 46.
61. Kaplan, *Our American Israel*, 212.
62. Fallas, "El Pueblo de Israel."
63. AIPAC's self-described mission is "to encourage and persuade the U.S. government to enact specific policies that create a strong, enduring and mutually beneficial relationship with our ally Israel." Anderson, "AIPAC." On AIPAC's origins, see Rossinow, "Edge of the Abyss," 23–43. On CUFI see Durbin, *Righteous Gentiles*.
64. Kaell discusses a tendency to overlook Catholic pilgrims in favor of Protestants in *Walking Where Jesus Walked*, 130, 203.

has enjoyed a remarkable capacity to set the terms of US public and political discourse, cracks in the consensus are emerging.

Whose Judaism? Refashioning the Boundaries of Legitimate Dissent

Legally and bureaucratically speaking, Israel is an independent state. Passports are required for US citizens to travel to Israel and vice versa. Affectively and charismatically, however, I have suggested that the US border with Israel is porous and inexact. It can be difficult to pin down. Amy Kaplan comes close to this argument when she observes that "what might have been the foreign policy concerns of a particular ethnic group came to have long-term symbolic associations with American national mythology."[65] Or, in the words of a 1956 editorial she discovered in Leon Uris's archive that captures the spirit of AmericaIsrael, "to help Israel today is to help ourselves."[66] Consequently, to question American support for Israel is not only to criticize Israeli treatment of the Palestinians, or to decry the inequities of the Israeli political system, or to challenge Zionist ideals, though it may be all of the above. It hits closer to home. To question American support for Israel is to question an American capacity for grace, salvation, and redemption. It is to question a set of American norms woven deeply into the tapestry of the United States as a religious and political project. To criticize AmericaIsrael is not only to risk being tarred as an enemy of the Jewish people, democracy, freedom, or Western civilization.[67] It is to risk being chastised or cast out as anti-American. AmericaIsrael is a US border-maintenance project as much as it is a security alliance.

Defenders of this project routinely denounce dissenting non- and anti-Zionists and their allies as anti-Semitic. Dissenters have pushed back against the liminal role to which they have been relegated in mainstream US discourse, forming a series of movements in which non-, anti- and post-Zionist Jews and their allies align themselves with antiracist and decolonial activists to call for a refashioning of political order in Israel and Palestine. These movements not only criticize the policies of the Israeli government but demand reconsideration of the foundations of Israeli ethnonationalism, including the

---

65. Kaplan, *Our American Israel*, 8.

66. See Kaplan's discussion of the "1776 analogy," used to galvanize American support for Israel by evoking Israel's founding as an anticolonial revolt against the British Empire akin to the American founding. Leon Uris, the author of *Exodus*, kept an editorial from the 1956 Congressional Record in a scrapbook in his archive that "likened the courage and stamina of the Israelis to that of the courageous Americans who declared their independence in 1776," concluding that "to help Israel today is to help ourselves" (Kaplan, *Our American Israel*, 80).

67. On the international politics of anti-Semitism, see Davis, "Faking Remembrance."

moral legitimacy, religious justification, and political viability of the Israeli State's claim to institutionalized Jewish political and legal supremacy.

Widespread protests on US college and university campuses erupted in the spring of 2024 in response to US public and private institutional and political complicity with the Israeli government's mass killings of civilians in Gaza. The protests were led by people of various ethnic and religious backgrounds, and included many Jewish protestors.[68] The protests called for universities and colleges to divest from Israel, for a multiethnic and democratic political order in the region, and an end to the war in Gaza. As one journalist who visited a pro-Palestinian encampment at the University of Chicago explained, for Jewish protestors "that means Seders and Shabbats (or Sabbaths), with non-Israeli kosher products, teaching about the pluralistic elements of Jewish traditions like the Moroccan Jewish Mimouna, and eating Palestinian food with Muslims and others in their coalition."[69] A Jewish student who was part of the Northwestern encampment told a reporter that "this encampment is the time at Northwestern where I've felt most connected to and supported in my faith at Northwestern because it has given me the space to be both Jewish and anti-Zionist."[70]

US government efforts to silence these and other critics are a prominent feature of the contemporary politics of AmericaIsrael. This section explores how AmericaIsrael operates not only as a normative ideal but also as a mode of governance by examining the strategies used to discipline and silence dissent involving US support for Israel.[71] These interrelated efforts include public condemnation and official sanctioning of non- and anti-Zionist expressions and, implicitly, the varied forms of Judaism from which they draw sustenance; legislative efforts to criminalize the Boycott, Divestment, Sanctions (BDS) movement, a solidarity movement for Palestinian rights critical of the Israeli occupation; and third, executive and legislative efforts at all levels of government to codify government definitions of anti-Semitism to include criticism of Israel, thus collapsing the distinction between critiques of the State of Israel and anti-Semitism. For the purposes of the discussion, I adopt Hilla Dayan and Yolande Jansen's approach to anti-Zionism as referring to

---

68. On competing visions of the American "Black Church" and their modes of engagement with Israel and Palestine, see Baumann, *Visions of the Holy Land*.

69. Akbar, "At U. of C. Encampment."

70. Rivera, "Chicago-Area College Protest Organizers."

71. Each of these dynamics intensified in the context of widespread protests against US support for Israel during the Israeli invasion of Gaza following Hamas's attack on southern Israel on October 7, 2023.

forms of expression that recognize "responsibility for the dispossession and expulsion of the Palestinians (the *Nakba*) in 1948, [oppose] the occupation of the West Bank, and [oppose] the practice of privileging the Jews in Israel and the occupied Palestinian territories, especially over the Palestinians."[72]

The first strategy to defend AmericaIsrael involves the suppression of non- and anti-Zionist expression in the name of combating anti-Semitism. In 2019, cosmetics billionaire and president of the World Jewish Congress, Ronald S. Lauder, announced a new $25 million initiative called the Anti-Semitism Accountability Project (ASAP), "devoted to rooting out what he sees as the growing tide of anti-Semitism in American politics."[73] ASAP was to be composed of a nonprofit and a super PAC that would "hold antisemitic politicians' feet to the fire."[74] In an interview after his announcement, Lauder differentiated between critics of Israeli policies and those who questioned the existence of the State of Israel. "I think everybody has a right to disagree with Israel's policies and what they're doing," he told the *New York Times*. He added, however, that he is uncomfortable with the BDS movement, and that his group would "look into universities, and their professors, that he sees taking 'an anti-Semitic point of view' and pressure them by contacting major contributors."[75] Lauder and like-minded critics accused BDS of unfairly singling out Israel for criticism, threatening Israeli business and commercial interests, and spreading anti-Semitic views.

Though Lauder's initiative went dormant in 2020 during the pandemic,[76] it was one of more than three dozen groups created since 2015 to combat anti-Semitism and, in most cases, anti-Zionism. Robert Kraft's Foundation to Combat Anti-Semitism (FCAS), also created in 2019, sought, according to Kraft, "to counter the normalization of antisemitic narratives that question Israel's right to exist."[77] Two other campaigns, Shine a Light, spearheaded by Natie Kirsh, and JewBelong, "have condemned anti-Zionism as a form of antisemitism and made aggressive defenses of Israel a central part of their

---

72. Stable definitions are elusive. As these authors point out, "'anti-Zionism' is a narrow reduction of 'critique of Israel,' because that too can come in many shades" (Dayan and Jansen, "Antisemitism, Anti-Palestinian Racism, and Europe").

73. Goldmacher, "Ron Lauder Pledges $25 Million to Fight Antisemitism."

74. Rosenfeld, "Ronald Lauder Pledged $25 Million to Fight Antisemitism."

75. Goldmacher, "Ron Lauder Pledges $25 Million."

76. A Lauder spokesperson told the *Forward* that "the onset of a global pandemic may have permanently altered the course of ASAP in March 2020 . . . but Mr. Lauder's commitment and financial support of the fight against antisemitism only accelerated" (Rosenfeld, "Ronald Lauder Pledged $25 Million").

77. Rosenfeld, "Robert Kraft Will Spend $25 Million."

work."⁷⁸ In the words of Shine A Light spokesperson Carly Maisel, the connection between anti-Zionism and anti-Semitism "is front and center a part of Shine A Light . . . If that doesn't work for you, this isn't the campaign for you."⁷⁹ The JewBelong website advises that "in the vast majority of cases, being anti-Zionist is antisemitic."⁸⁰ Before founding Shine A Light, Kirsh, who made his fortune under apartheid in South Africa, donated to the British Council's anti-boycott project BIRAX: the Britain Israel Research and Academic Exchange Partnership.⁸¹

The conflation of anti-Semitism and anti-Zionism in these campaigns, and the condemnation of anti-Zionists as anti-Semites, is central to their mission. Shine A Light considers the claim that Israel is guilty of apartheid to be anti-Semitic. To express a preference for nonterritorial or nonstatist expressions of Jewish collective identity is considered outside the bounds of acceptable public or private discourse. It is portrayed not only as anti-Israel but as anti-Semitic, anti-American, and antidemocratic. The effect is to marginalize non- and anti-Zionisms by pushing them below the threshold of legitimate public discourse. In fact, non- and anti-Zionisms take diverse forms and many predate the movement to create a Jewish state that began in the 1890s.⁸² Examples include what Jewish studies scholar and rabbi Shaul Magid describes as "the theological anti-Zionism of ultra-Orthodoxy, the moral and antinationalist anti-Zionism of Hermann Cohen and Franz Rosenzweig, the secular anti-Zionism of the American Council for Judaism, the diasporist anti-Zionism of Judith Butler or Daniel Boyarin, and the anti-imperialist anti-Zionism of Noam Chomsky."⁸³ In conflating anti-Zionism with anti-Jewish racism, the Lauder, Kraft, and Kirsh initiatives erase the staggering variety of

---

78. Rosenfeld, "Robert Kraft Will Spend $25 Million." In another piece, Rosenfeld explains that "Shine A Light is one of more than two dozen new groups that have sprung up to fight antisemitism in the last decade, and is backed by eight major foundations including Schusterman Family Philanthropies, the Paul E. Singer Foundation and UJA-Federation of New York. It is the brainchild of the Kirsh family, led by 92-year-old patriarch Natie, a billionaire who built and lost a fortune in apartheid South Africa and has maintained strong ties to Israel for decades—experiences that may provide clues to the campaign's approach" ("Behind the TV Ads").

79. Rosenfeld, "Behind the TV Ads." Maisel was speaking on a Jewish Funders Network podcast in January 2023.

80. JewBelong, "Antisemitism Cheat Sheet."

81. See Aked, "Billionaire Donor Using British Council to Combat Israel Boycott."

82. For an introduction see Sanders, "Despite Conflation of Israel with Judaism, Anti-Zionism Is More Kosher Than You Think." On Jewish political thought and political theology see Vatter, *Living Law*.

83. Magid, "Enforcers." On counter-Zionism as an alternative to anti-Zionism, see Magid, *Necessity of Exile*.

Jewish traditions and perspectives. They blind Americans to the possibility that support for the Jewish people can mean different things, politically, and does not necessarily or inevitably entail support for a Jewish state. Even to entertain these views, from their perspective, is anti-Semitic. And yet it remains incontrovertible that, as Magid counters, "if we're to honor the way 'actual Jews do Jewishness,' then we'd have to honor it even when they do Jewishness in a non-Zionist, or even anti-Zionist, way."[84]

The AmericaIsrael consensus is fraying. Attempts to collapse anti-Zionism and anti-Semitism have encountered stronger headwinds in recent years. An example is Representative Jerry Nadler's opposition to the passage of a 2023 US House of Representatives resolution asserting that all anti-Zionism is anti-Semitism.[85] Representing one of the largest Jewish constituencies in the country, Nadler criticized the legislation for what he described as an effort to "to weaponize Jewish lives for political gains":

> The resolution suggests that ALL anti-Zionism is antisemitism. That is either intellectually disingenuous or just factually wrong. And it unfairly implicates many of my orthodox former constituents in Brooklyn, many of whose families rose from the ashes of the Holocaust . . . While most anti-Zionism is indeed antisemitic, the authors, if they were at all familiar with Jewish history and culture, should know about Jewish anti-Zionism that was, and is, expressly NOT antisemitic. This resolution ignores the fact that even today, certain orthodox Hasidic Jewish communities—the Satmars in New York and others—as well as adherents of the pre-state Jewish labor movement have held views that are at odds with the modern Zionist conception."[86]

The effort to sustain a cultural and political consensus in support of AmericaIsrael in the face of challenges such as Nadler's is also reflected in a second arena of contestation: legislative efforts to criminalize the Boycott, Divestment, Sanctions movement, or BDS. Anti-BDS efforts occur at all levels, from local to federal. Described by a group of US-based political theorists as "one of the most widespread instances of solidarity politics in the world today," BDS is a Palestinian civil society movement whose demands include "ending the Israeli occupation and colonization of all Arab lands and dismantling the Wall; recognizing the fundamental rights of the Arab-Palestinian citizens of Israel to full equality; and respecting, protecting and promoting the rights of Palestinian refugees to return to their homes and properties as stipulated in

---

84. Magid, "Enforcers."
85. US House of Representatives, H.Res. 894.
86. Nadler, "Congressman Nadler's Floor Speech."

UN resolution 194."⁸⁷ An example of a legislative attempt to quash BDS is the Israel Anti-Boycott Act, first introduced in Congress in 2018 and designed to allow and encourage US states to enact laws requiring contractors with the government to pledge that they will not boycott goods from Israel lest their contracts be terminated.⁸⁸ Before the bill was introduced, twenty-six states had already passed similar legislation or had gubernatorial executive orders restricting boycotting of Israeli goods by state contractors. Critics of the proposed law claimed that participation in boycotts is a form of free speech protected by the First Amendment. In 2019, Marco Rubio introduced the Combating BDS Act, which was also intended to counter the call for boycotts, divestment, and sanctions against Israel by lending the federal government's support to state efforts to pass anti-boycott legislation. The proposed bill was blocked from moving forward by Democrats who argued that it violated First Amendment free speech protections. Rubio reintroduced the legislation in the Senate in 2023.⁸⁹

The aim of anti-BDS legislation is to criminalize anti-Zionist and pro-Palestinian speech, action, and organizing by conflating criticism of Israel with anti-Semitism and support for terrorism. These efforts police the terms of US public and political discourse concerning Israel and Palestine. They encourage unwarranted accusations of anti-Semitism against anti-Zionists and defenders of Palestinian rights. These efforts have been largely successful at the state level. As of 2019, more than 250 million Americans, or 78 percent of the US population, lived in states with anti-boycott laws or policies in place.⁹⁰ As of 2022, more than thirty US states had enacted legislation targeting boycotts for Palestinian rights. Thirty-five states had adopted laws, executive orders, or resolutions designed to discourage boycotts against Israel. As explained in the film *Boycott*, between 2015 and 2021, thirty-three US states passed legislation or executive orders that allowed for punishing individuals or companies that express support for boycotting Israel.⁹¹ Darryl Li describes these laws as falling in two categories: "Some preclude state pension funds from investing in companies that boycott Israel. Others prevent state governments from

---

87. Bruyneel et al., "Boycott, Divestment and Sanctions (BDS) and Political Theory," 450. See also BDS Movement, "Palestinian Civil Society Call for BDS."

88. US Congress, "Strongly Condemning."

89. US Congress, Combating BDS Act of 2023; US Congress, Combating BDS Act of 2017.

90. Human Rights Watch, "US: States Use Anti-Boycott Laws to Punish Responsible Businesses." See also Just Vision, "Anti-Boycott Legislation Tracker."

91. Mansour, "Laws Preventing Boycotts of Israel." The documentary referred to is Julia Bacha's *Boycott*.

contracting with entities that boycott Israel."[92] Although the ACLU, Palestine Legal, and the Council on American-Islamic Relations (CAIR) have successfully challenged anti-boycott orders and regulations on First Amendment grounds, many remain in place and new legislation is being proposed.

US politicians also use the powers of the executive to enforce the normative consensus underlying AmericaIsrael. The day after Lauder's announcement, then president Trump announced an Executive Order formalizing the US government's conflation of anti-Zionism with anti-Semitism in the name of protecting Jewish students who were alleged to have suffered discrimination on US college campuses.[93] According to the directive, anti-Semitism falls under Title VI of the Civil Rights Act, which prohibits discrimination on the basis of race, color, and national origin.[94] The order reads: "Discrimination against Jews may give rise to a Title VI violation when the discrimination is based on an individual's race, color, or national origin. It shall be the policy of the executive branch to enforce Title VI against prohibited forms of discrimination rooted in anti-Semitism as vigorously as against all other forms of discrimination prohibited by Title VI."[95] Biden's inauguration brought calls for a similar order,[96] and in May 2023, his administration released a National Strategy to Counter Antisemitism that "reaffirms the United States' unshakable commitment to the State of Israel's right to exist, its legitimacy, and its security—and makes clear that when Israel is singled out because of anti-Jewish hatred, that is antisemitism."[97] The accompanying Biden-Harris Fact Sheet noted that "Title VI of the 1964 Civil Rights Act prohibits discrimination based on shared ancestry or ethnic characteristics, including certain antisemitic and related forms of discrimination and bias in federally funded programs and activities."[98] Trump's order not only designated Jews as part of this class of protected subjects but also expanded the official government

---

92. Li, "Who's Afraid of the Big Bad Anti-Boycott Laws?"

93. White House, "Executive Order on Combating Anti-Semitism."

94. The novelty of this protection is debated. In 2011, under President Obama, Assistant Attorney General Thomas E. Perez of the Civil Rights Division of the Justice Department wrote a letter to the assistant secretary for civil rights in the Department of Education explaining that "although Title VI does not prohibit discrimination on the basis of religion, discrimination against Jews, Muslims, Sikhs, and members of other religious groups violates Title VI when that discrimination is based on the group's actual or perceived shared ancestry or ethnic characteristics, rather than its members' religious practice" (Perez to Ali).

95. White House, "Executive Order on Combating Anti-Semitism."

96. Marcus, "Time for Biden to Issue Executive Order on Antisemitism."

97. White House, "Fact Sheet: Biden-Harris Administration."

98. White House, "Fact Sheet: Biden-Harris Administration."

definition of anti-Semitism to include certain anti-Israel sentiments, such as proclaiming that "that the existence of a State of Israel is a racist endeavor." The Biden-Harris Strategy proclaimed similarly that "the U.S. Government, led by the Department of State, will continue to combat antisemitism abroad and in international fora—including efforts to delegitimize the State of Israel."[99]

The Education Department is required by law to rely on these definitions of anti-Semitism in assessing whether incidents or activities violate Title VI.[100] Other federal executive departments and agencies are also obligated to employ them in investigating civil rights complaints that allege anti-Semitism on university campuses.[101] In November 2023, three Jewish students sued New York University alleging that a hostile environment on campus had allowed anti-Semitism to go unchecked. The complaint argued that NYU violated Title VI. Though denying the charges, NYU immediately announced that it would create a Center for the Study of Antisemitism to "research both classical forms of antisemitism as well as the 'new antisemitism' and its links to anti-Zionism."[102]

While some Jewish individuals and organizations support these efforts, others denounce the conflation of anti-Zionism and anti-Semitism.[103] Kenneth Stern, lead drafter of the American Jewish Committee's working definition of anti-Semitism and a critic of Trump's order, notes that there is "a debate inside the Jewish community whether being Jewish requires one to be a Zionist. I don't know if this question can be resolved, but it should frighten all Jews that the government is essentially defining the answer for us."[104] Max Fisher explains that many Jews "are sensitive to implications that their religion carries a distinct nationality. Centuries of European anti-Semitism were built on the belief that Jews were foreigners within. As late as the 1980s, Soviet passports designated 'Jewish' as a nationality akin to Russian or Ukrainian."[105] Masha Gessen criticizes the attempt to redefine anti-Semitism to equate

---

99. White House, "U.S. National Strategy to Combat Antisemitism."

100. Ward and Levin, "Anti-Semitism or Free Speech?"

101. Palestine Legal Director Dima Khalidi suggests that it "enlists universities as censors of a growing student movement led by Palestinians and their demands for equality and freedom in their homeland in order to avoid federal consequences" ("Expert Q&A").

102. New York University, "NYU to Create Center for the Study of Antisemitism."

103. See, for example, Diaspora Alliance, which describes itself as "an international organization dedicated to fighting antisemitism and its instrumentalization by promoting the values of multiracial, pluralistic democracy" (Diaspora Alliance official website).

104. Stern, "I Drafted the Definition of Antisemitism."

105. Fisher, "In Era of Hardening Identities."

hatred of Jews with criticism of Israel, explaining that "Kushner and the executive order refer to the definition of anti-Semitism that was formulated, in 2016, by the International Holocaust Remembrance Alliance (IHRA); it has since been adopted by the State Department. The definition supplies examples of anti-Semitism, and Kushner cited the most problematic of these as the most important: 'the targeting of the state of Israel, conceived as a Jewish collectivity'; denial to 'the Jewish people their right to self-determination, e.g. by claiming that the existence of a state of Israel is a racist endeavor'; and comparing 'contemporary Israeli policy to that of the Nazis.'"[106] Gabe Stutman agrees that "the IHRA examples of anti-Semitism are overbroad and threaten to punish actions that are not inherently anti-Semitic—including not only garden-variety criticism of Israel, but some sharp critiques, as well."[107]

In the eyes of many of these critics, these policies and initiatives, undertaken in the name of fighting anti-Semitism, serve to perpetuate anti-Semitic tropes that set Jews apart as a separate nation, or even a separate race, in a move reminiscent of the Soviet Union's policies. This points toward a darker side of the consensus that sustains AmericaIsrael: the racial and religious othering of the Jewish people. J. Kameron Carter's notion of the "religion of Whiteness" is helpful here.[108] Citing DuBois, Carter proposes a concept of Whiteness linked not primarily to skin color but to what he describes as a "planetary structure of governance driven by Christian liberal humanism with western man at its apex." Building on Dietrich Bonhoeffer's critical reading of the reproduction of this "architecture of Whiteness" in his theological vision in *Ethics*, Carter suggests that the post–World War II international order enacts an "inclusionary supersessionism" vis-à-vis the Jewish peoples that engulfs them in the "Whiteness" of the West. Incorporating Jews into Western humanism aligns Jewishness with Whiteness and with colonial practice. One (paradoxical) implication of that incorporation is that the State of Israel emerges as a "Christian" nation-state, in continuity with post–World War II

---

106. Gessen, "Real Purpose of Trump's Executive Order on Anti-Semitism." For the State Department definition of anti-Semitism see https://www.state.gov/defining-antisemitism/. For an alternative definition adopted in response to the IHRA definition of 2016, see the Jerusalem Declaration on Antisemitism. Gessen argues, however, that the latter "has barely made a dent in the growing influence of the I.H.R.A. definition," noting that in 2021, "the European Commission published a handbook 'for the practical use' of the I.H.R.A. definition, which recommended, among other things, using the definition in training law-enforcement officers to recognize hate crimes, and creating the position of state attorney, or coördinator or commissioner for antisemitism" ("In the Shadow of the Holocaust").

107. Stutman, "Completely Wrongheaded."

108. Carter, *Religion of Whiteness*.

Western statist internationalism.[109] Carter is not the first to explore the effects of the alignment of Jewishness and Whiteness; Pankaj Mishra describes how, decades ago, "James Baldwin sought to profane what he termed a 'pious silence' around Israel's behaviour when he claimed that the Jewish state, which sold arms to the apartheid regime in South Africa, embodied white supremacy not democracy."[110]

AmericaIsrael thus draws on an older American tradition of *pro*-Zionist anti-Semitism, or anti-Jewish racism. This simultaneous incorporation and refusal of Jewishness comes across in discussions that racialize Jewish Americans as others who may be (or should be considered as) clandestine Israelis. The simultaneous reification and denigration of Jewish difference lies just below the surface of a speech to Jewish Americans by former president Trump, who referred to Benjamin Netanyahu as "your prime minister," implying either that Israel is an extension of US Jewish communities or that Jewish Americans are a satellite of Israel. In either case, he implied that Jewish Americans have "dual loyalties."[111] This accusation affirms Jewish Americans' standing as less than fully American and, by implication, as less than fully white. Jewish Americans are contingently accepted while remaining ultimately unassimilable. As Eric Goldstein shows in *The Price of Whiteness*, in the United States Jews were not considered "white" until after the Second World War.[112] Doubts about Jewish whiteness continue to circulate among partisans of white power and white nationalism.[113]

To enact a government policy that singles out Jews as racially and nationally distinct at a time when white nationalist movements founded on similarly racist premises are on the rise puts the weight of the US government

---

109. Carter, "Jews and the Religion of Whiteness."

110. Mishra continues, "Muhammad Ali saw Palestine as an instance of gross racial injustice. So, today, do the leaders of the United States's oldest and most prominent Black Christian denominations, who have accused Israel of genocide and asked Biden to end all financial as well as military aid to the country" ("Shoah after Gaza"). On the centrality of race in the constitution of international order, see O. Brown, "Underside of Order."

111. In 2019 and 2024, Trump stated that Jewish Americans who vote for Democrats are being disloyal to Jewish people and to the State of Israel. In 2024, he claimed that "any Jewish person that votes for democrats hates their religion. . . . They hate everything about Israel, and they should be ashamed of themselves because Israel will be destroyed" (Cameron, "Trump Says Jews Who Support Democrats 'Hate Israel' and 'Their Religion'").

112. E. Goldstein, *Price of Whiteness*.

113. Ward, "Skin in the Game." On white power movements in the United States and their connections to the Vietnam War, see Belew, *Bring the War Home*.

behind anti-Semitic tropes that represent Jews as (non- or dubiously white) outsiders to the American nation. It posits (all) Jews as racialized others and suspected clandestine Israelis. This inclusionary supersessionism has a long history in the United States and is at the core of the mainstream AmericaIsrael policy program. As Kaplan explains, "even advocacy for Zionism often had anti-Semitic undertones, a connection that has now been largely obscured by the mainstream story that in championing the Jewish state, Americans like [American civil rights attorney Bartley] Crum were rejecting anti-Semitism and trying to make amends for the Holocaust." Early American Zionists, such as Crum, believed that Jews raised in Palestine were stronger, blonder, bluer-eyed, more Western, and whiter than earlier generations raised in eastern Europe.[114]

White supremacy runs quietly below the surface of AmericaIsrael. In her discussion of the convergence of anti-Semitic, Alt-Right, and pro-Zionist views in US politics,[115] Atalia Omer explains that "the Alt-Right's longing for an ethnic state analogous to Israel (where whites can live securely) is, in effect, entirely consistent with modern anti-semitism. It reflects a rearticulation of the 'Ein Volk, Ein Reich' Nazi principle and the aspiration to relocate the Jewish diaspora away from the sites of white European societies where they supposedly, activating familiar antisemitic tropes, masterminded the decay and collapse of patriarchal values, and forms of authority."[116]

The government of Israel is a willing participant in this political alchemy of whiteness. Sharing with the United States a national interest in policing the limits of religiously and politically acceptable expressions of Judaism, Israel has constructed a discriminatory religio-national hierarchy that privileges certain understandings of what it means to be Jewish.[117] The Israeli establishment inoculates itself against criticism of this arrangement with the suggestion that any attempt to question it amounts to an anti-Semitic dismissal of the Jewish people's right to self-determination. Neve Gordon explains how the discourse of anti-anti-Semitism works: "whereas traditional antisemitism has been used as an instrument to justify the introduction of draconian

---

114. Kaplan, *Our American Israel*, 31.

115. Omer, *Days of Awe*.

116. Omer, *Days of Awe*, 227. Omer explores possibilities for Jews to "finally disengage from Zionism and its monopoly over the narrative about Jewish safety and survival," a process that will require "exposing the common roots of anti-black racism, Islamophobia, and antisemitism in Europe" (236–37).

117. Dalsheim, *Israel Has a Jewish Problem*.

laws and policies aimed at subjugating and even annihilating Jews, the new antisemitism accusation has been mobilized to protect a form of racial governance that subjugates and dispossesses Palestinians. The first form of antisemitism justifies the domination of Jews; the second uses the accusation of antisemitism to justify Jewish domination of another people."[118] Israel's "Basic Law: Israel as the Nation-State of the Jewish People," enacted by the Knesset on July 19, 2018, exemplifies the attempt to legalize Jewish supremacy in Israel.[119] The Basic Law constitutionalizes the principle of Jewish supremacy by foreclosing on the possibility of self-determination for the 20 percent of Israel's citizens who identify as Palestinian Arabs, legitimizing housing and planning policies that discriminate in favor of Jews and ending the status of Arabic as an official language.[120]

Some scholars have directly confronted efforts to reduce Judaism to the Israeli state's interpretation of Zionism. Yaacov Yadgar asks, "How does the Israeli nation-state's theopolitics—constituted, as it is (symbolically, at least), on an 'invented' national tradition—approach Jewish traditions that preceded it and continue to live alongside it?" He finds that "the 'problem' with those Jewish traditions is that they do not fit easily, if ever, into the commonly used categorical frameworks such as 'nation,' 'ethnicity,' 'race,' and, perhaps most importantly, 'religion,' which originate in modern Western discourse."[121] Yadgar reads Zionism as a counterreaction to the transformation of Judaism into a "religion," a process that, he explains, "has to do with the modern ideological innovation and practical transformation that originated in Europe, mostly in Germany, from the eighteenth century onward, which allegedly sought to reinterpret Jewish traditions so as to render them applicable to the allegedly universal (and, again, essentially European Protestant) category of religion, in itself a contemporaneous invention."[122] A tragic result of this history is that Jewish Israeli secularism is unable to conduct meaningful dialogue with the Jewish traditions from which it emerged.[123] Zionism, in short, is deaf to

---

118. Gordon, "Antisemitism and Zionism."

119. Knesset, "Basic Law." For a critique of the Basic Law, see Dubnov, "Israel's Jewish and Democratic Balance."

120. For alternative perspectives, see Omer, *Days of Awe*; Dalsheim, *Israel Has a Jewish Problem*; Yadgar, *Sovereign Jews*; and Magid, *American Post-Judaism*.

121. Yadgar, "On the Uses and Abuses of Tradition," 101.

122. Yadgar, "On the Uses and Abuses of Tradition," 102. See also Batnitzky, *How Judaism Became a Religion*.

123. Yadgar, "On the Uses and Abuses of Tradition," 107.

dissenting Judaisms. Amnon Raz-Krakotzkin agrees, observing that Israel "denies important aspects of even the country's Jewish past."[124]

America after AmericaIsrael?

Some Americans, particularly liberals and progressives, oppose the criminalization of "political" critiques of the State of Israel on free speech grounds. For many of the same people, however, criticism of Israel on "religious" grounds—in other words, criticism of Zionism itself—is seen as "crossing a line." This liberal-secular blind spot foregoes an opportunity for meaningful engagement with the "insubordinate religiosities" described in this chapter.[125] To the extent that dissenters are silenced on the pretense that they are anti-Semitic, antidemocratic, and anti-American, liberals and progressives continue to cede the terms of the debate about Judaisms, Zionisms, and US policy to AmericaIsrael. Its bipartisan gravitational pull congeals around an unspoken collective investment in Israeli/American state interpretations of Zionism. And Judaism.

And yet, to question Zionism as embodied by the Israeli State *does* delegitimate the State of Israel. This is not necessarily because such questioning is anti-Semitic, however, but because it carves out spaces in which what it means to live in community with others does not hinge on the existence of the Jewish state in its present form or, perhaps, on any Jewish state whatsoever.[126] These alternatives draw on long-standing traditions of nonnationalist Jewish thought and practice; as Lewis Siegelbaum explains, antinationalist Jews "are the legatees of a long Jewish tradition going back to the 17th-century Portuguese-Jewish philosopher Baruch Spinoza and carried forward by the German-Jewish poet Heinrich Heine, by Karl Marx, Rosa Luxemburg, and Leon Trotsky."[127] This tradition is carried forward by US advocacy groups that represent alternative Jewish collective and communal aspirations such as Jewish Voice for Peace and IfNotNow. It was expressed in certain corners of Senator Bernie Sanders' 2020 presidential campaign, which approached US-Israel relations as an opportunity to reconsider what it means to be American, Jewish, and Christian, and the complex relations between these ways of

---

124. Raz-Krakotzkin, "Religion and Nationalism in the Jewish and Zionist Context," 47.
125. Manrique, Caicedo, and Hurd, "Religiosidades Insumisas, Protestas Sociales y Democracias Hoy."
126. Boyarin, *No-State Solution*.
127. Siegelbaum, "On Anti-Zionism and Antisemitism."

life and various expressions of Zionism. It is also maintained in a flourishing critical scholarship.[128] Successful legal challenges to anti-BDS legislation in Texas and Arizona[129] and the increasingly vocal dissent of many Americans to the Israeli State's treatment of Palestinians are beginning to shift the needle.[130]

To envision alternatives requires acknowledging that, as is also the case in other traditions, political, territorial, and religious expressions of Judaism take different forms.[131] Support for Jewish individuals and communities may entail *opposition* to certain forms of political Zionism. Examples are the expulsion of Iraqi Jews after the creation of Israel, the Israeli government's limitations on nonorthodox forms of Judaism within Israel, and the 2023–24 Israeli mass killing of civilians in Gaza.[132] To see these alternatives requires that social scientists become attuned to a broader spectrum of political-religious possibility. The academic social sciences remain tethered to a separationist approach to the study of religion and politics, and often struggle to break free of its epistemological stranglehold over the modern category of religion conceived as private, volitional, and centered on belief and unbelief. Sensing that something is missing from the diplomatic and strategic accounts that dominate the field, scholars turn in vain to Christian and Jewish Zionisms to locate the missing piece of the puzzle. They will not find it there.

AmericaIsrael is, in part, the product of a productive tension between Americans' attraction to a rules-based international order and an irresistible impulse to transcend that order in the name of something bigger, to override the confines of state sovereignty in the name of a "religion that can be beyond

---

128. Neve Gordon, for example, criticizes the IHRA definition of anti-Semitism as "the Zionist definition of antisemitism" and "an Israeli counterinsurgency tool used primarily outside of Israel, in Europe and North America" ("Antisemitism and Zionism," 10).

129. As illustrated in the film *Boycott*, legal challenges to anti-boycott legislation at the state level have been successful in Texas and Arizona, where state laws have been struck down on First Amendment grounds. However, in February 2023, the Supreme Court declined to revive the *Arkansas Times*'s challenge to an Arkansas anti-boycott law requiring state government contractors to pledge not to boycott Israel, a policy the newspaper's lawyers described as a threat to a constitutionally protected form of collective protest. In its review of the case, the Eighth Circuit found that the legislation "does not ban *Arkansas Times* from publicly criticizing Israel, or even protesting the statute itself. It only prohibits economic decisions that discriminate against Israel" (Chung, "U.S. Supreme Court Spurns Challenge to Arkansas Law").

130. See the 2023 documentary *Israelism*, directed and written by Eric Axelman and Sam Eilertsen, chronicling efforts by young American Jews to redefine Judaism's relationship with Israel.

131. See Davis, "International Relations and the Jewish Question."

132. Thanks to Emma Davis.

religion."[133] It will be difficult to refashion this shared fantasy of supra-national redemption. Yet the bluster that surrounds it belies the fragility of the political and religious projects that it upholds. Though they may not speak as loudly or as forcefully, alternatives that attest to the ambivalence of the religious as a political force are bringing into view new possibilities for thinking, and living, the religious and political together. Returning to the words of Madame Mountford, "to American energy all things are possible."

---

133. Carter, "Unlikely Convergence," 179.

INTERLUDE III

Crossing

Our flight from Paris landed at Chicago O'Hare on a hot July afternoon in July 2019. With three exhausted kids in tow, we arrived at customs and were directed to an interview with a Customs and Border Protection (CBP) agent as part of the Global Entry Trusted Traveler Enrollment on Arrival program. Global Entry is a program for frequent border crossers that grants expedited clearance through customs for preapproved, low-risk travelers at selected airports upon arrival to the United States. Applicants are required to be interviewed in person. The interview appeared to be a formality, and we were anxious to move through it quickly and pick up our luggage. The agent asked about my job. I told him that I taught foreign policy and border politics, sidestepping the word *religion*. We chatted amicably for a few minutes. I had grown up hearing stories from my father about the summer in 1971 that he spent as an immigration agent in North Troy, Vermont, on the Canadian border. I was a baby, and he was in law school. Money was tight, and my parents were grateful for the fruits and vegetables that people had to leave behind at the border crossing.[1]

---

1. My father, Stephen Shakman, held a summer job with the Immigration and Naturalization Service at the North Troy-Highwater border crossing in 1971. It was a tense period because of the activities of the Front de libération de Quebec (FLQ), a militant Quebecois separatist group known for violent attacks, including the 1970 kidnapping and murder of Deputy Prime Minister Pierre Laporte. There was concern that armed members of the FLQ might try to cross the US-Canada border, in which case my father had been instructed to call Border Patrol. His superiors showed him a gun in a holster in a drawer at his station but gave him no firearms training, telling him to "go shoot rats in the dump" for practice. The original US station in North Troy, one of ten surviving 1930s station buildings in Vermont, was built in 1937. In 2014, it was nominated to the National Register of Historic Places. There are fifteen border crossings between Vermont and Quebec.

Sensing that the interview was coming to an end, I asked the agent, "Do we need to go back through the line for the kids?" "Do you want to go through that line?" he laughed, gesturing in the direction of a seemingly endless queue for foreign passport holders and another for US citizens without Global Entry. As I waited for him to return our documents, his expression suddenly changed, and his body language became tense. "You teach about the border," he said. "You know, everything you've seen on TV about what's happening on the border is a lie, right?" He had caught me off guard. "Really?" I said. "Yeah, you know, all that crap about kids being held in cages, and all that. It's all lies. I know because I saw with my own eyes. I spent six weeks down there, at the border in Texas, down south, just got back a couple weeks ago." I was speechless. I knew his statement conflicted with overwhelming public evidence, including a series of revelations about horrific detention conditions in Texas for child migrants documented in a report published the previous week by his own employer, the Department of Homeland Security (DHS).[2] The report, unambiguously titled "Management Alert—DHS Needs to Address Dangerous Overcrowding and Prolonged Detention of Children and Adults in the Rio Grande Valley (Redacted)," makes for difficult reading. It includes several full-page color photos of families with children in cages.[3]

The Homeland Security Department Office of the Inspector General (IG) published the report after visiting five Border Patrol facilities and two ports of entry in south Texas in June 2019, where they encountered "dangerous overcrowding and prolonged detention of children and adults."[4] The authors confirm that in the facilities visited, "there were more than 50 UACs ('Unaccompanied Alien Children') younger than 7 years old, and some of them had been in custody over two weeks while awaiting transfer."[5]

Though legally responsible for providing long-term detention, Immigration and Customs Enforcement (ICE) had run out of beds. During the week of the IG's visit, ICE had approximately fifty-four thousand beds occupied nationwide, but it was only funded for forty-two thousand. The report noted that unaccompanied children were being held in closed cells. Some adult detainees had resorted to protest by "clogging toilets with Mylar blankets and

---

2. US Department of Homeland Security, "Management Alert." For an internal US government report on conditions for detained migrant children published in 2022, see US Department of Health and Human Services, "Operational Challenges."

3. US Department of Homeland Security, "Management Alert."

4. US Department of Homeland Security, "Management Alert"; Roldan, "Homeland Security Report."

5. US Department of Homeland Security, "Management Alert," 6.

socks in order to be released from their cells during maintenance." The authors of the report explained that "at one facility, detainees who had been moved from their cell during cleaning refused to return to their cell. Border Patrol brought in its special operations team to demonstrate it was prepared to use force if necessary."[6] While CBP's standards on transport, escort, detention, and search (TEDS) emphasize humane treatment, hygiene and nutrition were abysmal: "although TEDS standards require agents to remain cognizant of detainees' religious and other dietary restrictions, many single adults had been receiving only bologna sandwiches. Some detainees on this diet were becoming constipated and required medical attention."[7]

The disparity in border-crossing experiences between those with Global Entry and migrants crossing from Mexico is stark. I do not know why the agent at O'Hare denied the reality of the deplorable situation in Texas. I was unable to muster the courage to challenge his account. His ability to speak and act in the name of the state deterred me from openly disagreeing with him. He was holding our five passports and spoke with conviction. I was tired. I resolved to push back next time. But that was the last time I spoke to a human being upon reentry to the United States. Since 2019, the questioning agent has been replaced with a "thinking" machine. At O'Hare, everything is biometric.

CBP is proud of its paperless facial recognition kiosks. The agency boasts that "to date, CBP has processed more than 300 million travelers using biometric facial comparison technology and prevented more than 1,800 impostors from entry to the U.S.";[8] 238 US airports use the technology. Once approved, travelers can cross into the US without showing a passport, speaking to an agent, or, in most cases, even slowing down to stop at a desk and register their crossing with a human being. CBP describes the process: "When the traveler presents him or herself for entry, or for exit, the traveler will encounter a camera connected to CBP's cloud-based TVS facial matching service via a secure, encrypted connection. This camera matches live images with existing photo templates from passenger travel documents. Once the camera captures a quality image and the system successfully matches it with historical photo templates of all travelers from the gallery associated with that manifest, the traveler proceeds to inspection for admissibility by a CBP Officer or

---

6. Roldan, "Homeland Security Report: Tensions Rising," 7–8.

7. Roldan, "Homeland Security Report: Tensions Rising," 9. On TEDS, see US Customs and Border Protection, "National Standards on Transport, Escort, Detention, and Search."

8. US Customs and Border Protection, "Say Hello to the New Face of Security, Safety and Efficiency."

exits the United States."⁹ The inspection involves walking past an agent waving you through. The program is popular. In the words of one enthusiastic traveler, "That is a fantastic invention to be able to do that, to be able to come into America and to go straight through with the facial to come in through the customs. As far as I'm concerned, the more the better, the better security that we can put universal, the better it can be for all of us." Another traveler exclaimed, "We did this today, let me say it is awesome!! Through customs and outside in under one minute."[10]

CBP also uses biometric facial comparison technology at sea points of entry. In 2022, working in partnership with Princess Cruise Lines, the agency announced that facial biometrics will be used at the Port of San Francisco, adding to fourteen other seaports across the United States that rely on the technology. The San Francisco CBP Field Office covers ports of entry in Alaska, northern California, Colorado, Hawaii, Idaho, northern Nevada, Oregon, Utah, and Wyoming as well as Guam and the Commonwealth of the Northern Mariana Islands. The collaboration with Princess Cruise Lines was announced with a flourish: "as of September 2022, CBP has leveraged facial biometrics to prevent more than 1,600 impostors using genuine travel documents from illegally entering the United States at air and land Ports of Entry."[11]

Yet CBP faces challenges from within. In January 2024, twenty-eight US state attorneys general signed a letter to President Joe Biden and Homeland Security secretary Alejandro Mayorkas in support of "Operation Lone Star," Texas governor Greg Abbott's controversial effort to secure the Texas-Mexico border. In a revival of tropes popularized in the early 2000s by the Minutemen, the letter of the attorneys general described the situation on the border as an existential threat to the United States due to the federal government's failure to secure the border. "Millions of people illegally coming into Texas as part of a coordinated assault on our border is an invasion," they warned, and "without a border, we would quickly cease to be a nation at all."[12] The attorneys general framed the situation in apocalyptic terms. Either Operation Lone Star receives the federal support it deserves, or the border will be

---

9. US Customs and Border Protection, "Say Hello to the New Face of Security, Safety and Efficiency."

10. US Customs and Border Protection, "Say Hello to the New Face of Security, Safety and Efficiency."

11. US Customs and Border Protection, "CBP, Princess Cruise Line Introduces Facial Biometrics at Port of San Francisco."

12. Quotations in this paragraph are from Texas Office of the Attorney General, "Supporting Texas' Efforts to Secure the Border."

open to cartels, slavers, terrorists, and rapists. "It is this Administration's deliberate refusal to enforce immigration law—indeed, its deliberate subversion of that law to grant to illegal immigrants benefits to which they are legally barred—that has encouraged millions of people to place themselves in hock to murderous criminal cartels; at the mercy of rapists; and into the hands of modern-day slavers, as these sex- and child-traffickers are more properly called." The letter concludes, menacingly, "If you cannot bring yourselves to enforce the law, get out of the way so Texas can."

The Oglala Sioux tribe in South Dakota responded by barring South Dakota governor Kristi Noem from the Pine Ridge Reservation because her attorney general, Marty Jackley, had signed the letter. "Due to the safety of the Oyate, effective immediately, you are hereby Banished from the homelands of the Ogala Sioux Tribe!" wrote Frank Star Comes Out, the president of the tribe.[13] He explained that "many of the people coming to the southern border of the United States in search of jobs and a better life are Indian people from such places as El Salvadore, Guatemalan and Mexico [sic] and don't deserve to be dehumanized and mistreated . . . they don't need to be put in cages, separated from their children like during the Trump Administration, or be cut up by razor wire furnished by, of all places, South Dakota."[14]

It is easy to be frustrated with CBP. At the same time, as Francisco Cantú's account of life in the Border Patrol attests, border enforcement is tasked with managing the unmanageable.[15] Border security has become a convenient repository for a host of existential fears including climate emergency, rising economic inequality, the demise of white supremacy, challenges to old-school expressions of masculinity and "proper" gender roles, threats to US (and Israeli) military supremacy, and anxiety about uncontrolled lawlessness and violence. Harel Shapira's study of the Minutemen in southern Arizona showed as much. The border's elusive yet tantalizing promise of exclusivity, order, community, and transcendence attracts liberals, conservatives, Christians, non-Christians, and the religiously indifferent. It is not only Christian nationalists.[16] It is not only the Minutemen. The promise of the border animates the work of religious asylum discussed in chapter 1. It is expressed through rituals of institutionalized legal discrimination such as the Muslim ban and

---

13. Shabad, "South Dakota Tribe Bans Gov. Kristi Noem from Reservation."
14. Oglala Sioux Tribe, "Statement of Oglala Sioux Tribal President Frank Star Comes Out."
15. See Cantú, *Line Becomes a River*.
16. On the threat to US democracy posed by Christian nationalists, see Gorski and Perry's *Flag and the Cross*. I see this "threat" in broader terms as compared to these authors, not confined to what they describe as Christian nationalism.

its antecedents that legalized discrimination in the name of national security, public order, and public health. It is part of the gravitational pull of AmericaIsrael and its false promise of stability, security, and superiority. The elusive promise and peace of the ideal border is constantly undermined by fear of various disruptive presences, including the countermagic of the outlaw saint Santa Muerte.

CHAPTER 4

Refusing

Holy Death in the Borderlands

> Against the magic of the border, there is counter-magic.
> SHAHRAM KHOSRAVI AND MAHMOUD KESHAVARZ,
> "The Magic of Borders"

Novelist and cultural anthropologist Hilary Cunningham observed that "borders, as perimeters of state authority, are not only significant arenas of state power, but also important loci of resistance to state sovereignty."[1] US borderlands are important sites for the emergence of countersovereigns.[2] Among them is La Santa Muerte, or Holy Death, popular patron saint of the marginalized, threatened, and poor. Maligned by the Catholic Church as a form of idol worship and veneration of death, vilified by Mexican and American law-enforcement officials as a folk saint—alongside Jesús Malverde and Juan Soldado—of the drug cartels, and criminalized as a "death cult" by the US Foreign Military Studies Office and a form of "deviant spirituality" and source of "spiritual insurgency" by law enforcement, devotion to the saint has nonetheless grown in spectacular fashion in the twenty-first century:

> Santa Muerte's popularity in Mexico exploded after 2001. Two very public sites emerged: a public sanctuary/shrine created by Enriqueta Romero in Tepito, a large, poor neighborhood in Mexico City, and a Santa Muerte sanctuary founded by David Romo of the Traditional Apostolic Catholic Church Mexico-USA in Colonia Morelos, a rough neighborhood of Mexico City near Tepito. The Bony Lady now claims some ten to twelve million followers in Mexico, Central America, and the US; religion historian Andrew Chestnut claims it is the fastest growing religious movement in the Americas.[3]

---

1. Cunningham, "Sanctuary and Sovereignty," 372.
2. Spencer Dew describes Santa Muerte as a countersovereign in his essay "The Treachery of Sovereignty," November 2021, on file with the author.
3. Lorentzen, "Saint of the Dispossessed."

Offering protection from harm in an unforgiving world, and drawing on the image and reality of death, *la flaquita* (the skinny girl) serves as an uncanny reminder that no one—not even Customs and Border Protection officers—can escape death.[4]

This chapter introduces the saint and her followers as agents of borderlessness. Always on the move, they challenge US norms of sovereignty and territoriality. Her followers are a fugitive, resistant, runaway series of communities with certain parallels to the intentionally stateless peoples of upland Southeast Asia described by James Scott in *The Art of Not Being Governed*.[5] Devotion to la Santísima is a form of what Carter characterizes as "unstately" religion.[6] She enacts a bodily refusal of US borders.[7] The threatening aura that surrounds her cannot be captured within the terms of the study of popular religion,[8] or the study of border politics, political economy, or *narcocultura*. The movement is a popular political and religious insurgency that refuses borders of all kinds: between religion and superstition, the United States and Mexico, gay and straight, legal and illegal, Indigenous and settler, man and woman, territoriality and flight, black and white, and life and death.

Introducing Santa Muerte and her followers into our story affords a better understanding of the lived practices of outsiders to American (border) religion and also reveals a new perspective on its most committed insiders. US law-enforcement officials fear Santa Muerte's real presence. Her material presence, and the primitive and demonic forms of devotion that it is said to

---

4. "La protección que se le supone a la imagen, aunque está construida desde éticas muy diversas, tiene el común denominador de referirse a la muerte y ésta contiene siempre la idea de *fin*, de *límite*, de *frontera*; dicho contenido es el que se resalta en todos los casos, sugiriendo un lema más o menos como éste: 'la muerte está conmigo, y si está conmigo puede estar contra ti, por tanto es mejor que no me molestes'" (Castells Ballarin, "La Santa Muerte y la cultura de los derechos humanos," 20). Shrines to Santa Muerte are found throughout the United States, including in Los Angeles, Chicago, Miami, New York, Houston, and Tucson.

5. Scott, *Art of Not Being Governed*.

6. Carter, "White Messianic." Carter argues for conceiving of the sacred otherwise, asking, "Can we imagine a form of we-ness, forms of life together, solidarity, sociality, social life that are unhinged from the charismatic messianic dynamics of the logics of the state? Is there a way to think an 'otherwise, we'? Might we invoke an un-stately religion, illiberal religion, the sacred otherwise, not predicated upon the logic of polis. Not delimited, bordered, and border-protecting 'we the people.'"

7. Thanks to Greg Johnson for this phrase and for the connection to Native Hawaiian resistance to US sovereignty. See Johnson, "Domestic Bones, Foreign Land, and the Kingdom Come."

8. "Creo que la de la religiosidad popular no es una categoría suficiente para estudiar el fenómeno del amplio culto a La Santa Muerte" (Castells Ballarin, "La Santa Muerte y la cultura de los derechos humanos," 20).

inspire, allegedly renders her devotees incapable of distinguishing between spirituality and criminality. This blurring of the boundaries, these authorities suggest, aggravates devotees' susceptibility to the temptations of the drug trade. The deep-seated fear of Santa Muerte among law enforcement and anxieties about the effects of her presence have led to clumsy attempts to manage her alleged incursions on public order, "good" religion, impermeable borders, and Western civilization. I discuss three examples of attempts to curb her appeal and criminalize her followers: in the courts, in a master's thesis, and in the work of a government consulting firm. I conclude that interpreting devotion to Santa Muerte through conventional categories of religion, law, and politics falls short. Rather than forcing her into these categories, it is worth considering her potential to teach us something new.

Meet the Saint

Santa Muerte is difficult to pin down.[9] Her devotees invoke a dizzying mixture of precolonial, Catholic, Indigenous, Caribbean, and African traditions. A composite figure incorporating characteristics and powers from a seemingly endless list of disparate times and places, her genealogy is complex, shrouded in mystery, and perennially contested. That is part of her appeal. Santa Muerte shares certain characteristics with the Brazilian female trickster Pomba Gira, among other figures.[10] Laura Roush describes the rise of Santa Muerte devotion as a set of "dispersed and vague practices [that] gained the appearance of a coherent rite in the wake of accusations against a 'cult' that did not yet exist."[11] Lois Lorentzen describes her as a Catholic-African mélange incorporating aspects of Haitian Vodou Cuban Santería, and Brazilian Palo

---

9. La Santa Muerte goes by many names, including the Skinny Lady (*la flaquita*), the Bony Lady (*la huesuda*), the White Girl (*la niña blanca*), the White Sister (*la hermana blanca*), the Pretty Girl (*la niña bonita*), the Powerful Lady (*la dama poderosa*), the Godmother (*la madrina*), Lady of the Shadows (*señora de las sombras*), White Lady (*señora blanca*), Black Lady (*señora negra*), Holy Girl (*niña santa*), Saint Sebastienne (*Santa Sebastiana*), and Beautiful Lady Sebastienne (*Doña Bella Sebastiana*).

10. Like Santa Muerte, Pomba Gira offers protection to devotees and materializes in "liminal zones that both connect and demarcate the spaces in which humans compartmentalize the world—where directions converge, day turns to night, and the world of the living encounters that of the dead." She is "a trickster figure known for ignoring limits and exceeding boundaries, whether of social comportment or moral action" (Hayes, *Holy Harlots*, 51, 65). Thanks to Ayodeji Ogunnaike.

11. Roush, "Santa Muerte, Protection, and *Desamparo*," 147.

FIGURE 9. Santa Muerte shrine, Nogales. Photo by Mauro Trejo, 2022.

Mayombe.¹² Howe, Zaraysky, and Lorentzen point to the influence of a pre-Hispanic cult of death dating back three millennia and later merging with Catholicism, citing death figures revered by Maya, Zapotecos, and Totonacas and highlighting ritual practices of the Aztecs and the Mexicas. They also describe a belief that the Holy Death came from Yoruba traditions brought by African slaves, passing through Vodou, Santería, or Palo Mayombe, and later merging with Catholicism.¹³ Anthropologist Katia Perdigón Castañeda traces Santa Muerte's origins to medieval Europe, suggesting that the figure is based on a European archetype of death seen in religious art.¹⁴ Desirée Martín encapsulates her political and religious genealogy as follows:

> Many argue that the cult to Santa Muerte has existed for hundreds of years and is linked to pre-Hispanic goddesses such as Coatlicue, the goddess of life,

---

12. Lorentzen, "Saint of the Dispossessed." Vargas Gonzalez ("¡Oh Muerte Sagrada!") also associates Santa Muerte with "Afro-Caribbean and Brazilian spiritual traditions, and specifically with the goddess Orisha (also known as Oya, goddess of war and the ruler of cemeteries and funeral rites)," cited in Martín, *Borderlands Saints*, 187.

13. Howe, Zaraysky, and Lorentzen, "Devotional Crossings," 26–27.

14. Howe, Zaraysky, and Lorentzen, "Devotional Crossings," 27.

death, and rebirth, or Mictecacihuatl, the queen of the underworld and goddess of death. Anthropologist Alfredo Vargas Gonzalez affirms that the image of Santa Muerte has been present since the Spanish conquest. He cites her historical association with San Pascual Bailon (also known as San Pascual Rey or San Pascualito, as well as Santo Esqueleto [Saint Skeleton], since he is sometimes represented as a skeleton), a Catholic saint with a long cult history in Chiapas and Guatemala (Vargas Gonzalez 103). Lomnitz cites Serge Gruzinski's description of colonial religious sodalities or *cofradías* in Mexico, including one from the eighteenth century that developed a cult to Santa Muerte and employed the saint's image 'to gain political power' by granting the miracle 'of handing [the group] the rods of justice [*bara de govierno (sic)*]' (*Death* 486).[15]

Santa Muerte's kaleidoscopic Indigenous and settler-colonial histories are a source of power, and part of her strength and appeal. This situates her firmly in Mexican history. In his retelling of the history of Mexican republicanism, Arturo Chang tracks the "transformative influence of indigeneity, religion, and plebeian politics on republican political thought."[16] Describing Mexican revolutionaries' efforts to reclaim and remake Catholicism as simultaneously Indigenous, Mexican, and pan-American,[17] Chang describes the revolution as a critical juncture in the popular indigenization of Catholicism in the Americas, marking the creation of a unique form of Mexican Catholicism that was always indigenized in significant ways. Santa Muerte is another popular contemporary indigenization of Mexican Catholicism. William Calvo-Quirós describes her as "a peculiarly Mexican vernacular saint."[18] Pilar Castells Ballarin observes that "sin que importe demasiado la falta de unanimidad en cuanto a su fuente originaria (prehispánica, colonial, sincrética o actual). Es una construcción cultural de gran vitalidad y dotada de una fuerza" (The lack of unanimity with regard to her origins [pre-Hispanic, colonial, syncretic, or present] matters little. She is a cultural construction with great vitality and is gifted with strength.)[19] Her appeal cannot be explained away as a side effect of economic discontent, political disenfranchisement, or religious exclusion. Devotion to the saint is part of a longer tradition of the indigenization of Mexican spiritual life that works outside of, while also

---

15. Martín, *Borderlands Saints*, 186; Vargas González, "¡Oh Muerte Sagrada!"; Lomnitz, *Death and the Idea of Mexico*.
16. Chang, "Restoring Anáhuac," 9.
17. Chang, "Restoring Anáhuac."
18. Calvo-Quirós, *Undocumented Saints*, 230. Calvo-Quirós offers an excellent ethnographic and historical account of the ritual repertoires associated with worship of Santa Muerte.
19. Castells Ballarin, "La Santa Muerte," 16.

riffing on, logics of nation-state sovereignty. She is, in the words of Calvo-Quirós, "a traveling enclave of imaginary and spiritual nationhood."[20]

Devotees pray for the saint's active intercession to overcome life challenges, including soliciting her help with punishing enemies and rivals, finding employment, ensuring good health and safety for those crossing borders, and finding or reviving romantic love. Some call on her alongside other popular saints; as Pansters explains, "when she is called upon to support migrants attempting to cross into the United States, she stands close to Juan Soldado, the poor soldier from Tijuana who was believed to be unjustly tried and executed in 1938 and later became a folk saint."[21] Many of her followers approach worship through the notions of *paro* and *amparo*, words derived from the Spanish verb *parar*, meaning "to stop." Bigliardi explains: "The Diccionario del español de México registers three meanings: (i) interruption or suspension of an activity (incl. the medical expression paro cardíaco), (ii) temporal suspension of work as a form of protest, (iii) colloquially, 'to do somebody a paro' (*hacerle el paro*) means helping somebody to get out of some difficulty. But also a difficulty can consist of some kind of undesired interruption; thus the term displays an intrinsic ambiguity. This, in my interpretation, deeply resonates with the symbolic ambiguity of la Santa."[22]

This emphasis on stopping, aversion, and avoidance of difficulty also aligns with certain practices in O'odham Sonoran Catholicism. "Within Saints Way [*Sasaznto Himdag*], or O'odham Sonoran Catholicism," explain Seth Schermerhorn and Lillia McEnaney, "saints themselves are often spoken of and treated as powerful entities in their own right, or at least as an extension of their O'odham owners, who are capable of both helping and hurting O'odham."[23] Many devotees to la Santísima consider themselves Catholic.[24] Others reject the church and Christianity altogether.[25] There are many In-

---

20. Calvo-Quirós, *Undocumented Saints*, 235.

21. Pansters, *La Santa Muerte*, 30.

22. "Due acknowledgement should be given to the term paro (pl. paros, cf. the verb parar, to stop)—a favour consisting in the stoppage or inversion or avoidance of an undesirable or unfavourable situation, analogous to favours usually exchanged among human beings" (Bigliardi, "La Santa Muerte and Her Interventions in Human Affairs," 317–18).

23. Schermerhorn and McEnaney, "Through Indigenous Eyes," 43.

24. As Calvo-Quirós explains, "relations between the LSM movement and the Catholic Church are contentious and muddy—sometimes even to those following LSM. LSM's followers understand her as being part of a much larger and interconnected matrix of spiritual entities, a matrix that includes some traditional recognized Catholic saints such as the Virgin Mary and others, and others of whom are not" (Calvo-Quirós, *Undocumented Saints*, 256).

25. Using these categories risks oversimplifying the complex history of Christianity. On the

digenous practitioners, and Indigeneity is often projected onto the figure of Santa Muerte. There is a complicated Indigenous/mestizo history at work among devotees. Affiliations are complex and vary over time. Devotion to the saint is also deeply commercialized, offering a simultaneous celebration and parody of late capitalist subjectivity. She invokes more than a mere logic of exchange, while also participating in that logic.[26]

Santa Muerte refuses the terms of the war on drugs, in which she is depicted as a "tool of the trade" alongside cartels and guns. She defies the organized hierarchy of the Catholic Church by standing in solidarity with the LGBTQ+ community.[27] Many return the favor. She denies sovereignty to law-enforcement authorities who forcefully claim it, standing with the undocumented, the poor, and the border crossing. Her following is characterized by what Martín describes as "the transgression of all manner of boundaries, whether spatial, temporal, legal, ethical, sexual, racial, or class-based."[28] She embraces those in limbo. She loves the "naco/naca"—a Mexican term used to denote "all that is tacky, low-class, vulgar, uncultured, dark-skinned, or indigenous-looking."[29] She is the great equalizer.[30] She embraces otherness, including the otherness of death, because she personifies it: "La Santa Muerte is not identified with a deceased person; rather, she is the personification or sanctification of death itself, and this imbues her with extraordinary power."[31] She is also selective when it comes to whom she wants to help; not all petition-

---

refiguring of Christianity by Indigenous peoples in the wake of a catastrophic epidemic in the sixteenth century that left the colonial church in ruins, see Jennifer Scheper Hughes's counter-history, *Church of the Dead*.

26. As Mara Epstein and Sarah McFarland Taylor explain, "traditionally, discomfort in dealing with the intertwined dynamics of religion and marketing has been rooted in a cultural assumption that commodified or transactional religion is somehow 'inauthentic' religion, as this represents a transgression of a perceived binary between the 'sacred' and the 'secular'" (Epstein and Taylor, *Selling the Sacred*, 5).

27. See Calvo-Quirós, *Undocumented Saints*, 261–67. Calvo-Quirós notes that Santa Muerte has become popular among LGBTQ+ Latinx communities "because she reflects their subjugated reality—the slow violence of social death in the eyes of the state and other institutions like the Catholic Church" (266).

28. Martín, *Borderlands Saints*, 190.

29. Martín, *Borderlands Saints*, 192.

30. "This saint's immense power is epitomized by her great equalizing capacity, all the more so in a society as deeply unequal as neoliberal Mexico, for death undoes the differences between rich and poor, the included and the excluded, the neo-liberal tycoon and the market woman, mestizo and indigenous, and criminals and law-abiding citizens" (Pansters, *La Santa Muerte*, 18).

31. Pansters, *La Santa Muerte*, 29.

ers are taken under her wing. One devotee describes her as "a jealous deity who is prone to revenge and discriminating in her choice of devotees; these are precisely the reasons she is valued."[32] For her followers, "Santa Muerte's dark side is not exclusively or even primarily linked to the criminal underworld or the drug wars. Instead, it manifests itself through the death saint's purported jealousy and the price she supposedly exacts from believers who dare to use her powers recklessly or who fail to pay her proper tribute."[33] Santa Muerte has a dark side. But it is not the one on which law enforcement insists.

Commentary on the saint is divided between two camps: historians and scholars of popular religion tend to be sympathetic to her followers as "underdogs," on the one hand, and law enforcement, governmental, and church authorities are almost uniformly suspicious and hostile, on the other. Examples of the former include Castells Ballarin, who attributes Santa Muerte's popularity to the suffering caused by an indifferent neoliberal Mexican state that neglects the needs of ordinary people,[34] and Martín, who detects racist, classist, and anti-Indigenous sentiment behind the denigration of the saint's followers. According to Martín, "Accusations on the part of many middle- or upper-class Mexicans and others that La Santisima Muerte and her devotees are satanic or criminal conceals their true disdain for the impoverished, transient, migrant, indigenous, and naco masses who worship the death saint."[35]

The racialized denigration of Santa Muerte and her devotees by governmental and clerical authorities is part of a long history of the criminalization of forms of spiritual work defined as magic, superstition, sorcery, devil worship, "not religion," and so on. In *Experiments with Power*, J. Brent Crosson examines these dynamics in the context of the practice of obeah, a form of spiritual work popular in Trinidad and across the Caribbean.[36] Criminalized under Spanish (1592–1707) and British (1797–1962) rule, obeah was a crime in Trinidad until 2000 and remains one in much of the anglophone Caribbean. Although Crosson initially set out to redeem obeah as a legitimate religion, his interlocutors challenged the terms of this attempt: "rather than making

---

32. Howe, Zaraysky, and Lorentzen, "Devotional Crossings," 33.

33. Martín, *Borderlands Saints*, 196.

34. "En México se estaría dando un traspaso de las peticiones que normalmente se hacen al Estado hacia La Santa Muerte: trabajo, vivienda, una vida mejor, seguridad, educación, salud, como parte del repertorio que citan sus fieles, son asignables a las funciones del Estado, a través de sus aparatos. Se transfieren a La Santa Muerte las peticiones que, se supone, son exclusivas del Estado" (Castells Ballarin, "La Santa Muerte y la cultura de los derechos humanos," 19).

35. Martín, *Borderlands Saints*, 193.

36. Crosson, *Experiments with Power*, 3.

obeah into a religion, they made me ask how spiritual work challenged the hegemonic limits of the category of religion."[37] After reconsidering his terms,[38] Crosson settled on a definition of obeah as a "healing-harming engagement with esoteric power."[39] The misalignment between obeah and Western categories of religion results from the fact that the act of defining religion and secularism excludes African-identified practices on racial grounds.[40] As Crosson explains, "the identification of evil with African (not-)religion has been a key part of Western modernity's moral and racial discourse, particularly in popular representations of obeah and 'voodoo' for American, British, French, and West African audiences."[41]

US imperial practices are saturated with this moral and racial discourse. The American occupation of Haiti between 1915 and 1934, for example, identified "sorcery" with rebellion. Haitian spiritual practices were seen as forms of political insurgency, not as religion.[42] As historian Kate Ramsey explains, the US enforced laws against *les sortilèges* (spells) in Haiti in the name of moral decency and the consolidation of political control.[43] On their face, such regulations did not involve the repression of religion but were seen as promoting universal values, a free market, modern scientism, public health, the rule of law, and religious freedom. The othering of African religion is central to law enforcement's fear of Santa Muerte and her followers. Religious freedom, American-style, was never intended for sorcerer insurgents or outlaw saints.[44]

Summoning One's "Spiritual Armor": Santa Muerte in the Crosshairs

Santa Muerte's location outside of the secular-religious grid of intelligibility raises deep suspicion on both sides of the US-Mexico border. In 2009, then

---

37. Crosson, *Experiments with Power*, 5.

38. "To describe it as either 'healing' or 'sorcery' were both moves of translation that wedged African-identified religious practices into Western categories rather than focusing on the ways these practices could 'recursively' transform a scholar's categories of analysis" (Crosson, *Experiments with Power*, 21).

39. Crosson, *Experiments with Power*, 22.

40. "The race-based exclusion of African-identified practices from both sides of this [secular-religious] dialectic was a foundational act in the making of religion and secularism as modern 'universals'" (Crosson, *Experiments with Power*, 8). Vincent Lloyd and Jonathan Kahn make a similar point in their introduction to *Race and Secularism in America*.

41. Crosson, *Experiments with Power*, 10.

42. Ramsey, *Spirits and the Law*.

43. American-sponsored antisuperstition campaigns against in Haiti targeting vodou, materialism and paganism also targeted Catholicism per Ramsey.

44. Hurd and Sullivan, "Introduction: Religion, Law, and Politics, American-style," 1–16.

Mexican president Felipe Calderón ordered the Mexican army to bulldoze nearly forty shrines to the saint along the border, many of which had been created to ensure safe passage into the United States and for general protection.[45] A few years earlier, the Mexican government had stymied devotees' attempts to obtain formal legal recognition as a religion: in 2002, the Traditional Apostolic Catholic Church Mexico-USA founded the Sanctuary of Holy Death in Mexico City and registered as a religious organization the following year. But in 2005, the government of Vicente Fox, under pressure from the Catholic Church, revoked its official status as a religious organization in a twenty-five-page resolution "claiming that the group did not meet the qualifications of a religion, citing theological doctrine dating back to the Council of Trent in 1570."[46] In 2016, the Mexican government registered and recognized the first nonprofit organization affiliated with Santa Muerte veneration, Santa Muerte Universal (SMU, or Rosita de Natanahel AC), though the movement remains unrecognized as an official religion.[47]

Both church and state locate Santa Muerte as "superstition" in Storm's tripartite division between the secular, the religious, and the superstitious.[48] As a result of devotees' alleged failure to modernize religiously, they are presumed to be overly affected by the saint's material presence. Being under her sway inclines them toward criminality. Devotion to Santa Muerte is, in the eyes of the authorities, either not religion or it is "bad" religion. As one pair of analysts put it, "Who can say if those who are willing to compromise their values—and in a sense have already darkened their souls—are not willing to complete the transformational process taking place and accept criminally derived forms of spirituality and religion into their hearts?"[49]

For law enforcement, Santa Muerte is unrecognizable as the sympathetic would-be saint of the downtrodden depicted by anthropologists and scholars of religion. Instead, these authorities describe her as a "tool of the trade" of drug dealers and smugglers and a form of devil worship that both emerges from and conduces to criminality. Campaigns to criminalize her followers evoke national security, good religion, and law and order; one journalist "tracked down more than a dozen instances nationwide where law enforcement officials have used Santa Muerte practice as an indicator, targeting worshippers as criminals. Court records show that prayer books, statuettes, even

45. Lorentzen, "Saint of the Dispossessed."
46. Howe, Zaraysky, and Lorentzen, "Devotional Crossings," 29.
47. Calvo-Quirós, *Undocumented Saints*, 246–47.
48. Storm, *Invention of Religion in Japan*.
49. Bunker and Bunker, "Spiritual Significance," 2–3.

skeleton-emblazoned air fresheners have been used as evidence in efforts to detain, search, convict and sentence people."[50] David Metcalfe, a researcher tracking law-enforcement reactions to Santa Muerte devotion, explained to journalist Matt Smith that "linking Santa Muerte to crime persists as a sort of legend repeated from officer to officer, without any real research to back up their beliefs."[51]

Writing in the *FBI Law Enforcement Bulletin*, Robert Bunker (of the "darkened their souls" quotation two paragraphs previous) describes devotion to Santa Muerte as a "spiritual insurgency": "Enough ritualistic behaviors, including killings, have occurred in Mexico to leave open the possibility that a spiritual insurgency component of the narcotics wars now exists. Not all of the narcotics leaders, their foot soldiers, and assassins have remained religious or, alternatively, embraced secularism. But, evidence suggests that the numbers of defections to the cults that worship a perverted Christian god (e.g., La Familia Michoacana and Los Caballeros Templarios) and the various unsanctioned saints (e.g., Jesús Malverde, Juan Soldado, and Santa Muerte) have grown for years." He continues, "While the adherents of a more benign drug saint, such as Jesús Malverde, can engage in nonreligious killing, others who worship Santa Muerte increasingly appear unable to separate their criminality from their spiritual beliefs."[52] Pamela and Robert Bunker develop a longue durée approach to religious history in an essay in *Small Wars Journal*:

> This insurgency has at its basis a spiritual, if not religious, component that threatens the underlying foundations of our modern Western value system. This component is derived from the well known cartel technique of offering an individual ¿Plata O Plomo?—take our silver or we will fill you with our lead. As a tactic taken by groups with a theological bent, such as La Familia, this offer becomes Faustian, join us and in the process give up your soul or die, a choice historically associated with incidents of religious conversion at the tip of a sword. That technique is typically carried out by young religions, such as militant Christianity and Islam, during their expansionistic phases. These post-battlefield mass conversions are considered by the victors as actually saving the souls of those joining the righteous ranks of God's chosen. A side benefit of such practices is of course to replenish the ranks of the fallen and to vastly increase the size of a religious movement via an ever-expanding holy war. Compare the size and power of Islam in the 7th century to that of the religion a couple of centuries later and the historical benefits of this process

50. Smith, "Modern-Day Witch Trials."
51. Smith, "Modern-Day Witch Trials."
52. Bunker, "Santa Muerte."

become readily apparent. Even Christianity, with Emperor Constatine's [sic] conversion prior to the Battle of the Milvian Bridge in the early 4th century, has benefited from a similar process with the subsequent mass religious conversion of the Roman state and its legions.[53]

These authors conclude that police need wellness and spirituality programs, "to provide 'spiritual armor' against dark ritualistic crime scenes and altars containing human remains."

In an analysis of the misperceptions that led to the botched 1993 Bureau of Alcohol, Tobacco, Firearms, and Explosives raid on the Branch Davidian compound in Waco, Texas, Nancy Ammerman observes that "the tendency to discount the influence of religious beliefs and to evaluate situations largely in terms of a leader's individual criminal or psychological motives is, I believe, very widespread in the FBI. In our initial briefings with negotiators and tacticians, the consensus around the table was that when they encountered people with religious beliefs, those beliefs were usually a convenient cover for criminal activity."[54] While the presumption among law enforcement is that religious implements connected to Santa Muerte are problematic "tools of the trade" that conduce to violence, it may be more accurate to describe guns and drugs as devotional objects in this context.

Private consulting firms such as C/O Futures, LLC, founded by Robert Bunker, also criminalize Santa Muerte and her followers. C/O Futures describes itself as "providing specialized research and analytical consulting services that facilitate client knowledge solutions for addressing future socio-political and operational environment shaping and response."[55] The firm's mission is "to further and protect liberal-democratic values and institutions—both public and private—in the face of the disruptive systemic level change taking place during the transition from the modern to post-modern epochs of human civilization." Among their five "client service areas" is "Narratives," which they describe on their website next to a photo showing an array of "tools of the [drug] trade" that includes a Santa Muerte figurine. The page reads:

> Research and analysis related to the Narratives service area pertains to constructed realities and cultural norms held by nonsecular threat group members and their organizations, as well as secular authoritarian ideologies, that are in variance to liberal-democratic values. C/O Futures, LLC principals and associates have extensive professional experience related to narratives analysis. This service area includes the following functional groupings:

53. Bunker and Bunker, "Spiritual Significance."
54. Ammerman, "Waco, Federal Law Enforcement, and Scholars of Religion," 292.
55. Quotations in this section are from the C/O Futures website.

- *Radical Islamist Culture*—Salafi-jihadist and Shia extremist values and world views that may include ritual killing and self-sacrificial (cult of the martyr) elements.
- *White Nationalism and Neo-Nazi Culture*—far right extremist and hate groups espousing racial purity, white supremacy, and governmental and ethnic conspiracy theories; can manifest fringe Christian, Satanic, or pagan (Odinist) spiritual forms.
- *Violent Leftist & Anarchist Culture*—neo-Marxist, naturalistic, and nihilistic ideologies in violent opposition to liberal-democracy and capitalism.
- *Narco and Mara Cultura*—Latin American derived cartel and gang culture steeped in violence, brutality, and illicit activities.
- *Dark Spirituality & Occultism*—forms of dark (human sacrificial and death magic linked) spirituality and occultism found predominately, but not exclusively, with some cartel and gang members and their larger groups.
- *Deradicalization Narratives*—approaches and programs to deradicalize VNSA members and promote liberal-democratic norms.
- *Authoritarian Narratives Undermining Liberal-Democratic States*—primarily foreign (Russian and Chinese) social media based propaganda and information operations targeting liberal-democratic institutions and values for societal disruption and authoritarian shaping purposes.
- *Epochal Narrative Change*—liberal-democratic narratives protection and furtherance strategies and programs as a component of post-modern civilizational conflict.

The site links to publications on Santa Muerte authored by C/O Futures associates, with a note specifying that "research and analytical products provided by C/O Futures, LLC can range from research notes and essays through larger monographs, customized studies, threat analysis and projections, and book length publications and anthologies. Additionally, response and mitigation guidance, as well as opposing threat group programs and doctrinal and policy support, can be supplied."

Writing in PoliceMag.org, Richard Valdemar reinforces C/O Futures's portrayal of devotion to Santa Muerte as a perverse form of idol worship associated with drug-related crime and violence. In an example of the anti-Indigenous strain of efforts to criminalize the saint and her followers, Valdemar posits a connection between worship of Santa Muerte and a revival of human sacrifice. He connects the saint to worship of the female Aztec god of the dead, Mictecacihuatl, celebrated in Mexico on the Day of the Dead, and connects this worship to the exclusion of what he describes as "traditional Catholic saints":

> What is far more disturbing is the growing acceptance of this perverse idol worship among the general Mexican population. Thousands attend processions

and celebrations to honor Santa Muerte and the traditional Catholic saints are ignored. Some human sacrifices to Santa Muerte have been claimed in Tijuana and Nuevo Laredo in 2006. In 2008, 11 headless bodies were found in the Yucatan and the heads were said to have been burned in honor of Santa Muerte. Perhaps Mexico is returning to the practice of human sacrifice to a new Mictecacihuatl, the female Aztec god of the dead.[56]

To follow Santa Muerte is antireligious, antiorthodoxy, and anti–law and order. While some in the drug trade may engage in "nonreligious" killing, it is impossible for followers of Santa Muerte. Their deviant religion contaminates everything. Devotees have fallen prey to bad religion that is exacerbated by poverty, lack of education, poor governance, and a childlike attraction to pagan ways. Beyond that, devotion to the saint is a form of devil worship, as suggested by Valdemar's spiritual warfare epigraph from Ephesians 6:10–12:

> Finally, draw your strength from the Lord and from His mighty power. Put on the armor of God so that you may be able to stand firm against the tactics of the devil. For our struggle is not with flesh and blood but with principalities, with the powers, with the world rulers of this present darkness, with evil spirits in the heavens.[57]

Law-enforcement authorities on both sides of the border depict Santa Muerte as a spiritual and material threat to US and Mexican national security that commands dangerous and subversive (read: Indigenous, pagan, dark-skinned) forces against the righteous defenders of (the borders of) modernity and civilization. These officials fear Santa Muerte's real satanic presence in an echo of the 1980s Satanic panic, a modern-day set of Salem witch trials that involved accusations of a satanic entity that stood behind an alleged "vast conspiracy" of ritual child abuse that became the focus of concern.[58] One

---

56. Valdemar, "Patron Saints of the Mexican Drug Underworld." Anthropologist Kirby Farah explains the history glossed in this passage: "Spanish conquerors faced difficulty in convincing native peoples to give up their rituals honoring death goddess Mictecacihuatl. The compromise was to move these indigenous festivities from late July to early November to correspond with Allhallowtide—the three-day Christian observance of All Saints' Eve, All Saints' Day and All Souls' Day. With this move, the holiday was nominally connected to Catholicism. But many practices and beliefs associated with the worship of the dead remained deeply indigenous" ("Day of the Dead").

57. Valdemar, "Patron Saints of the Mexican Drug Underworld."

58. Nearly two hundred people were charged with crimes involving occult ritual abuse over the course of this collective hysteria, and dozens were convicted. See Beck, *We Believe the Children*. Among the more widely publicized episodes in the panic was a lawsuit filed against Proctor & Gamble by a couple from Kansas, James and Linda Newton, accusing the company of supporting "the church of Satan" by funneling profits from P&G's household goods business

journalist reporting on Santa Muerte observed that "many law enforcement agents actually believe in Santa Muerte as a supernatural entity that has the power to influence human action and events."[59] The materiality of her presence—in the form of statues, air fresheners, screen savers, prayers, and so on—is seen as truly disruptive. She actively incites criminality and violence. She has agency.

Fear of Santa Muerte participates in a longer, often implicitly anti-Catholic, history of shunning what Robert Orsi describes as the "real presence" of the gods. To acknowledge such presence is taken as a sign of irrationality, superstition, and magical thinking. "Modern theories of religion," writes Orsi, "were written over the accounts of the gods really present, submerging them in a theoretical underworld, while on the surface the gods were reborn as symbols, signs, metaphors, functions, and abstractions."[60] Making "good religion" involves classifying, condemning, and criminalizing that which is denominated as superstition, magic, and witchcraft, as was done a century ago in Trinidad and Haiti. To the extent that the authorities can criminalize certain powers as dangerous, premodern, thuggish, and demonic, the state and its official religions assume the mantle of rationality, law, and "good religion."[61]

Law enforcement's response to Santa Muerte and her followers also can be interpreted through the construct of "governmateriality." This concept draws attention to the intersection of governmentality and materiality to illuminate a set of actions, modalities of presence, and materializing processes visible in a variety of locations and contexts. These include not only law enforcement but also museums, archives, academic production, ritual acts, and military bases, among others.[62] In the case at hand, it prompts us to consider Santa Muerte as

---

into devil worship, citing P&G's moon and stars trademark as a satanic symbol. (The *New York Times* notes that the logo dated to 1882 and the stars referred to the thirteen original colonies.) In 1994, "researchers with the National Center on Child Abuse and Neglect found that investigators could not substantiate any of roughly 12,000 accusations of group cult sexual abuse based on satanic ritual." Court cases related to the panic continued until 2007 (Yuhas, "It's Time to Revisit the Satanic Panic").

59. Smith, "Modern-Day Witch Trials," citing Andrew Chesnut.
60. Orsi, *History and Presence*, 2.
61. Crosson, *Experiments with Power*.
62. The concept of governmateriality "allows us to investigate how instances of indigenous religions materalise as acts of governance in struggles over the definition and control of subjects, objects, and environments, and to address the ambivalent effects of these manifestations: Their ability to generate rights and privileges for bodies, practices, and spaces that come across as indigenous and religious, but also the risk of rejection or persecution since there are those who still believe that such bodies, practices, and spaces are primitive and irrational" (see Arctic University of Norway, "GOVMAT").

a complex material entity who, in the words of Bjørn Ola Tafjord, "contributes to the governing of her own constituent parts, of other actors who become involved with her, and of their shared environments."[63] Law enforcement wants to contain Santa Muerte not only because her material presence encourages her *followers* to conflate genuine spirituality and criminality but also because it exceeds and confounds their *own* capacities to manage her spiritual energies. This leads to their awkward attempts to don amateur theologians' hats to establish Santa Muerte's heterodoxy vis-à-vis mainstream Christianity. Kevin Freese's analysis for the US Foreign Military Studies Office is a case in point: "These rituals resemble the pagan concept of *do ut des*, or giving a favor in hopes that another favor might be given (lit. "I give so that you might give") which, although present in Christianity, is not standard practice. Furthermore, most of the objectives of these prayers would be incompatible with Christian doctrine, which explains why an alternative saint is needed. In this sense, *Santa Muerte* is more akin to primitive Western polytheistic adorations. It also resembles modern esoteric practices such as Voodoo, Santeria, Palo Mayombe, and Wicca."[64]

The religious classification cum criminalization of Santa Muerte and her followers is also deeply racialized. According to Martín, "the most important reason for much of the criticism of the death saint and her devotees is the pervasive prejudice and racism against the lower classes and anyone perceived to be dark-skinned or 'Indian.'"[65] She continues, "Her presence along the U.S.-Mexico border is also threatening because she influences and symbolizes two of the most transgressive, ambivalent identities from the perspective of the Mexican and U.S. states—that of migrants and impoverished barrio residents. Both groups fall outside the parameters of national citizenship and represent a form of refusal of the state."[66] The idea that the Indigenous and Afro-descendant elements of devotion to Santa Muerte make devotion to her especially disruptive and violent threads through these accounts. As a commentator for the *American Conservative* recounted, "I had a liberal Protestant churchgoing friend once who would embrace and display things like this, because the friend believed it was exotic and showed solidarity with Latin American and Caribbean cultures. The friend had zero knowledge of the real spiritual powers behind this stuff, nor did my friend want to know. . . . This stuff is real—and really dangerous."[67]

63. Bjørn Ola Tafjord on Santa Negrita, on file with the author.
64. Freese, "Death Cult of the Drug Lords," 10.
65. Martín, *Borderlands Saints*, 192.
66. Martín, *Borderlands Saints*, 191.
67. Dreher, "Santa Muerte."

These fears are palpable in Antonio Cervantes Jr.'s master's thesis, "Santa Muerte: Threatening the U.S. Homeland," written in 2011 for the US Marine Corps University in Quantico.[68] Warning that "the U.S. has taken no action to thwart the religious movement," Cervantes finds that "Santa Muerte is in and of itself a religion incompatible to good order and discipline. Its ideologies and esoteric practices in its absolute essence evidently promotes a society of lawbreakers." He traces the devious roots of Santa Muerte devotion, which, like Valdemar, he attributes to a failure to codify Aztec religion in contrast with the development of "cannon [sic] law in Catholicism": "The Aztec religion, on the other hand, had no written doctrine, but rather traditions passed on through word of mouth and ritualistic practices making the belief system susceptible to the damaging effects of individual interpretation. . . . In time, that also evolved into various syncretic practices among the Mexican people, but the one sentiment that remained deeply embedded within the principles of their belief was the obsession with death and mysticism." In this view, the problem with Santa Muerte is that "lack of doctrine is generating various interpretations, thereby aggravating the metamorphic state presently occurring. In other words, due to the lack of doctrine, the narco-cultures have developed their own innovative ways of revering Santa Muerte." If this slippery cult were pinned down and codified, then the rightful authorities could take charge, and the obsession with death, drugs, and guns would subside. As it stands, the renegade saint is contributing to the erosion of state authority if not societal collapse.

Cervantes also fears Santa Muerte's real presence. Rather than tempering devotees' faith, he explains, a failure to achieve their objectives only leads to more extreme forms of devotion. It's a vicious circle. Contravening modern understandings of rational religion, in this account, Santa Muerte infuses the worshipper with perverse forms of empowerment: "When their transactions or major drug operations were unsuccessful, adherents did not see it as a failure by Santa Muerte, but as a necessity to provide the icon with greater offerings. The psychological empowerment that the icon infused on the worshiper reinforced 'social fissures that eventually contributed to the erosion of the state authority.'" These fissures stand in contrast to the modern ideal of political and religious subjectivity that is implicit in Cervantes's analysis, in which subjects are understood to be free to the extent that they exercise rational individual agency, as Webb Keane has shown. "What is at stake is not just the transmission of correct doctrine," writes Keane, "but also the production of human subjects who are (relatively) free because they fully grasp the

---

68. Cervantes, "Santa Muerte." All quotations in this section are from this document.

agency that is rightly theirs."⁶⁹ Followers of Santa Muerte fail to grasp the agency that is rightly theirs.

This agentic shortfall facilitates the association between the materiality of "narco saint" iconography and deviant behavior among "iconic worshippers" such as drug trafficking. Cervantes warns that "talismans, amulets, stickers, colored rosaries, scapulars, and other trinkets have gained significant popularity among these iconic worshippers who place their trust in them for guidance and protection . . . US law-enforcement agencies are concerned that the demand of these items directly reflects the violence and the growing trend of adherents, particularly within the narco gang communities." These deviant forms of material religion require heightened scrutiny and suspicion on the part of law enforcement. In this framing, the question, "what is the actual connection between devotion to Santa Muerte and criminality?" can never be satisfactorily answered because the saint's association with the drug trade renders those who worship her suspect *prior* to questioning. Hanging a Santa Muerte air freshener from the rearview mirror is sufficiently damning. In turn, those involved in criminality also may find themselves attracted to Santa Muerte as a protective force, thus creating the very connection that the authorities expect to find.⁷⁰ And so Santa Muerte finds herself in court.

"Suspicious Circumstances": La Santísima in Court

In *US v. Medina-Copete*, one of the two defendants, Maria Vianey Medina-Copete, was alleged to have been praying to Santa Muerte during a traffic stop.⁷¹ A translation of her prayer was introduced at trial:

For protection during a trip

> Holy Spirit of Death, I invoke your Holy Name to ask you to help me in this venture. Make my way over the mountains valleys and paths an easy one, never stop bestowing upon me your good fortune weave the destiny so that bad instincts vanish before me because of your powerful protection. Prevent Santa Muerte problems from growing and embracing my heart, my Lady, keep any illness from embracing my wings [illegible]

---

69. Keane, *Christian Moderns*, 76.
70. Thanks to Terje Østebø.
71. Officer Arsenio Chavez, who initiated the traffic stop, testified that the defendant "was fidgeting around, her legs were shaking, and . . . she was reading [a] document during the course of the stop." He said that the document "looked like some type of prayer of some sort" (*US v. Medina-Copete*, 2–3).

Glorious Santa Muerte be my protector and light my path. Be my advocate before the redeemer. Be my truth in times of darkness

Grant me the strength and faith to invoke your name and to thank you now and forever for all your favours

Amen

Oh miraculous Santa Muerte, Niña Blanca of my heart and right arm of god our lord. Today I come to you with infinite devotion to implore you for health, fortune and luck

Remove from my path [illegible] that hurts me, envy and misfortune; don't allow my enemy's slander reach and harm my spirit

may no one prevent me from receiving the prosperity that I am asking of you today

my powerful lady bless the money that will reach my hands and multiply it so that my family

lacks for nothing and I can outreach my hand to the needy that crosses my path

keep tragedy pain and shortage away from me

this votive candle I will light so that the radiance of your eyes forms an invisible wall around me

grant me prudence and patience holy lady, Santa Reina de las Tinieblas ["Holy Queen of Darkness"] strength, power and wisdom tell the elements not to unleash their fury wherever they cross paths with me take care of my happy surroundings that I want to adorn in my Santa Muerte amen.

The legal controversy hinged in part on whether this prayer should be accepted by the court as a "tool of the trade" of drug smugglers. Is testimony involving so-called narco saints admissible evidence?[72]

The confrontation began with a routine traffic stop on Interstate 40 in New Mexico. Officer Arsenio Chavez stopped Medina-Copete and her codefendant, Rafael Goxcon-Chagal, for following too closely, issued a traffic citation, and then, "based on [his] training and experience and indicators that [he] had noticed," requested that Goxcon answer a few additional questions. The indicators, according to Chavez, included the odor of air freshener, Goxcon's and Medina's nervousness, Goxcon's inability to identify the truck's owner, Medina's reading from the prayer, and inconsistencies in their initial stories. Chavez also remarked that Goxcon's attire struck him as "kind of odd . . . like he was trying to fit in with the innocent motoring public" because people "typically don't wear an Army shirt with an Air Force hat."[73] In a subsequent

---

72. The district court admitted US marshal and self-described expert Robert Almonte's expert testimony but required that he refrain from using the term *narco saint* in his testimony.

73. *US v. Medina-Copete*, 5.

search, Chavez discovered a hidden compartment in the vehicle containing roughly two pounds of 90 percent pure methamphetamine in a secret compartment behind the dashboard.[74] He arrested both suspects and charged them with drug trafficking and possession of illegal firearms.

In the proceedings that followed, a judge for the New Mexico District Court had to decide whether to admit testimony from US marshal Robert Almonte, a self-described expert on Santa Muerte described by the government as a "cultural iconography hobbyist."[75] At stake was whether evidence related to what Almonte called "narco saints" could serve as legitimate, legally admissible evidence that drug trafficking had occurred. Prior to trial, Medina and Goxcon had filed a joint motion in limine to exclude Almonte's testimony.[76] In response, the trial court issued a sixty-seven-page memorandum opinion order in *United States v. Goxcon-Chagal*, concluding that Almonte *was* qualified to provide testimony about Santa Muerte and that his testimony would be admissible as evidence.[77] The Tenth Circuit summarized these developments:

> The district court concluded that Almonte could testify as an expert because Santa Muerte veneration "relates to the tools of the narcotics trade, which the 10th Circuit has recognized may require expert assistance to aid the jury." Because "[e]xpert testimony is liberally admissible under the Federal Rules of Evidence," and because Almonte had "considerable qualifications for a law enforcement officer," the district court permitted him to testify as an expert. The court deemed his opinion to be "sufficiently reliable" largely based on other courts' conclusions that "the presence of personal items related to so-called narco saints can support a conclusion that a defendant was engaged in drug trafficking."[78]

---

74. Miera-Rosete, "Officers at the Gate," 184.

75. "Almonte . . . has more than 25 years' experience in law enforcement, primarily with the El Paso, Texas Police Department. He has published two books: Evolution of Narcotics Investigations and Managing Covert Operations. Almonte produced a law enforcement training video entitled Patron Saints of the Mexican Drug Underworld based on his 'extensive research' beginning in 2003 and 'comprising hundreds, if not thousands[,] of hours of study' regarding 'how the Mexican drug traffickers involve the spiritual world in their activity.' He is currently writing a book on the same topic and is a frequent lecturer at state law enforcement associations. The government described Almonte as a 'cultural iconography hobbyist'" (*US v. Medina-Copete*, 8).

76. *US v. Medina-Copete*. A motion in limine (on the threshold) is a motion discussed outside of the presence of the jury to request that certain testimony be excluded or included.

77. Miera-Rosete, "Officers at the Gate," 194, citing *United States v. Goxcon-Chagal*. As Miera-Rosete notes, on appeal the party's names are switched so that the case becomes Medina-Copete not Goxcon-Chagal.

78. *US v. Medina-Copete*, 8–9.

The district court had maintained that "various courts have found the general proposition that the presence of personal items related to so-called narco saints can support a conclusion that a defendant was engaged in drug trafficking . . . the Eighth Circuit noted that the presence of a 'Santa Muerte figure' was one of the 'suspicious circumstances' that justified the investigative detention."[79] The New Mexico court's theological reasoning merits quoting at length:

> Defendant asserts that Marshal Almonte's (who was to testify as an expert witness on Santa Muerte) opinion is not reliable because it is too huge a leap "to go from cell phones [and] pagers to religious belief as a 'tool of the trade.'" (Tr. at 76, cited at 20). Defendant argues that such a broad definition of "tool of the trade" would allow the Government to target individuals who wear the Christian cross as drug traffickers because a large number of people who are Christians wear crosses. The Government aptly finds the holes in this argument. *Drug trafficking does not have the same connection to the Christian cross as does Jesus Malverde paraphernalia. The cross, or the worship of legitimate saints, are common symbols used for a multitude of purposes.* They both have a "less frequent appearance" in drug trafficking cases than does paraphernalia associated with Jesus Malverde or Santa Muerte. There is no indication that the wearing of a Christian cross occurs in the context of drug trafficking frequently enough to infer a connection between the two, so there is no danger that individuals will be targeted for their religious beliefs, as Defendant contends. Moreover *prayer to Jesus Malverde, as opposed to legitimate saints, holds the dubious distinction of seeking protection from law enforcement.* As the Government noted at the hearing, *"Jesus Malverde is for people that operate outside the law."*[80]

Those who follow the law worship legitimate saints, not illegitimate ones. Jesús Malverde and Santa Muerte are for people who operate outside the law. According to the district court, then, Almonte's proposed testimony did not violate Fed. R. Evid. 704(b) (prohibiting expert testimony on "a mental state or condition that constitutes an element of the crime charged or of a defense"), was not improper profile evidence, and was not precluded by the First Amendment or the Federal Rules of Evidence (Fed. R. Evid. 610, prohibiting admission of evidence of "a witness's religious beliefs or opinions . . . to

---

79. *US v. Goxcon-Chagal*, 19, citing *US v. Pena-Ponce*, 588 F.3d at 584. In *US v. Favela-Lujan*, US district judge Robert C. Brack wrote, "In that these authorities demonstrate that cultural icons such as the Santa Muerte and Jesus Malverde are associated with drug smugglers, evidence of the prayer to the Santa Muerte would be highly relevant to the issue of knowledge" (*US v. Favela-Lujan*).

80. *US v. Goxcon-Chagal*, 19–20, emphasis added.

attack or support the witness's credibility"). The jury found both defendants guilty on all charges.[81]

Goxcon and Medina protested the government's conflation of spirituality and criminality and appealed their sentences. On appeal, the Tenth Circuit vacated and remanded the decision due to the inadmissibility of Almonte's testimony,[82] holding that "the trial court abused its discretion, under Fed. R. Evid. 702, by admitting Almonte's expert testimony about the meaning of Medina's prayer."[83] As Judge Lucero of the Tenth Circuit reasoned:

> During the trial, the district court allowed a purported expert on certain religious iconography to testify that veneration of a figure known as "Santa Muerte" was so connected with drug trafficking as to constitute evidence that the occupants of the vehicle were aware of the presence of drugs in a secret compartment. In addition to qualifying a law enforcement official as an expert on Santa Muerte, the district court allowed the witness to wander far afield and render theological opinions about the "legitima[cy]" of Santa Muerte vis-à-vis other venerated figures. We conclude that the law enforcement officer was improperly vetted under Fed. R. Evid. 702, Daubert v. Merrell Dow Pharmaceuticals, 509 U.S. 579 (1993), and Kumho Tire Co. v. Carmichael, 526 U.S. 137 (1999), and that the testimony thus proffered was both impermissible and prejudicial, requiring us to reverse the convictions and order a new trial.[84]

Although the appeals court noted that other factors contributed to their decision, including Officer Chavez's limited Spanish ("The record reveals that

---

81. "Medina was sentenced to a total of 180 months' imprisonment: three concurrent 120-month sentences for conspiracy, possession with intent to distribute, and being an illegal alien in possession of a firearm; a 24-month sentence (also concurrent) for illegal reentry; and a 60-month consecutive sentence for carrying a firearm during and in relation to a drug trafficking offense. Goxcon received 180 months' imprisonment: two concurrent 120-month sentences for conspiracy and possession with intent to distribute and a 60-month consecutive sentence for carrying a firearm during and in relation to a drug trafficking offense." (*US v. Medina-Copete*, 11–12).

82. In seeking to determine "whether a law enforcement officer and 'cultural iconography hobbyist' can testify as an expert on 'the use of Santa Muerte and drug trafficking,'" the appeals court held "that the district court abused its discretion by permitting Almonte's expert testimony" and that "missing from the district court's discussion of Almonte's qualifications is any discussion of how his Santa Muerte testimony could legitimately connect Medina's prayer to drug trafficking." The court also found that the government failed to explain how Santa Muerte iconography was a "tool of the trade", and that "the highly prejudicial nature of Almonte's testimony leaves us with grave doubt that the outcome of the trial would have been the same without it." *US v. Medina-Copete*, 21, 15, 17, 29.

83. Miera-Rosete, "Officers at the Gate," 185.

84. *US v. Medina-Copete*, 2.

Chavez had difficulty conjugating Spanish verbs outside of the first-person form, leading him to ask questions such as, 'I don't have any illegal firearms in this truck?'"), their decision ultimately hinged on the inadmissibility of Almonte's testimony on Santa Muerte as a "tool of the trade."

In the decision to vacate and remand, the Tenth Circuit focused on the substance of Almonte's testimony on the presence of Santa Muerte in relation to criminality. Of particular significance was Almonte's claim that the prayer found in Medina's hands, even without other evidence of criminal activity "would be a very good indicator of possible criminal activity based on that one statement there about making some—some money. Absolutely." Contrasting the Santa Muerte prayer with a hypothetical prayer to St. Jude, which would not "be an indicator unless the officer observed other suspicious behavior or items in the vehicle," Almonte said that "St. Jude is a legitimate Catholic saint," and that a criminal praying to St. Jude would be "misusing him."[85]

In dissent, the Tenth Circuit found that Almonte's "expert testimony characterizing the mere presence of the prayer as 'a very good indicator of possible criminal activity' approaches psychobabble and substantially influenced the outcome."[86] They concluded that "Almonte should not have been permitted to testify under Fed. R. Evid. 702 because his experience did not render him qualified as an expert on the connection between Santa Muerte worship and drug trafficking, his knowledge did not assist the jury, and his opinion was not based on the proper application of reliable principles and methods."[87] As noted by Calvo-Quirós, rather than retrying the case, however, the state accepted plea bargains resulting in prison sentences of ninety months for Goxcon-Chagal and forty-eight months for Medina-Copete.[88]

Not all cases that have relied on expert testimony about Santa Muerte have led to such results.[89] In 2013, Christian Ramiro Mireles appealed a life

---

85. *US v. Medina-Copete*, 11.
86. *US v. Medina-Copete*, 30.
87. *US v. Medina-Copete*, 23.
88. Calvo-Quirós, *Undocumented Saints*, 222.
89. For a ruling that admitted Almonte's testimony, see the majority opinion in *US v. Holmes*, a case summarized as follows:

> Defendants Holmes and Rendon appealed their convictions for conspiracy to possess with intent to distribute methamphetamine. The court concluded that the district court did not abuse its discretion in admitting 'narco-saint' testimony where, without the testimony, the significance of such evidence would not be familiar to average jurors with no previous exposure to the drug trafficking business; because the narco-saint evidence was relevant to establish the existence of the conspiracy, its admission was proper for both parties, and no limiting instruction was necessary; the evidence was sufficient

sentence on the grounds that it was unfair for the jury to have heard about his Santa Muerte worship as evidence of guilt in a sentencing hearing.[90] On appeal to the Fifth District Court of Appeals, Mireles's attorney contended that "the trial court abused its discretion by not declaring a mistrial and giving curative instructions when the State presented evidence that he worships Santisima Muerte, or Santa Muerte, and that followers of Santisima commit violent acts. The State argues that a mistrial was not required because the trial court instructed the jury to disregard the evidence, and the trial court's refusal to give a curative instruction after some of the testimony was harmless error."[91] At trial, the prosecution had called as a witness Texas police investigator Leo Pena, known for his seminars for law enforcement in which he describes Santa Muerte as a "narco saint." Pena testified in Mireles's trial that "understanding Santa Muerte provides a look inside the heads of vicious criminals."[92] Although Mireles's sister had testified that her entire family worshipped "Santisima Muerte as a part of (her) Catholic religion"[93] and that she was unaware of any violent practices associated with that worship, a Texas state court justice rejected Mireles's appeal, concluding that "a person's affiliation with a certain religion or cult may be relevant to punishment."[94]

Conclusion

Santa Muerte and her followers' refusal of borders recalls an oft-cited passage from Gloria Anzaldúa's text, *Borderlands/La Frontera*:

---

for a reasonable jury to find that Holmes was guilty beyond a reasonable doubt; and Holmes' sentence was reasonable.

The relevant passage from the decision is here:

Law-enforcement officers may testify about the drug trafficking connection of otherwise innocuous household items. In [one past case], an officer testified as an expert about the significance of Ziploc bags in the drug trade. Although most users of Ziploc bags are not drug dealers, the bags have drug-trade application. Similarly, even if many with Malverde statues are not affiliated with the drug trade, narco-saint iconography may be an indicator of drug trafficking. The reliability of such evidence comes not from scientific foundations but from Almonte's personal knowledge and experience. The district court did not abuse its discretion in finding Almonte's expert testimony reliable.

90. Smith, "Modern-Day Witch Trials."
91. *Mireles v. State*, 16.
92. Smith, "Modern-Day Witch Trials."
93. *Mireles v. State*, 10.
94. *Mireles v. State*, 20, citing *Davis v. State*, 805–6.

> The sea cannot be fenced,
> *el mar* does not stop at borders.
> To show the white man what she thought of his arrogance,
> *Yemayá* blew that wire fence down.
> This land was Mexican once. Was Indian always
> And is.
> And will be again.[95]

In doing research for this book, I encountered a sense among certain borderland communities that, as Anzaldúa implies, US sovereignty is a temporary inconvenience. In the words of Javier Loera, war captain and tribal preservation officer of the Ysleta del Sur Pueblo, a community that has lived on both sides of the Rio Grande/Rio Bravo since before the creation of the United States or Mexico: "To me [the border] is just a geopolitical division among these two relatively new nations that have come in existence. We have lived through the Mexican and the Spanish colonialisms . . . this river is just a political barrier that divides two sides of the earth that have always been here."[96] Empires come and go. These communities are willing to "wait out the state," as Greg Johnson writes of the Indigenous Hawaiian activists with whom he collaborates. Justin Richland describes a related practice of "cooperation without submission" in his work with the Hopi in Arizona.[97] For communities that see their lifeways as destined to outlast the current regime, the US is no more than a temporary overseer indebted to a particular linear understanding of history and progress that is not universally shared. Luis Léon describes an alternative, cyclical epistemology and eschatology that he associates with the Mexican Americas:

> Religion and culture in the Mexican Americas are based on a cyclical model of mythical history and the inscription of Mexican cultural memory into the Southwest represents a fundamental challenge to a Protestant vision of a linear American history of progress and, subsequently, to the foundations of the imagined American community itself. The characteristic back and forth patterns between symbolic systems and national jurisdictions that characterize borderland religion undercut notions of a progressive civilization. It is within this arena, therefore, that the mythos of American society is most severely

---

95. Anzaldúa, *Borderlands/La Frontera*, 24–25.
96. Loera, " Boundary." Loera died in November 2022 at the age of sixty-six.
97. Johnson, "At Home and Abroad"; Richland, *Cooperation without Submission*.

critiqued. And, moreover, this cyclical model of history proposes new expansive visions for social organization—the meaninglessness of borders.[98]

Devotion to Santa Muerte invokes temporalities and time horizons that put US borders in their place. Her following attests to Sullivan's remark that "modern state law and rule of law ideology do not in fact enjoy, and do not deserve, the monopoly they claim for themselves."[99] Santa Muerte is more than a cultural icon, demonized icon of death, or pitiable pseudo-saint of the dispossessed. She is an agent of political and spiritual solidarity that recalls earlier revolutionary figures such as Our Lady of Guadalupe, who, as Léon reminds us, appeared in 1531 "as a swarthy Catholic madrecita" to the newly colonized Indigenous population of Mexico on the outskirts of Mexico City. Guadalupe became associated with the Nahuatl deity Tonantzin and, like Santa Muerte, "decimated the border between European and (native) American religions through processes of syncretism, continuity, and transformation."[100]

It is for these reasons, and not only due to her alleged associations with narcocultura, that authorities on both sides of the border fear Santa Muerte. Confounding the line between pure and impure religion, a line that breaks down under her gaze, rituals in her honor are marked by an openness to the exorbitant, the unsettled, and the monstrous.[101] Indifferent and at times openly hostile to US racial, religious, sexual, and settler-colonial lifeways, she riffs on and reacts against dominant modes of mediation between humans and gods, humans and objects, and living and dead.[102] Inhabiting while also refiguring nation-state and church sovereignty, she and her followers are unable to break free of the present system entirely. Yet they also invoke an "unstately religion, illiberal religion, the sacred otherwise, not predicated upon the logic of polis. Not delimited, bordered, and border-protecting 'we the

98. Léon, "Metaphor and Place," 567.
99. Sullivan, "... You're Doing It Right Now."
100. "Guadalupe appeared first as a swarthy Catholic madrecita to the newly colonized indigenous population of Mexico in 1531. She requested that a church be built on the site of her apparition, a hill called Tepeyac on the outskirts of Mexico City—previously the abode of the Indian mother goddess (Elizondo; Lafaye). Instantly she became associated with the Nahuatl deity, Tonantzin—who had a number of avatars—and as a result she decimated the border between European and (native) American religions through processes of syncretism, continuity, and transformation. Throughout history she has symbolized the power to overcome barriers, from Mexican Revolutionaries to Chicana feminists" (Léon, "Metaphor and Place," 546).
101. Winters, "Race and Religion beyond the State."
102. Handelman and Oliphant, "On France, Violence, and Religious Media."

people."[103] Challenging conceptual frameworks, temporalities, and critical terminologies—and *dotada de una fuerza*—Santa Muerte keeps her distance from church and state. Offering solidarity when other sources of protection have failed, she galvanizes an incipient Indigenous-Catholic *ekklesia*.[104] For members of her church, the US-Mexico border is relevant only in passing. Other forces are at play. To the authorities, that is the real threat.

---

103. Carter, "White Messianic."

104. Johnson, Klassen, and Sullivan use the term *ekklesia* "to open an inquiry into the ways collectives in the Americas have been forged from an ill-defined yet powerful church@stateness composed of the interpenetrating and mutually constitutive forces of religion, law, and politics. Christian ideas and motivations have played a fundamental role in generating these collectives, the body of Christ and the body politic together working to constitute the people as chosen, celebrated, and accorded the right to exercise will" (*Ekklesia*, 3).

INTERLUDE IV

Walking
Pilgrimage to Magdalena

> When we celebrate Kino/Saint Francisco there is no border.
> PILGRIM TO MAGDALENA IN ALEX LA PIERRE AND JERRY HAAS,
> "The Pilgrimage to Magdalena"

The Pilgrimage to Magdalena, also known as the Camino de Kino, is an annual Indigenous-Catholic pilgrimage commemorating Father Eusebio Francisco Kino and his patron saint and namesake, Saint Francis Xavier. The pilgrimage is not especially well known beyond the US-Mexico borderlands. Even for O'odham pilgrims, there are rival destination pilgrimages, including fiestas for Saint Francis at Mission San Xavier in southern Arizona, the O'odham village of San Francisquito in Sonora, and a rotating feast of Saint Francis that moves across the eleven districts of the Tohono O'odham Nation.[1] Yet every October, thousands of pilgrims, or *peregrinos*, trek between sixty and one hundred miles along the Juan Bautista de Anza National Historic Trail to and from Magdalena (figure 10). They depart from the San Xavier del Bac mission, Nogales, several Native American communities in southern Arizona, and other locations around Sonora, and walk together toward the church known as Santa María Magdalena (or Magdalena de Kino) in Magdalena, Mexico, where Father Kino died in 1711.[2]

Upon arrival in Magdalena de Kino, pilgrims present offerings to a reclining wooden statue of Saint Francis de Xavier inside the mission church, which was rebuilt by the Franciscans in 1830–1832.[3] They stand in line to pay homage to the saint, taking turns kissing his face, caressing him, and gently

---

1. Schermerhorn, *Walking to Magdalena*, 33.
2. Brandon Flowers has a song about the pilgrimage entitled "Magdalena," a recording of which is available on YouTube: https://www.youtube.com/watch?v=TA84NSp-hdU.
3. The original church is no longer standing but was dedicated by Father Kino in 1711 to Saint Francis Xavier. It was the reason for Kino's visit to Magdalena.

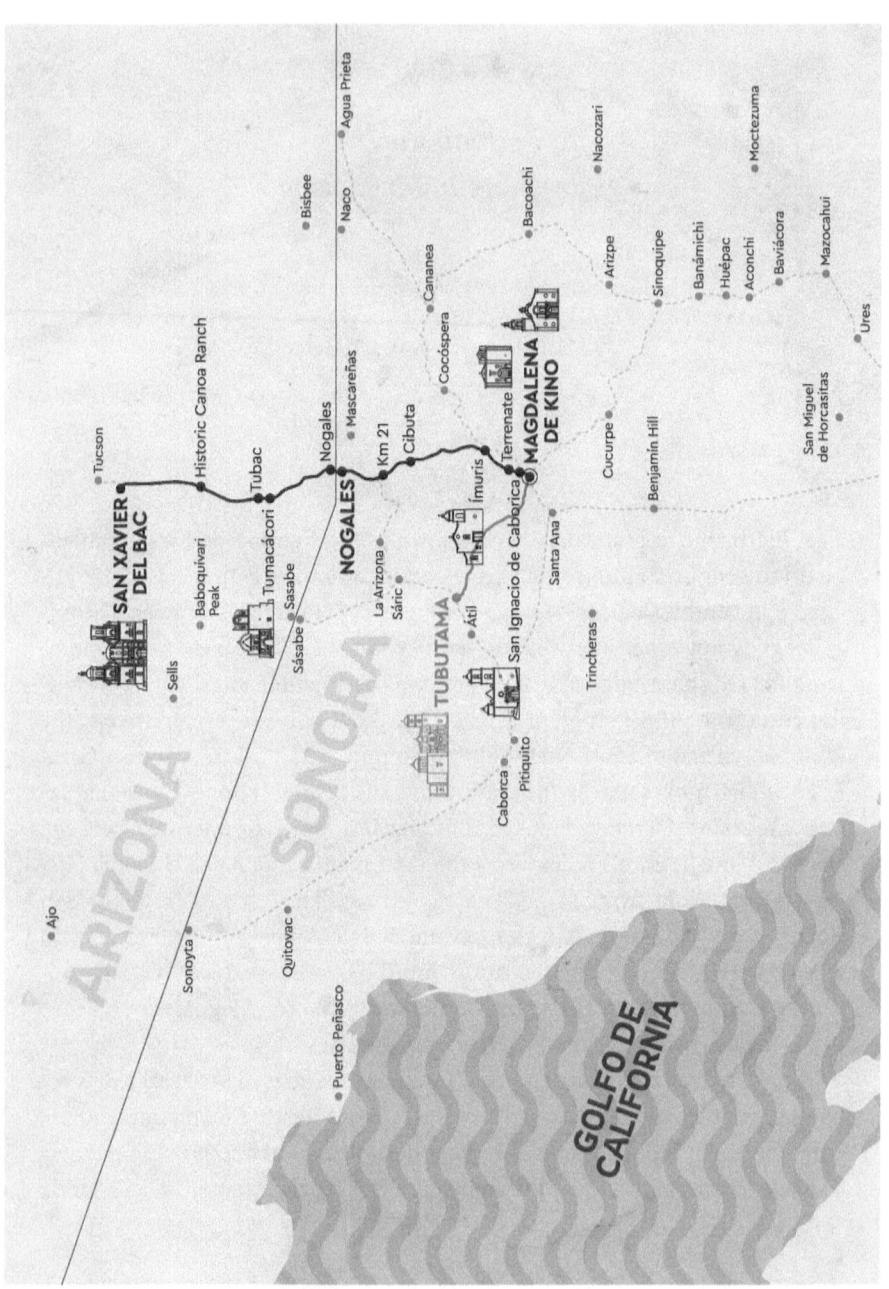

FIGURE 10. Pilgrimage to Magdalena.
Image courtesy Border Community Alliance (BCA); artwork by Rocío LaPierre.

FIGURE 11. Saint Francis, Church of Santa María Magdalena. Photo by author.

lifting his head for good luck (figure 11). It is said that if you can lift him, you are free of sin.[4]

Pilgrims also visit Padre Kino's tomb in the public plaza next to the church. They then partake in the Fiesta de San Francisco, a street festival featuring music, food, and dance.

These festivities have been taking place since at least the early eighteenth century. John Russell Bartlett, commissioner of the United States and Mexico Boundary Commission, charged with demarcating the border as provided by the Treaty of Guadalupe Hidalgo, visited Magdalena on a festival day in October 1851. Bartlett recalled extensive gambling and expert card shuffling by (in his words) "unattractive women": "Whole ranges of booths were devoted to this exciting amusement; and crowds of every age, sex, and class were assembled about them. . . . Some of the tables were attended by women, selected,

---

4. I took this photo of Saint Francis during my first visit to Magdalena in 2020. When I returned in 2023 the statue of Saint Francis had been encased in glass due to the pandemic, making it impossible for pilgrims to fulfill their duties to touch his feet or lift his head.

not on account of their personal beauty, but for their expertness in shuffling the cards."[5]

Father Kino's bones have been on display in the plaza next to the church under a glass dome since they were excavated by a team of determined archaeologists in 1966. That same year, the town of Santa María Magdalena de Buquivaba was renamed Magdalena de Kino in his honor. Kino was a Tyrolean Jesuit, missionary, geographer, explorer, cartographer, and astronomer whose missions in the Pimería Alta profoundly shaped the political and religious landscape of the borderlands from the late 1600s until his death of fever in 1711.[6] As mentioned, his patron saint was Saint Francis Xavier, a sixteenth-century Jesuit missionary and cofounder of the Society of Jesus, born in 1506 in Navarra, Spain. After a life of evangelizing in India, Southeast Asia, and Japan, Saint Francis Xavier died in 1552 on an island off the coast of China. The patron saint of missionaries and Kino's Jesuit order, Saint Francis Xavier was buried in what was then Portuguese Goa, in India, after being packed in lime for transport. His body remained uncorrupted when removed from the lime, a miracle that is said to have played a part in his canonization in 1622.[7]

On the Catholic calendar, the feast of Saint Francis Xavier is December 3. The fiesta in Magdalena, however, is celebrated on the feast day of Saint Francis of Assisi, October 4. This discrepancy is likely a result of the fact that in 1767, the Spanish king Carlos III expelled the Jesuit order, of which Father Kino was a member, from the Spanish dominions, or New Spain, to be replaced in northern Sonora by the Order of Friars Minor, or the Franciscans.[8] The Franciscans' patron saint was Saint Francis of Assisi.[9] So there were two saints by the name of Francis, one whose feast day was October 4 (Assisi) and the other who was celebrated on December 3 (Xavier). Since at least as early as 1828, the feast day in honor of San Francis Xavier is celebrated in Magdalena on the feast day of Saint Francis de Assisi, October 4, the focus of which is a statue of Saint Francis Xavier.[10] In its early days, the pilgrimage was carried out primarily by Pima, Mayos, Yaquis, and O'odham.

---

5. Cited in Fontana, "Pilgrimage to Magdalena," 43.

6. Kino's legacy is honored by the nonprofit Kino Border Initiative, which works on behalf of humane and workable migration policy between Mexico and the United States.

7. Fontana, "Pilgrimage to Magdalena," 41.

8. On the modes of presence of the (absent) Jesuits after their expulsion, see Molina, *Inventories of Ruin*.

9. Griffith, "Pilgrimage to Magdalena and The Festival de San Francisco."

10. Fontana, "Pilgrimage to Magdalena," 42. To complicate matters further, replicas of the reclining Jesuit Saint Xavier sold in Magdalena are garbed in the brown habits worn by Franciscans in the late nineteenth century.

For pilgrims, the trek is as much about the experience of walking as it is about reaching the destination. Roberto Lopez describes why he began walking:

> After a newborn relative was given last rites, [Roberto] Lopez promised he would walk to the Magdalena mission if the baby survived. Miraculously, the baby did, and come October that year [1978], Lopez walked. Lopez, now 48, strode from his house near Reid Park, planning to head out to Magdalena alone. He stopped at his parents' home near Pueblo High School, where his brother-in-law John Robles decided to go with him. Walking day and night for about 120 miles, they made it. "By the third year, more people came along with us. It kind of snowballed," Lopez says. Year after year since then, Tucson's Lopez and Robles clans, plus friends and acquaintances, have gathered to make the pilgrimage to Magdalena. They do it not just for religious reasons, but also to renew their bonds with one another, Lopez said. Striding down the edge of Mexico's Highway 15, they join a dispersed flow of Mexican, Mexican-American, Tohono O'odham and Yaqui pilgrims. All are taking part in a tradition of Sonoran Desert Catholicism that dates back at least to the 1800s. They walk to the mission churches—either San Xavier del Bac south of Tucson or, more often, to Magdalena's mission—to fulfill a promise or give thanks.[11]

Like other lived spiritualities, the pilgrimage fits uneasily into the mutually exclusive categories of modern world religions.[12] It escapes the grid. Though often described as a Catholic ritual, as in the previously quoted passage from the *Arizona Daily Star*, Seth Schermerhorn observes that the O'odham have made Christianity their own by embedding and emplacing it within O'odham ancestral and conceptual landscapes, transforming and reinventing it in the process.[13] Walking is central to their practice. Like the Samaritans, for whom walking in the desert to provide aid to migrants is also understood as a religious pilgrimage, it is the walking that matters.[14] Walking sacralizes past and present community. Steps are chronicled with walking sticks that are festooned with ribbons, indicating the number of times a pilgrim has completed the pilgrimage and memorializing the connection to the landscape and to those who walked before.

Temporally, as suggested by the ribbons on the walking sticks, the pilgrimage encompasses both past and present. One O'odham leader explained

---

11. Steller, "Prayerful Pilgrimage."
12. See Schermerhorn, *Walking to Magdalena*.
13. Schermerhorn, *Walking to Magdalena*, 6, 23. See also J. Hughes, *Church of the Dead*.
14. "The trope of walking as a religious experience of pilgrimage is an important one in the Samaritans' understanding of what they are doing when they 'hike in the desert'" (Shapira, *Waiting for José*, 141).

to Schermerhorn that to understand the walk he would have to understand that it was not a recent development. "This walk was here in the time of I'itoi," he explained. I'itoi, who lives in a cave below the peak of Baboquivari Mountain, is the creator of the O'odham people. He formed their bodies and endowed them with *himdag*, their way of life. For many O'odham, the himdag encompasses Christian practices. "In this view," explains Schermerhorn, "what Tohono O'odham have made of Christianity was made for them by I'itoi."[15] The implication is that "Tohono O'odham did not make Christianity their own within the last 150 years or so, as Western scholars of all stripes have assumed; I'itoi made Christianity for them at the time of the establishment of the O'odham homelands."[16] It was not brought to them by Padre Kino; it was embedded in the land at the founding of the O'odham cosmos. It was always there.[17]

While strengthening communal bonds and connections to the land, the pilgrimage also affords an opportunity to reinforce bonds with other pilgrims and with the saints through the practice of making *mandas*—petitions or promises made in exchange for the fulfillment of a request. Mandas can be requests for health or healing, or expressions of gratitude to Padre Kino and Saint Francis. Pilgrims forge communal bonds not only with other pilgrims walking in community but also with the missionaries to whom they direct their mandas, with loved ones to whom they dedicate their mandas, with the local roadside communities that welcome and encourage them, with the sacred spaces and places traversed during the journey, and with community and family members who have made the journey previously. "Past, present, and future seem simultaneously tangible."[18] The spirit of the pilgrimage is bottom-up, communal, and relational rather than top-down, centralized, and institutionalized. A person returning from the pilgrimage is understood to be a different and more mature one than the individual who embarked on it.[19] Movement transforms individuals in body and mind: "Walking simultaneously produces persons and places, or socially significant spaces, which in turn produce well-practiced, disciplined, 'ripe' persons . . . a particular O'odham way of walking is related to the incremental production of *siakam*, an O'odham notion of maturity pertaining to 'ripening' or 'ripeness.'" If

---

15. Schermerhorn, *Walking to Magdalena*, 124.
16. Schermerhorn, *Walking to Magdalena*, 124.
17. Schermerhorn, *Walking to Magdalena*, 124, 153.
18. Schermerhorn, *Walking to Magdalena*, 43.
19. Schermerhorn, *Walking to Magdalena*, 36.

O'odham refers to people, then *siakam* refers to "ripened, mature, modest individuals who subtly and stylishly exude O'odhamness."[20]

For pilgrims to Magdalena the border is superfluous. The pilgrimage predates its creation. Using the O'odham measure, today O'odham land encompasses a sixty-two mile strip (as the eagle flies) that straddles bordered land between Arizona and Sonora; Americans measure this border region as seventy-five miles long.[21] This makes O'odham land the second-longest border zone on a Native reservation, surpassed only by the US-Canada border zone in the Iroquois tribal nation on the shores of Lake Ontario.[22] As mentioned earlier, the border in the O'odham region reflects a settlement reached at the time of the 1854 Gadsden Purchase. The 1848 Treaty of Guadalupe Hidalgo had placed most O'odham lands in Mexico. In 1854, with the Gadsden Purchase, US president Franklin Pierce paid Mexico $10 million for 29,670 square miles of land, a settlement that divided O'odham land in two (figure 12). At the time, however, most O'odham north of that border were unaware of having officially become Americans, and they "continued to live as though the boundary did not exist for many years."[23] As vice chair of the Chukut Kuk District of the Tohono O'odham Nation, Kendall Jose, reminded journalist Todd Miller in 2022, "The O'odham people never consented to the United States' construction of the border in the mid-19th century."[24]

The pilgrimage to Magdalena underscores the contrast between Indigenous understandings of geography in this region and the enclosure and claiming that has come to define the idea of borders under US jurisdiction. In one sense, O'odham claims to sovereignty operate as a kind of shadow sovereignty, in parallel yet also subordinate to US claims. This claim is both derivative and limited; mirroring, riffing on, and at times aspiring to—and even reinforcing—state sovereignty. A 2017 official statement of the Tohono O'odham Nation observes that "[the nation] has worked closely for decades with U.S. Customs and Border Patrol and other agencies to secure the U.S. homeland."[25] In another sense, however, the O'odham claim to southern Arizona and northern Sonora as O'odham lands is timeless and the border meaningless. The tribe's traditional lands reach as far as Hermosillo to the

20. Schermerhorn, *Walking to Magdalena*, 122.
21. Schaeffer, *Unsettled Borders*, 56 and 163n7.
22. Schaeffer, *Unsettled Borders*, 58.
23. Schermerhorn, *Walking to Magdalena*, 161.
24. Miller, "After Years of Tribal Resistance."
25. Cited in Wiles, "Closed Border Gate."

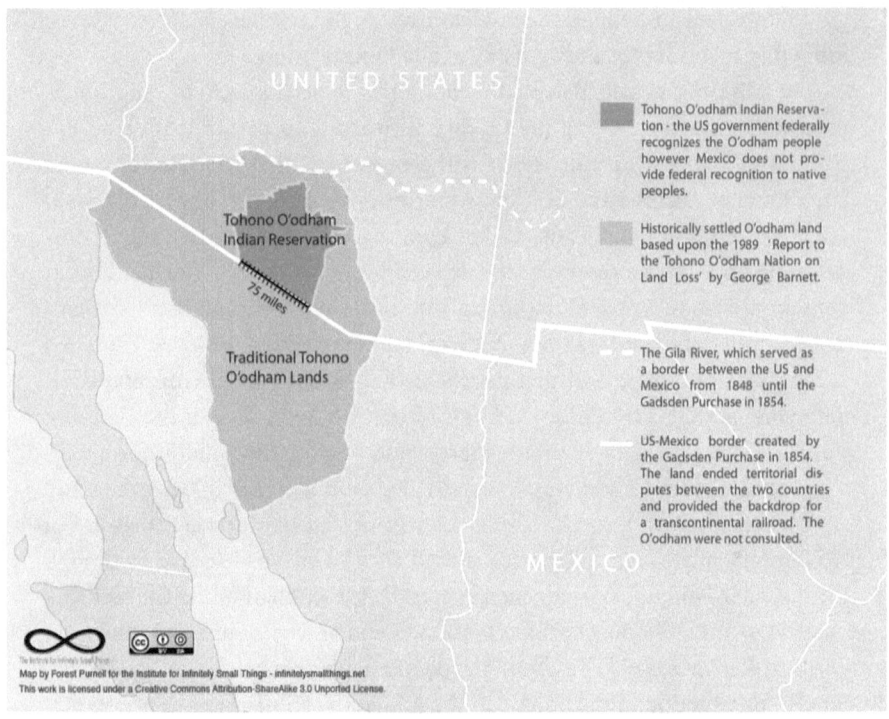

FIGURE 12. Historically settled Tohono O'odham lands.
Source: Forest Purnell for the Institute for Infinitely Small Things, CC BY-SA 3.0 via Wikimedia Commons.

south and the Sea of Cortez to the west. About two thousand of the tribe's thirty-four thousand members live in what is now Sonora on the Mexican side. Any divide between them is artificial and arbitrary; as Schermerhorn relates, O'odham continue to "think of Magdalena as existing with O'odham territory, both by actually walking to Magdalena themselves and by praying in their own homes for their loved ones who are making the journey for the people."[26] The O'odham way of life, or himdag, explains Felicity Amaya Schaeffer, "is inseparable from their sacred right to movement across land."[27] "For the O'odham and Apache today," she writes, "movement across land to hunt, to harvest, and to engage in pilgrimages connects them to a phenomenological orientation of belonging with ancestors who made similar journeys."[28] Some pilgrims experience ancestors as actually present with them during the

26. Schermerhorn, *Walking to Magdalena*, 32.
27. Schaeffer, *Unsettled Borders*, 58.
28. Schaeffer, *Unsettled Borders*, 7.

walk.[29] To the ancestors, and to their (future) descendants, the US-Mexico border and the configurations of sovereignty that it sustains was, is, and will be irrelevant. "O'odham land is defined not by maps or borders but by footprints marking the path of the ancestors from the past to the future, including plant and animal ancestors that have shaped O'odham existence, culture, and character as a desert people."[30]

Since the 9/11 attacks and the subsequent uptick in border militarization, US and Mexican authorities have obstructed pilgrims' movement to and from Magdalena.[31] No concerns have been voiced for their religious freedom. These restrictions intensified in 2006, when George W. Bush signed the Secure Fence Act, authorizing and partially funding seven hundred miles of border fencing. On Tohono O'odham land, the government replaced barbed-wire fencing with a line of thick metal posts.[32] As the border hardened, migrants from further south began to be diverted from easier points of crossing onto more remote O'odham lands to evade Border Patrol. In 2010, half of migrant deaths in Arizona occurred in the Tohono O'odham Nation.[33]

Since 9/11, members of the O'odham Nation crossing the border for any reason have been restricted to one entry point on the reservation, unless they choose to travel several hours to access other ports of entry off reservation. Since 2010, the Mexican government has required US citizens traveling below the kilometer 21 marker in Sonora to have a US passport, including those making the pilgrimage to Magdalena. To apply for a passport, one needs a birth certificate and a social security card. This is often difficult for O'odham elders, many of whom were born at home and lack a birth certificate. Border Patrol has begun to harass pilgrims during the crossing. Many carry statues of saints with them to Magdalena, and Border Patrol have been known to break them open on the suspicion that they contain drugs.[34]

In 2016, a controversy erupted on O'odham lands that brought all these concerns to a head. New private landowners on the Mexican side of the line had recently purchased traditional O'odham land in Sonora, just south of the San Miguel Gate. The San Miguel Gate, or Wo'osan Gate in the O'odham language (figure 13), is a popular crossing point for pilgrims to Magdalena.

---

29. Schermerhorn, *Walking to Magdalena*, 42. Pilgrims are connected to place, past pilgrimages, and deceased pilgrims through the staffs they carry and the stories linking the staffs with persons and places, past and present, living and dead (96). See *Walking to Magdalena*, chap. 3.

30. Schaeffer, *Unsettled Borders*, 147.

31. Schermerhorn, *Walking to Magdalena*, 168.

32. Nañez, "Border Tribe."

33. Morales, "Border Wall Would Cut across Land Sacred to Native Tribe."

34. Schermerhorn, "Pilgrimage to Magdalena."

FIGURE 13. San Miguel (Wo'osan) Gate, Tohono O'odham Nation.
Photo by Mamta Popat. © Arizona Daily Star.

The new owners on the Mexican side built a fence and posted bilingual "Private Property" signs announcing that neither "the Border Patrol, the Tohono O'odham Nation, nor any other agency of the United States Government has any jurisdiction over this land."[35] No longer able to cross at San Miguel, pilgrims have been forced to cross at Sasabe, adding several hours to their trip by car from Sells to Pozo Verde, before heading into Tubutama and then Magdalena.[36]

Wo'osan Gate is a traditional O'odham passageway that was created when the border was drawn to make it easier for tribal members to cross back and forth between Mexico and the United States. Most Americans and Mexicans cannot cross legally at this gate; it is intended only for O'odham tribal citizens with Tribal IDs. Mexico, however, does not offer federal recognition to Indigenous peoples and does not recognize O'odham sovereignty. As a result, the land south of the gate could be sold as private property.

US Border Patrol brushed aside the controversy surrounding the closure, describing it as "a private dispute between a landowner in Mexico and the

---

35. Schermerhorn, *Walking to Magdalena*, 169.
36. Schermerhorn, *Walking to Magdalena*, 169.

tribe."³⁷ While technically it was a private property owner that closed the gate, Kenneth Madsen, a professor at Ohio State, explains that "Border Patrol has blocked everything else except these 15 feet, so all the private land owner had to do was build a fence on 15 feet of his property." The welded gate, according to journalist Tay Wiles, "was built to blend in with the border fencing around it, in a rusty metal bollard style." The landowner, "painted the sign in Border Patrol green to make it look as official as possible."³⁸ The O'odham tore the gate down, but it was again welded shut by the Mexican landowner. Wiles notes that "it was not clear why the owner wanted to stop traffic; rumors circulated that it had something to do with drug cartel influence."³⁹

As a result of the closure of the crossing to vehicles, three O'odham villages on the Mexican side of the border, Wo'osan, Kuwith Wahia, and Kom Wahia, could no longer access their food supply in Arizona. The closest grocery store on the Mexican side is three hours by car from the villages, in Caborca. The villagers share one Chevy Suburban. Many speak only O'odham and do not carry passports, complicating the crossing at the next-nearest crossing point at Sasabe.⁴⁰ Reduced to hunting rabbits and conserving what little food they had, some tribal villagers began to suffer from malnutrition after the gate was welded shut. One elder was hospitalized. Arizona-based Tohono O'odham tribal elder and activist Ofelia Rivas began collecting donations to buy food in Tucson and deliver it by car to the isolated villagers.

San Miguel Gate, "once a regularly trafficked route for O'odham to see relatives, sell goods, and travel to medical appointments or to traditional ceremonies,"⁴¹ was the last of five original border gates on O'odham land to be welded shut. The first was the gate nearest to Ofelia Rivas's hometown, farther west, also used for travel to traditional ceremonies. As Wiles explains, "in 2016, the San Miguel gate was the next stitch in the steady sewing shut of a border dividing a nation of people who never wanted it in the first place."⁴² Gabriella Cázares-Kelly, a Tohono O'odham woman who lives in Tucson and works as a teacher on the reservation, explained that when San Miguel was welded shut, "it affected us as a larger community. The traditional routes have been a big part of our community for hundreds and hundreds of years. That

37. Marizco, "Tohono O'odham's San Miguel Gate May Be Closing."
38. Wiles, "Closed Border Gate."
39. Wiles, "Closed Border Gate."
40. "The families all shared one Chevy suburban that sometimes broke down, and the dirt roads to the villages were incredibly rough. The closed gate just added to the challenges" (Wiles, "Closed Border Gate").
41. Wiles, "Closed Border Gate."
42. Wiles, "Closed Border Gate."

was a very normal part of our history to be making the journey to the ocean or traditional villages in what is now Mexico."[43]

The militarization of the reservation continues apace. In 2019, the US subsidiary of the Israeli military contractor Elbit Systems—which touts its products as "field-proven" on Palestinians—was awarded a $26 million contract by Customs and Border Control to build a series of surveillance towers on the Tohono O'odham reservation.[44] Despite protests, one of the new towers, described as "a 160-foot surveillance tower capable of continuously monitoring every person and vehicle within a radius of up to 7.5 miles," was built at the base of a hill overlooking Ofelia Rivas's home.[45] The towers are outfitted with cameras that have night vision, thermal sensors, and ground-sweeping radar, all of which feed real-time data to Border Patrol in Ajo, Arizona.[46] Investigative journalist Will Parrish reports that, "according to Bobby Brown, senior director of Customs and Border Protection at Elbit Systems of America, the company's ultimate goal is to build a 'layer' of electronic surveillance equipment across the entire perimeter of the U.S. 'Over time, we'll expand not only to the northern border, but to the ports and harbors across the country,' Brown said."[47] Nellie Jo David, a tribal member and participant in a 2017 delegation of activists from the borderlands to the West Bank, organized by the Palestinian civil society group Stop the Wall, described the towers as "just one more target on our culture and way of life . . . We can't really have the same ceremonies if there are going to be eyes on us, coming from an operational control room with likely a white male agent looking into what it is to be O'odham."[48]

As a child in the 1960s, Ofelia Rivas recalls "walking through washes across the border to visit family on a regular basis." Today, however, "when she drives through checkpoints in and around the reservation, she doesn't

---

43. Cited in Wiles, "Closed Border Gate."

44. Parrish, "U.S. Border Patrol.'" According to a press release from Elbit Systems, "The IFT [integrated fixed towers] system comprises a command and control center and a networked multi-tower, multi-sensor system that continuously monitors portions of the U.S. southern border. Information from the towers is sent to the command and control center at a Border Patrol Station providing agents with long-range, persistent surveillance and situational awareness that allows them to dispatch an appropriate response." Elbit Systems, "Elbit Systems U.S. Subsidiary Awarded Additional $26 Million Contract."

45. Parrish, "U.S. Border Patrol."

46. Parrish, "U.S. Border Patrol."

47. Parrish, "U.S. Border Patrol."

48. Cited in Parrish, "U.S. Border Patrol." Stop the Wall describes itself as a "Palestinian grassroots anti-apartheid wall campaign" (https://stopthewall.org/).

speak English to the authorities. She considers it a form of protest. On a recent drive through a checkpoint, a Border Patrol agent asked if she was a US citizen. She responded, as she usually does, exclusively in O'odham. The agent repeated the question several times before waving her through. As soon as she was out of view, Rivas smiled. 'I'm not a U.S. citizen,' she says. 'This is O'odham land as far as the eye can see. . . . These mountains only know O'odham words.'"[49]

49. Wiles, "Closed Border Gate." As is common among the O'odham, Rivas was born at home and does not have a birth record. David Ortega, an O'odham Marine Corps veteran who served in Lebanon in the early 1980s, also was born at home in Mexico and does not have US citizenship, and thus cannot receive veteran's benefits. See Dougherty, "One Nation, Under Fire."

CONCLUSION

The Ideal Border

In a 2019 essay, artist and professor Nicole Antebi describes the joy of discovering a set of "meander maps" created by Harold Fisk in 1944.[1] Fisk, an Army Corps of Engineers cartographer and geologist, had drawn the maps to depict the Lower Mississippi's meanders from southern Illinois to southern Louisiana (figure 14). A *meander* is a turn or winding of a stream or river. As Antebi explains, it refers to "the ribbon-like waveform that a powerful river can take when sediment builds up on the inside edge of its flow, bending its course. Over time, as more dirt and rocks pack on, the river keeps meandering, pushing the water into fresh curve shapes. Sometimes the bend will complete as a loop, known as an oxbow."

Antebi hung the meander map in her living room and looks at it every day, "marveling at the way the Mississippi is tangled up in a way that undercuts the simplistic authority of other maps." As a native of El Paso, she was curious to find a meander map of her hometown river, the Rio Grande/Rio Bravo del Norte, which serves as the border between El Paso, Texas, and the Mexican city of Juárez. She decided to make her own.[2]

The United States and Mexico intended to use the Rio Grande/Rio Bravo to define the border in the 1848 Treaty of Guadalupe Hidalgo. As Alana de Hinojosa explains, however, in 1952 "when a binational team of engineers and cartographers mapped this river through the towns of Franklin (later renamed El Paso) and Paso del Norte as the new U.S.-Mexico boundary, the Rio Grande's meandering was perceived as nothing short of anarchy: a river

---

1. Antebi, "Between Texas and Mexico."

2. Antebi's digital animation of the historical meanders of the Rio Grande/Rio Bravo from 1827 through 1960 can be viewed in her essay "Between Texas and Mexico."

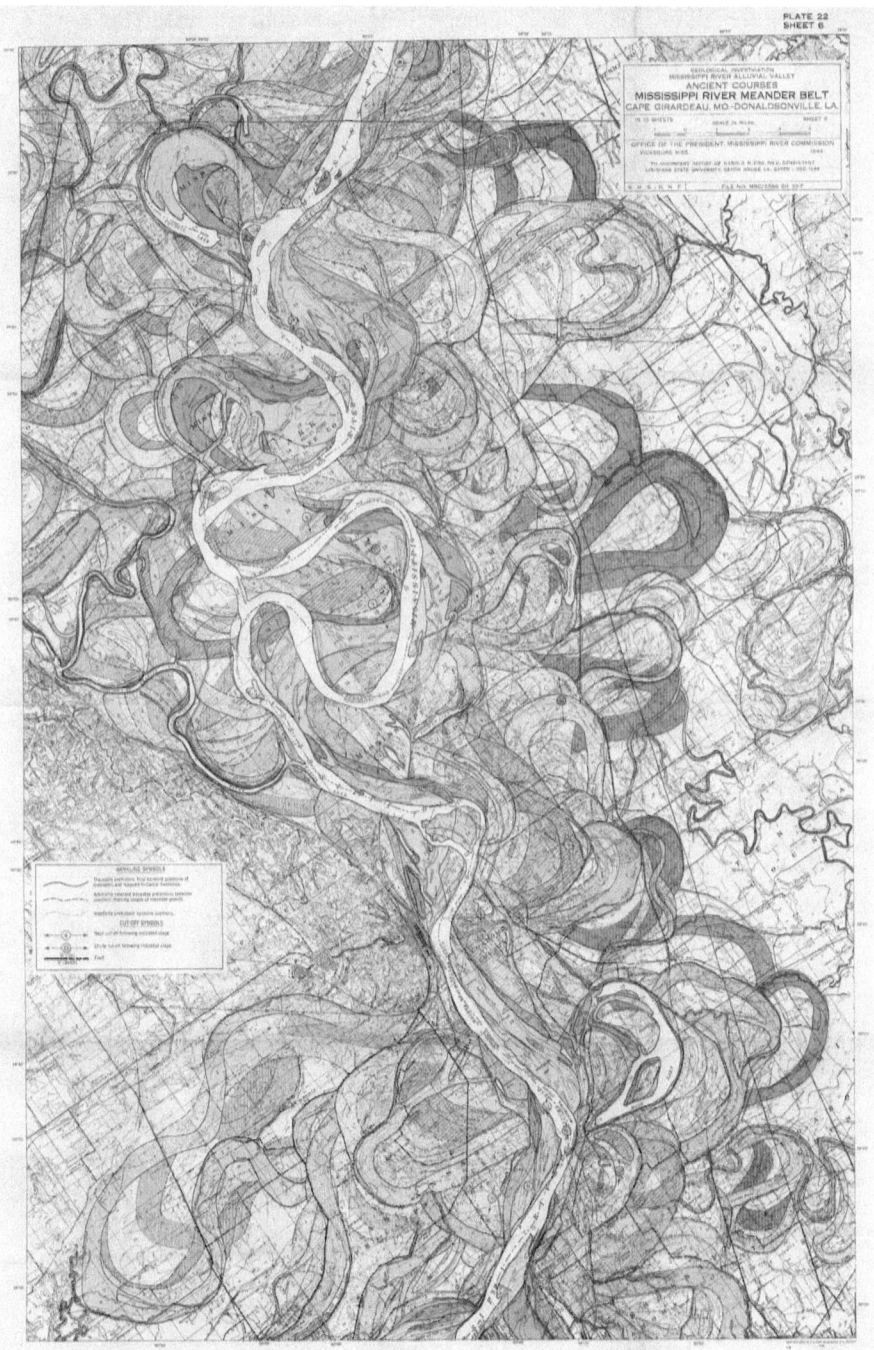

FIGURE 14. One of Harold Fisk's 144 Mississippi meander maps for the US Army Corps of Engineers, USAC.
Science History Images / Alamy Stock Photo.

in open rebellion against the boundary commission and a threat to the sanctity of the U.S.-Mexico border."[3] As the "river with two names" continued to move, so did the border. A severe flood in 1864 left several hundred acres of disputed Mexican territory to the north of the river—the result of the abrupt change in course. This led to complications. As Antebi explains, "by 1864 the river had shifted southward almost 600 acres across the international boundary marker; one of its oxbows, known as Cordova Island, was surrounded on three sides by the United States. It would take a century before the two countries would resolve that land dispute."[4] Two decades later, the US and Mexico signed the Treaty of 1884 to "avoid difficulties which may arise through changes of [river] channel."[5] The treaty prescribed that the border would run down the middle of the Rio Grande/Rio Bravo along the deepest channel, regardless of natural alterations in the banks or channels, from El Paso to the Gulf of Mexico. It specified that any alterations had to result from gradual natural causes, and not by floods or avulsions.[6] "In what seemed almost like an attempt to parse the intentions of the river itself," writes Paul Kramer, "it was decided that gradual changes in its course would move the border, while hasty ones would leave the boundary where it was."[7] The 1884 treaty provided:

> Article I.—The dividing line shall forever be that described in the aforesaid treaty and follow the center of the normal channel of the rivers named, notwithstanding any alterations in the banks or in the course of those rivers, provided that such alterations be effected by natural causes through the slow and gradual erosion and deposit of alluvium and not by the abandonment of an existing river bed and the opening of a new one.
>
> Article II.—Any other change, wrought by the force of the current whether by the cutting of a new bed or when there is more than one channel by the deepening of another channel than that which marked the boundary at the time of the survey made under the aforesaid treaty, shall produce no change in the dividing line as fixed by the surveys of the International Boundary Commissions in 1852, but the line then fixed shall continue to follow the middle of

---

3. de Hinojosa, "El Chamizal Is Ours Forever," 94.
4. Antebi, "Between Texas and Mexico."
5. Coerver, "Treaty of 1884."
6. An *avulsion* is a sudden change of course in a river. The Mississippi is known for its dramatic avulsions: "over the course of about twenty-four hours, in 1876, the Mississippi abandoned its old channel on one side of Reverie, Tennessee, and started running on the other, cutting the town off from its old state and connecting it to dry land in Arkansas" ("Ancient Courses").
7. Kramer, "Border Crosses."

the original channel bed, even though this should become wholly dry or be obstructed by deposits.[8]

The Texas State Historical Association explained that "this provision followed the long-established doctrine of international law known as 'the law of accretion' that stipulates when changes in the course of a boundary river are caused by a deposit of alluvium (a process called accretion), the boundary changes with the river, but when changes are due to avulsion, the old channel remains the boundary."[9] As Kathy Velikov and Geoffrey Thün observe, "this rendered the border an unstable condition, as its line needed to be redefined by the International Boundary Commission each time floods caused the river to relocate."[10] Alana de Hinojosa emphasizes, however, that the law of accretion is based on precedents from other parts of the world, and that in this case "a combination of the river slowing down in the lower valley and depositing sediment over centuries had built up an extensive alluvial plain over which the river moved outside the neat definitions of accretion and avulsion."[11] The river defied the law of accretion.[12] An additional convention in 1889 set up the International Boundary Commission to process disputes arising out of changes in the river.[13] In 1908, a US-Canada boundary commission—the International Boundary Commission de la Frontière Internationale—was created. It describes itself as "quietly effective at maintaining the boundary line between the United States and Canada."[14]

The dispute between the United States and Mexico over the land carved away from Mexico during the flood of 1864 became known as the "Chamizal

---

8. US Department of State, *Papers Relating to the Foreign Relations of the United States.*
9. Gregory and Liss, "Chamizal Dispute."
10. Velikov and Thün, "How the Rio Grande Came to Separate the U.S. and Mexico."
11. de Hinojosa, "El Chamizal Is Ours Forever," 100.
12. de Hinojosa, "El Chamizal Is Ours Forever," 100.
13. In 1944, its name was changed to the International Boundary and Water Commission ("About Us"). On the discursive displacement of the possibility of El Paso's illegitimate possession of El Chamizal see de Hinojosa, "El Chamizal Is Ours Forever."
14. Their unusually poetic website is worth a read. Under "The Boundary and You" it says: "For most of us, the border, or boundary, as it should be called, is nothing but an abstract line, sometimes straight, sometimes impossibly jagged, laid out on a road map, a globe or on our GPS navigation devices. For others, the boundary is a very real part of daily life. It is a granite obelisk that stands out in the middle of a front lawn next to a garden gnome. A 6-metre vista, clear cut through a maple grove. A length of electrician's tape that runs through the middle of a library that straddles the Quebec/Vermont boundary or, a curious landmark between the 18th hole and clubhouse of a golf course on the Prairies. Its monuments can also be seen as lonely sentinels atop some of the continent's highest peaks" (International Boundary Commission de la Frontière Internationale, "Boundary and You").

dispute," after the shrubs growing in the area.[15] The flood had created large land protrusions, called "bancos," and the six-hundred-acre banco known as "El Chamizal" was among them. During Prohibition, a bar emerged named Hole in the Wall, built at the foot of Eucalyptus Street on Cordova Island, a land tract in the Chamizal where the river looped back toward the United States. The loop created a Mexican alcove on the US side, where for twenty-five cents Manuel Munguia would serve patrons whiskey and bottled beer.[16] Like the Prohibition-era bars in Ambos Nogales and Vermont/Quebec mentioned earlier, Hole in the Wall customers could enter on the US side, where alcohol was illegal, walk to the Mexican side, and drink a beer.[17] So many similar establishments popped up along the Rio Grande during this era that former El Paso mayor R. E. Sherman reputedly described the Rio Grande as the "longest river in the world, wet on one side and dry on the other."[18]

The Chamizal dispute was formally resolved in July 1963,[19] with the signing of the Chamizal Convention in Mexico City by US ambassador Thomas C. Mann and Mexican foreign minister Manuel Tello.[20] The two countries agreed to relocate the Rio Grande into a custom-built concrete 4.3-mile channel in accordance with an engineering plan recommended in "Minute 214" of the International Boundary and Water Commission, United States and Mexico of August 28, 1963, which was annexed to the Convention. Designed to carry a flood of 18,000 cubic feet per second, "the river channel shall be relocated so as to transfer from the north to the south of the Rio Grande a

---

15. Alana de Hinojosa explains that both US and Mexican claims to El Chamizal are settler-colonial in nature: "Spanish and Mexican mestizo settlers first stole El Chamizal (and this region more broadly) from the Manso, Suma, and Mescalero Apache peoples. But when this region became the U.S.–Mexico borderlands in 1848, U.S. property law and racial logics relegated the landed, mixed-race Mexicanos—including the elite 'Spanish' families who owned property in El Chamizal—into a racially inferior and landless category that was 'Other' to Anglo Americans" ("El Chamizal Is Ours Forever," 95).

16. Kramer, "Border Crosses."

17. *Pulso* staff, "Border Is Alive!"

18. Long, "El Pasoans Escaped Dry Times."

19. US Department of State, *Boundary: Solution of the Problem of the Chamizal*. The convention was ratified by the US Senate on December 17, 1963, and signed by President Johnson on December 20, 1963. In April 1964, the US Senate and House of Representatives passed Public Law 88–300, the "Chamizal Convention Act."

20. "The agreement awarded Mexico 366 acres of the Chamizal area and 71 acres east of the adjacent Cordova Island. Although no payments were made between the two governments, the United States received compensation from a private Mexican bank for 382 structures included in the transfer. The United States also received 193 acres of Cordova Island from Mexico" (US Customs and Border Protection, "Did You Know?").

THE IDEAL BORDER   173

tract of 823.50 acres composed of 366.00 acres in the Chamizal tract, 193.16 acres in the southern part of Cordova Island, and 264.34 acres to the east of Cordova Island. A tract of 193.16 acres in the northern part of Cordova Island will remain to the north of the river."[21] The center line of the new river channel, described in Minute 214, an annex to the convention, would serve as the international boundary. The level of detail in the engineers' description of the border's path through the channel is remarkable:

> The centerline of the proposed new channel would diverge from the center line of the present channel at point "A" shown on the Exhibit. Beginning at that point, the centerline is described as follows, with distances approximate: It would be aligned easterly along a curve of 2,300-foot radius and 0.44 mile in length, and a tangent of 0.62 mile, approximately parallel to the present channel and from 600 to 900 feet to the north of it; thence northeasterly along a curve of 1,640-foot radius and .32 mile in length, and a tangent of 0.22 mile; thence easterly along a curve 2,080 feet in radius und 0.35 mile in length and a tangent of 0.62 mile, crossing the west boundary of Cordova Island at a point 200 feet to the south of Monument No. 3 and approximately 1,000 feet to the south of the north boundary of said Island and 3,500 feet to the north of the present channel of the river; the line would continue to the southeast along a curve 1,910 feet in radius and 0.38 mile in length, which would cross the east boundary of Cordova Island 330 feet to the east of Monument No. 13 and thence also southeasterly along a tangent. 0.82 mile; thence easterly along a curve of 5,730 feet in radius and 0.53 mile in length to connect with the present channel.[22]

The costs of constructing the channel, including six rebuilt bridges, were borne equally by both governments. During construction, the border was effectively suspended: construction workers were not subject to immigration restrictions and project materials were exempted from import/export taxes.

Historians attribute the US motivation to reach the Chamizal agreement (figure 15) in the early 1960s to fear of Mexican sympathies with Cuba during the Cuban Missile Crisis, resulting in efforts by President Kennedy to cultivate anti-Communist goodwill with Mexico and other Latin American countries.

There is a sense of urgency in the documents. Chamizal National Monument park ranger Rodney Sauter reported that in the hasty process of

---

21. US Department of State, *Boundary: Solution of the Problem of the Chamizal*, 3.

22. US Department of State, *Boundary: Solution of the Problem of the Chamizal*, Annexes, "Authentic Copies of Minute 214 of the International Boundary and Water Commission, United States and Mexico, and Map Attached Thereto," 10.

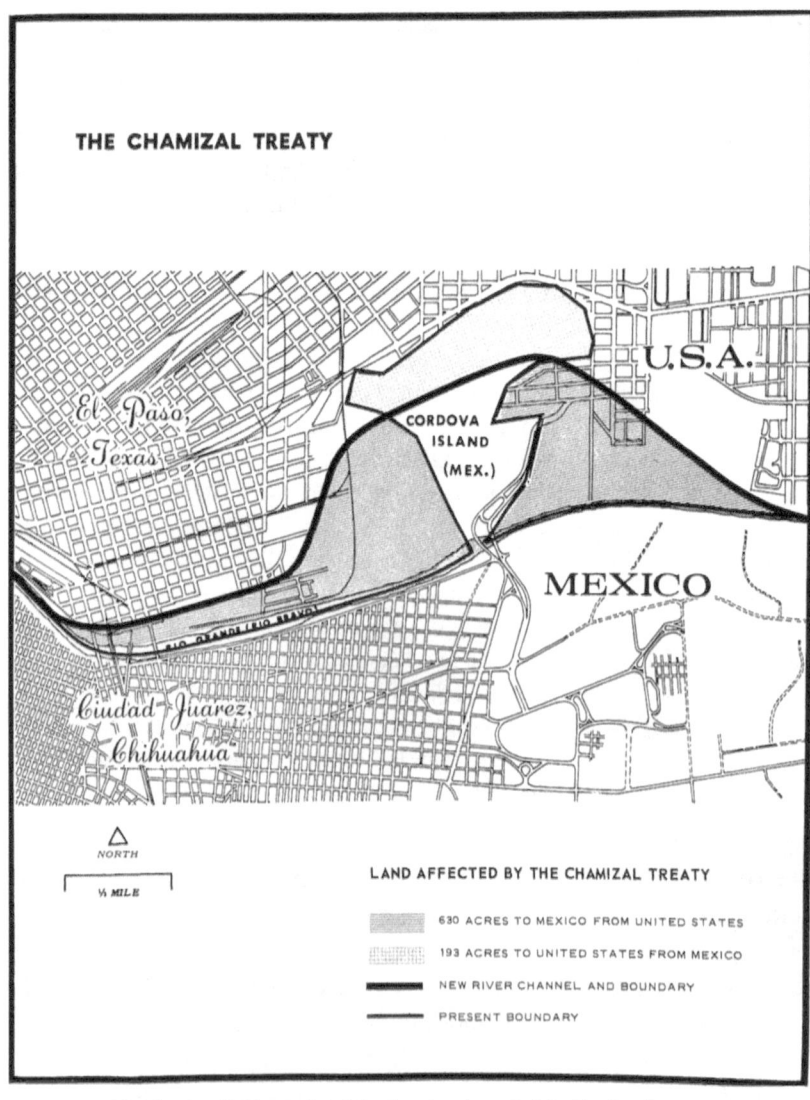

FIGURE 15. Map showing El Chamizal and the changing channel of the Rio Grande.

redrawing the boundary, Ambassador Mann and his team "went to the local Esso station and purchased one of their maps. And they drew lines and took them back and forth, between the United States and Mexico. So that there wasn't really like an official public record of the negotiations."[23] The upshot was that the disputed land, which had been considered part of El Paso

23. *Pulso* staff, "Border Is Alive!"

for nearly a century, was "returned" to Mexico and a concrete channel constructed to reroute the Rio Grande north to align it with the border.[24] According to the annex to the convention "Minute 214," "the new lined channel would provide a stable international boundary, would permit more effective sanitary control of the river and would contribute to improvement and beautification of the border between the two countries at El Paso-Ciudad Juárez."[25]

At a ceremony marking the resolution of the Chamizal dispute in December 1968, US President Lyndon B. Johnson and Mexican President Gustavo Díaz Ordaz met on the newly constructed Bridge of the Americas over the Rio Grande/Rio Bravo to celebrate the end of the dispute and witness the newly rerouted river-border in action. But like the neighbors in Frost's famous poem "Mending Wall," the two presidents had to use a spell to make the engineered concrete trough perform. They stood on the bridge overlooking the concrete channel. In front of them was a ceremonial black box with two red buttons (figure 16) that were supposed to trigger the explosion of a temporary dirt dam, releasing the Rio Grande/Rio Bravo into the Adolfo López Mateos River Channel, a 4.3-mile-long concrete trough that was the new international boundary.[26]

The International Boundary and Water Commission had built the dirt dam for the occasion. The presidents were to turn a key to arm the box, causing a light to come on. They were then to push the red buttons, detonating an explosive charge that would blow up the dam, causing a gush of water to flow through the channel. The crowd would cheer. But the ceremony did not go as planned: at the last minute, the Secret Service would not allow the necessary wiring to be so close to the presidents. An engineer was placed on standby. When he saw the presidents push the buttons, the engineer radioed down to another engineer who detonated the charges. There was nothing but a puff of smoke. Engineers hastily bulldozed the dam so that the river would trickle into the channel.

The former riverbed on the Juárez side became home to the dusty playgrounds of the Parque Chamizal, while the US side features the Cesar Chavez elevated highway next to the fifty-five-acre Chamizal National Memorial, a

---

24. Velikov and Thün, "How the Rio Grande Came to Separate the U.S. and Mexico."

25. US Department of State, *Boundary: Solution of the Problem of the Chamizal*, Annexes, "Authentic Copies of Minute 214 of the International Boundary and Water Commission, United States and Mexico, and Map Attached Thereto," 12.

26. The channel was named after the previous Mexican president who had been part of earlier negotiations. This paragraph draws on National Park Service, "Little Black Box," and Kramer, "Border Crosses."

FIGURE 16. Ceremonial black box.
LBJ Library photo by Yoichi Okamoto.

National Park Service monument commemorating what the Park Service describes as the "harmonious settlement" of the boundary dispute.[27] While it may have been harmonious for some, that was not the case for the primarily Mexican American families, many of them Korean War veterans, living in border limbo who found themselves forcibly relocated and their homes razed to create the concrete channel.[28] As Kramer explains, "people scattered throughout El Paso, finding themselves in strange and sometimes unwelcoming neighborhoods.... According to one woman, where Chamizal residents moved in, Anglos moved out. Some boundaries shifted more easily than others."[29]

27. National Park Service, Chamizal: National Memorial Texas.
28. The convention called for the "orderly evacuation of the occupants of the lands referred to in paragraph (a)" (US Department of State, *Boundary: Solution of the Problem of the Chamizal*, 5). US Korean War veterans had built houses in the area with money from the GI Bill, and the Chamizal became a community of about 5,600 primarily Mexican American residents, all of whom had lived in a border limbo and were eventually evicted when the US government forcibly sold off their properties to return the land to Mexico.
29. Kramer, "Border Crosses."

The Rio Grande/Rio Bravo in this area today is either a quiet stream or series of puddles in a sandy and desolate concrete channel. The combined effects of the river's rerouting, border militarization, and extensive upstream dam projects have led to a rather bleak scene on the riverbanks. As Antebi describes: "The barrier that the river provides is joined by real border fences, reinforced by razor-wire-topped pylons and cameras that run right along the water's natural flow and its concrete channels. The U.S. government watches every move below, while the people living along the river with two names can barely see the water, or our neighbors on the other side. Each day brings new policies to block or detain asylum seekers and migrants from legal entry, adding new challenges and terror imposed on the *fronterizx*—people from both El Paso and Juárez—who have always crossed and made a life on both sides."[30]

The quixotic attempt to enforce a border in the middle of a river that refuses it remains a source of controversy. In 2023, the State of Texas installed a border barrier made up of four-foot-wide connected buoys anchored to the riverbed in a one-thousand-foot-long barrier running down the middle of the Rio Grande/Rio Bravo between Eagle Pass, Texas, and Piedras Negras, Mexico. The buoys had nets below them to prevent swimmers from passing underneath and were designed to roll over if anyone tried to climb over them.[31] The river refused to cooperate: the International Boundary and Water Commission found that by mid-August, 787 feet (79 percent) of the 995-feet-long buoy line installed by Texas in July had drifted into Mexico, with only 208 feet of the line remaining in the United States.[32] The US federal government sued the State of Texas in 2023 for usurping federal control of the border by creating an "unauthorized obstruction to the navigable capacity of waters of the United States in violation of Rivers & Harbors Act (RHA) section 10."[33]

---

30. Antebi, "Between Texas and Mexico."

31. The state also placed razor wire—braided steel wire with sharp metal attachments—along the Texas side of the river.

32. Montoya-Galvez, "Nearly 80% of Texas' Floating Border Barrier Is Technically in Mexico."

33. Goodman, "Texas Patrols Its Own Border"; US Army Corps of Engineers, "Section 10 of the Rivers & Harbors Act." The complaint, filed in the US District Court for the Western District of Texas, charged that "defendants have built structures in the Rio Grande, a navigable water of the United States, without the Corps' authorization, in violation of RHA section 10, 33 U.S.C. § 403. These structures include a floating barrier and related infrastructure. Defendants' structures also constitute an unauthorized obstruction to the navigable capacity of waters of the United States in violation of RHA section 10,33 U.S.C. § 403" (*United States of America v. Abbott et al.*, 1–2). Texas governor Greg Abbott's response to the suit was "Texas will see you in court, Mr. President" (6).

In the preface to her book, *The Ideal River*, Joanne Yao writes that "the dream of taming rivers wove through the history of the modern world like a bright thread," lurking in a "desire for neatness, predictability, finite boundaries, and a straightened sense of political purpose."[34] Yao focuses on nineteenth-century efforts to use scientific and technical expertise to tame transboundary rivers in the name of civilization and rational authority, as expressed in attempts to create international commissions to govern the Rhine, the Danube, and the Congo—all transboundary rivers like the Rio Grande/Rio Bravo. The ideal river was meant to serve as "a rational and reliable highway for the seamless movement of goods, people, and ideas," that "enriches the state, enlightens the populace, and brings liberal progress."[35] The proper use of modern science and technology would allow for human mastery of nature's contingencies. It would usher in an era of global civilization and soften humanity's rougher edges. It would "civilize the natives." Writing in the same spirit as Yao but in reference to the Rio Grande's concrete channel, Kramer speaks of the "compelling illusion that nature could be made to carve mankind's self-divisions into the earth."[36]

The ideal river and the ideal border have a lot in common. Just as modern architects and river planners invested in a capacity to tame and regularize rivers, so have border planners and policymakers chased after an ideal of borders as lines of control that facilitate the seamless and safe movement of goods, peoples, and ideas to enrich American citizens, regularize border crossings, and guarantee national security. The dream of taming borders, like the dream of taming rivers, "weaves through the history of the modern world like a bright thread." Yet, also like rivers, borders are unwieldy and unpredictable. Human control is partial and incomplete. Borders are places of fantasy and also of extreme violence. Fear abounds. "Even Heaven itself is going have a wall around it," declared Robert Jeffress, Pastor of First Baptist Dallas Church and recipient of the 2023 Friends of Zion award in Jerusalem.[37] US borders are the site of efforts to escape the ordinary and find spaces outside of law, places of selective emancipation, even chosenness. They are more than a physical frontier. They are simultaneously closed and open, fortified and deferred, legalized and exceptionalized, sacred and secular.

---

34. Yao, *Ideal River*, ix. She describes her project as a consideration of "how our entangled human-river histories enabled the political possibilities of modernity" (x).

35. Yao, *Ideal River*, 3.

36. Kramer, "Border Crosses."

37. Cole, "Evangelical Pastor Robert Jeffress." The 133-year-old historic sanctuary at First Baptist Dallas was destroyed in a four-alarm fire on July 19, 2024. The cause of the fire remains undetermined.

Acknowledgments

To the colleagues, activists, family, and friends who shared their insights and experiences about borders and border crossing over the past several years, thank you. These conversations were essential to this project. To the amazing students in my US border seminars at Northwestern, you sparked my thinking and gave me hope for the future.

An ACLS/Luce Fellowship in Religion, Journalism and International Affairs supported a sabbatical to work on this project in 2019–20. When that leave was interrupted by the pandemic, a 2023 COVID-19 research recovery grant from the Weinberg College of Arts & Sciences at Northwestern helped compensate for lost time. The Weinberg Center for International & Area Studies supported a 2023 symposium at Sciences Po-CERI, where I received invaluable feedback from Maria Birnbaum, Iza Hussin, Yolande Jansen, and Nadia Marzouki. The Northwestern–Sciences Po short-term faculty exchange and the generosity of my CERI host, Nadia Marzouki, gave me much-needed time to complete a first draft.

To the GOVMAT collective (Bjørn Ola Tafjord, Greg Alles, Helge Årsheim, Greg Johnson, Arkotong Longkumer, Liudmila Nikanorova, and Terje Østebø), thanks for the discussions of my Santa Muerte chapter alongside your work. I enjoyed our meetings. Thanks to Spencer Dew, Arturo Chang, and Ayodeji Ogunnaike for their contributions and suggestions on that chapter.

Thanks to former Northwestern graduate student Christa Kuntzelman for her assistance with the asylum cases in chapter 1 and for our conversations about her work as a refugee and immigrant advocate in Chicago. Thanks to my undergraduate research assistants Mara Kelly, Addison Feldman, Callie Stolar, and Jane Clarke for your work on this project—working with each of you was a pleasure. I am also indebted to an amazing cohort of past and present Northwestern graduate students: Owen Brown, who compiled an early bibliography; Emma Davis, who offered suggestions on the AmericaIsrael chapter and also read through the entire manuscript; Nathalia Justo, for her thoughtful work on the moral politics of citizenship; and Juliana Sexauer, who proofread the manuscript. I am also grateful to Gina Giliberti, Emerson Murray, Ely Orrego, Hafsa Oubou, Shah Chaudhary, and Daniela Rosas for our conversations.

Other colleagues enriched this book in countless ways: Libby Anker, Osman Balkan, Iselin Frydenlund, Constance Furey, Dan Galvin, Geoff Levy, Melani McAlister, Matt Scherer, Peter Slevin, Winnifred Sullivan, and Erin Wilson all contributed to early stages of the project. James Bielo, Alana de Hinojosa, Ian Hurd, Brannon Ingram, Ángela Iranzo, Andrew Johnston, Carlos Manrique, Levi McLaughlin, Tornike Metreveli, Michelle Molina, Atalia Omer, Robert Orsi, Rocío Preciado, Diego Rossello, Noah Salomon, Ulrich Schmiedel, Ben Schonthal, Hannah Strømmen, Sarah McFarland Taylor, Mauro Trejo, Miguel Vatter, and Jessica Winegar all pitched in at later stages. I am grateful to Seth Schermerhorn for sending me a copy of his book, *Walking to Magdalena*, and for sharing his experiences crossing the border as a pilgrim. Thanks to Bill Ferris and Heidi Hamilton at Stantec for taking the time to explain how border crossings are built, and to Eddie Jones for discussing the design of the Mariposa Land Point of Entry.

A special thanks to Sarah Leavitt and Alex La Pierre. Sarah curated an exhibition, *The Wall/El Muro*, at the National Building Museum in Washington that inspired my thinking, visited my Northwestern classes virtually during the pandemic, shared her bibliography on borderlands history, and traveled with me to the borderlands. She is the traveling companion mentioned in the first pages of the introduction. This book would not be what it is without her intellect and intuition. Alex La Pierre is a public historian, cultural ambassador, and fount of borderlands experience whom I met several years ago when he was with Border Community Alliance. He now heads up his own group, Borderlandia, and continues the quiet yet essential work of educating and building bridges rather than walls. Thank you, Alex, for all that you do, and thanks also to Rocío Preciado, who designed the graphic in the interlude on the pilgrimage to Magdalena.

I want to acknowledge Border Community Alliance (BCA), and in particular Jerry Haas and Celia Bavier, for hosting speakers, collaborating on a screening of their documentary film *Pilgrimage to Magdalena* at the 2022 AAR annual meeting, and inviting Northwestern undergraduates to participate in BCA's work as summer interns. The support of the Weinberg Center for International and Area Studies, and particularly Associate Director Bianca

ACKNOWLEDGMENTS 181

Jimenez, has been crucial to the success of this collaboration. Thanks to the Borderlinks team in Tucson for including me in a weeklong immersion in border-related advocacy work. I will never forget our visit to the immigrant rights group Mariposas sin Fronteras to learn about efforts to end systemic violence against LGBTQ+ people in detention and provide opportunities for self-determination.

Thanks to Kyle Wagner at the University of Chicago Press for his enthusiasm and kindness from the moment I approached him with the proposal for this book, to the two anonymous reviewers for the press who engaged constructively and thoughtfully with the manuscript, and to the excellent production, design, and marketing teams at the press. Thanks to Marta Steele for her prompt and professional index.

Finally, thanks to Ian, Ally, Sophie, and Audrey—and our dogs Jake and Rafi—for reminding me to set work aside and have fun. To my parents, Steve and Susan, thank you for (among other things) modeling another way to relate to borders, as a pro bono asylum attorney and a volunteer ESL instructor, respectively.

This book is dedicated to border crossers and those who support them.

An earlier version of chapter 1 appeared as "Freedom, Salvation, Redemption: Theologies of Political Asylum," *Migration & Society: Advances in Research* 4 (2021): 110–23. Parts of the introduction appeared as "'Where People Come to Press Close to the Other Side': Religion, Politics, and the American Border," *American Religion* 3, no. 2 (Spring 2022): 108–16.

Sources

Abbott, Greg. "Anti-Israel Policies Are Anti-Texas Policies." Office of the Texas Governor. Press Release, May 2, 2017. https://gov.texas.gov/news/post/anti-israel-policies-are-anti-texas-policies.

Abu-Lughod, Lila. *Do Muslim Women Need Saving?* Cambridge, MA: Harvard University Press, 2013.

Ackerman, Spencer. "Bad Lieutenant: American Policy Brutality, Exported from Chicago to Guantánamo." *Guardian*, February 18, 2015. https://www.theguardian.com/us-news/2015/feb/18/american-police-brutality-chicago-guantanamo.

Adayfi, Mansoor. *Don't Forget Us Here: Lost and Found at Guantanamo*. New York: Hachette Books, 2021.

Agamben, Giorgio. *Homo Sacer: Sovereign Power and Bare Life*. Translated by Daniel Heller-Roaszen. Stanford, CA: Stanford University Press, 1998.

Agamben, Giorgio. "The State of Emergency as a Paradigm of Government." *Tablet*, May 6, 2020. https://www.tabletmag.com/sections/arts-letters/articles/state-of-emergency-giorgio-agamben.

Agrama, Hussein Ali. *Questioning Secularism: Islam, Sovereignty, and the Rule of Law in Modern Egypt*. Chicago: University of Chicago Press, 2012.

Akbar, Ahmed Ali. "At U. of C. Encampment, Jewish Organizers Explain Significance of Their Anti-Zionist Shabbat Service." *Chicago Tribune*, May 5, 2024.

Aked, Hillary. "Billionaire Donor Using British Council to Combat Israel Boycott." Electronic Intifada, March 14, 2016. https://electronicintifada.net/content/billionaire-donor-using-british-council-combat-israel-boycott/15991.

Allen, Lee. "Don't Leave Home without It." *Indian Country Today*, March 23–30, 2011, 38–39.

Allen, Lee. "State-of-the-Art Border Crossing Opens in Arizona." *Banderas News*, October 22, 2014. http://www.banderasnews.com/1410/nr-stateoftheartmariposabordercrossing.htm.

American Civil Liberties Union. "Customs and Border Protection's (CBP's) 100-Mile Rule." ACLU Washington Legislative Office, Washington, DC.https://www.aclu.org/sites/default/files/assets/14_9_15_cbp_100-mile_rule_final.pdf.

American Civil Liberties Union. "Guantánamo by the Numbers." Interactive graphic. May 2018. https://www.aclu.org/issues/national-security/detention/guantanamo-numbers.

American Civil Liberties Union. "Know Your Rights: 100-Mile Border Zone." Accessed August 26, 2024. https://www.aclu.org/know-your-rights/border-zone.

American Civil Liberties Union Michigan. "The Border's Long Shadow." March 25, 2021. https://www.aclumich.org/sites/default/files/field_documents/100_mile_zone_report-updated.pdf.

Ammerman, Nancy T. "Waco, Federal Law Enforcement, and Scholars of Religion." *Armageddon in Waco: Critical Perspectives on the Branch Davidian Conflict*, edited by Stuart A. Wright, 282–96. Chicago: University of Chicago Press, 1995.

"Ancient Courses: Harold Fisk's Meander Maps of the Mississippi River (1944)." *Public Domain Review*, July 21, 2020. https://publicdomainreview.org/collection/maps-of-the-lower-mississippi-harold-fisk/.

Anderson, Michael. "AIPAC." Access Jewish Cleveland. Accessed August 28, 2024. https://www.accessjewishcleveland.org/organizations/aipac/.

Antebi, Nicole. "Between Texas and Mexico, a Restless Border Defies the Map." *Bloomberg*, August 16, 2019. https://www.bloomberg.com/news/articles/2019-08-16/mapping-a-restless-river-at-the-u-s-mexico-border.

AnthroBoycott. "American Anthropological Association Endorses Resolution Supporting Palestinian Rights & Boycotting Israeli Apartheid." July 24, 2023.https://www.anthroboycott.org.

Anzaldúa, Gloria. *Borderlands/La Frontera: The New Mestiza*. San Francisco: Aunt Lute Books, 1987.

Apuzzo, Matt, and Michael S. Schmidt. "U.S. to Continue Racial, Ethnic Profiling in Border Policy." *New York Times*, December 5, 2014. https://www.nytimes.com/2014/12/06/us/politics/obama-to-impose-racial-profiling-curbs-with-exceptions.html.

Arctic University of Norway. "GOVMAT: The Governmateriality of Indigenous Religions." Bjørn Ola Tafjord, lead researcher. INREL research group, Department of Archaeology, History, Religious Studies, and Theology and the Faculty of Humanities, Social Sciences, and Education. Accessed August 26, 2024. https://en.uit.no/project/govmat.

Asma-Sadeque, Samira. "Shia Muslim Scholars Denied Entry into US Suspect Religious Bias." *Guardian*, April 3, 2023. Accessed August 26, 2024. https://www.theguardian.com/us-news/2023/apr/03/shia-muslim-scholars-denied-us-entry-no-given-reason.

Axelman, Eric, and Sam Eilertsen. *Israelism*. Somerville, MA: Tikkun Olam Productions, 2023. https://www.israelismfilm.com.

Aziz v. Trump. No. 1:17 CV 116, WL 580855 (E.D. Va. Feb. 13, 2017).

Bacha, Julia, dir. *Boycott*. Washington DC: Just Vision, 2021.

Baker, Kelcey, Katherine Freeman, Gigi Warner, and Deborah M. Weissman. *Expert Witnesses in U.S. Asylum Cases: A Handbook*. Chapel Hill, NC: University of North Carolina, 2018. http://www.law.unc.edu/documents/academics/humanrights/expertwitnesshandbook.pdf.

Bain, William. *The Political Theology of International Order*. Oxford: Oxford University Press, 2020.

Batnitsky, Leora. *How Judaism Became a Religion: An Introduction to Modern Jewish Thought*. Princeton, NJ: Princeton University Press, 2013.

Baudrillard, Jean. *America*. New York: Verso, 2010.

Baumann, Roger. *Visions of the Holy Land: African American Christian Engagement with Israel and Palestine*. New York: Columbia University Press, 2024.

Bayoumi, Moustafa. "Racing Religion." *New Centennial Review* 6, no. 2 (Fall 2006): 267–93.

SOURCES

BDS Movement. "Palestinian Civil Society Call for BDS." Open letter, July 9, 2005. https://bdsmovement.net/call.
Beaman, Lori G. *The Transition of Religion to Culture in Law and Public Discourse*. New York: Routledge, 2020.
Beck, Richard. *We Believe the Children: A Moral Panic in the 1980s*. New York: Public Affairs Books, 2015.
Belew, Kathleen. *Bring the War Home: The White Power Movement and Paramilitary America*. Cambridge, MA: Harvard University Press, 2019.
Bellah, Robert N. "Civil Religion in America." *Daedalus* 134, no. 4 (2005).
Bender, Courtney. "America Is Hard to See." In Hurd and Sullivan, *At Home and Abroad*, 91–112.
Bennett, Jane. *Vibrant Matter: A Political Ecology of Things*. Durham, NC: Duke University Press, 2010.
Berlit, Uwe, Harald Doerig, and Hugo Storey. "Credibility Assessment in Claims Based on Persecution for Reasons of Religious Conversion and Homosexuality: A Practitioners Approach." *International Journal of Refugee Law* 27, no. 4 (2015): 649–66.
Berger, Benjamin L. "Two Theologies of Chosenness." In *Theologies of American Exceptionalism*, edited by Winnifred Fallers Sullivan and Elizabeth Shakman Hurd. Bloomington: Indiana University Press, 2019. https://publish.iupress.indiana.edu/read/theologies-of-american-exceptionalism/section/e9b91e76-9033-4ed7-9c38-6f9a17d5a9ef.
Berger, Benjamin L. *Law's Religion: Religious Difference and the Claims of Constitutionalism*. Toronto: University of Toronto Press, 2015.
Beydoun, Khaled A., and Justin Hansford. "The F.B.I.'s Dangerous Crackdown on 'Black Identity Extremists.'" *New York Times*, November 15, 2017. https://www.nytimes.com/2017/11/15/opinion/black-identity-extremism-fbi-trump.html.
Bielo, James S. *Ark Encounter: The Making of a Creationist Theme Park*. New York: New York University Press, 2018.
Bielo, James S. *Materializing the Bible: Scripture, Sensation, Place*. Bloomsbury Studies in Material Religion. London: Bloomsbury Academic, 2021.
Bigliardi, Stephano. "La Santa Muerte and Her Interventions in Human Affairs: A Theological Discussion." *Sophia* 55 (2016): 303–23.
Blankholm, Joseph. *The Secular Paradox: On the Religiosity of the Not Religious*. New York: New York University Press, 2022.
Blumberg, Antonia. "Why Trump's Failed Attempt to Prioritize Christian Refugees Never Had a Chance." *Huffington Post*, March 10, 2017. http://www.huffingtonpost.com/entry/why-trumps-failed-attempt-to-prioritize-christian-refugees-never-had-a-chance_us_58bef9bae4b0d841663e3595.
Boumediene, Lakhdar. "My Guantánamo Nightmare." *New York Times*, January 7, 2012. https://www.nytimes.com/2012/01/08/opinion/sunday/my-guantanamo-nightmare.html.
Boumediene v. Bush. 553 US 723 (2008). https://casetext.com/case/boumediene-v-bush-5.
Boyarin, Daniel. *The No-State Solution: A Jewish Manifesto*. New Haven: Yale University Press, 2023.
Boyer, Paul. *When Time Shall Be No More: Prophecy Belief in Modern American Culture*. Cambridge, MA: Harvard University Press, 1994.
Brown, Candy Gunther. *Debating Yoga and Mindfulness in Public Schools: Reforming Secular Education or Reestablishing Religion?* Durham, NC: University of North Carolina Press, 2019.
Brown, Owen R. "The Underside of Order: Race in the Constitution of International Order." *International Organization* 78, no. 1 (2024). DOI:10.1017/S0020818324000018.

Bruyneel, Kevin, Jodi Dean, Jack Jackson, Dana M. Olwan, Corey Robin, William Clare Roberts, C. Heiki Schotten, and Jakeet Singh. "Boycott, Divestment and Sanctions (BDS) and Political Theory." *Contemporary Political Theory* 18, no. 3 (2019): 448–76.

Bunker, Pamela L., and Robert J. Bunker. "The Spiritual Significance of ¿Plata O Plomo?" *Small Wars Journal*, May 27, 2010. https://smallwarsjournal.com/blog/journal/docs-temp/444-bunker.pdf.

Bunker, Robert J. "Santa Muerte: Inspired and Ritualistic Killings." *FBI Law Enforcement Bulletin*. LEB, February 2013. https://leb.fbi.gov/articles/featured-articles/santa-muerte-inspired-and-ritualistic-killings.

Burla, Shahar, and Dashiel Lawrence, eds. *Australia & Israel: A Diasporic, Cultural and Political Relationship*. Brighton, UK: Sussex Academic Press, 2015.

Burlingame, Susan. "NEH Grant Will Help Scholars Challenge Current Views of Jews in the Middle East." Penn State News, November 3, 2021. https://www.psu.edu/news/research/story/neh-grant-will-help-scholars-challenge-current-views-jews-middle-east/.

Butler, Judith. *Bodies That Matter: On the Discursive Limits of "Sex."* New York: Routledge, 1993.

C/O Futures website. Accessed March 13, 2024. https://www.cofutures.net/epochal-change.

Calvo-Quirós, William E. *Undocumented Saints: The Politics of Migrating Devotions*. Oxford: Oxford University Press, 2022.

Cameron, Chris. "Trump Says Jews Who Support Democrats 'Hate Israel' and 'Their Religion.'" *New York Times*, March 18, 2024. https://www.nytimes.com/live/2024/03/18/us/trump-biden-election.

Cantú, Francisco. *The Line Becomes a River: Dispatches from the Border*. New York: Riverhead Books, 2018.

Carter, J. Kameron. "Jews and the Religion of Whiteness." Lecture, Herbert D. Katz Center for Advanced Judaic Studies, University of Pennsylvania, Philadelphia, February 11, 2021. Posted on YouTube. https://www.youtube.com/watch?v=PK-Ucq-4ZuQ.

Carter, J. Kameron. "The Politics of the Atonement." *Immanent Frame*, July 18, 2011. https://tif.ssrc.org/2011/07/18/the-politics-of-the-atonement/.

Carter, J. Kameron. *The Religion of Whiteness: An Apocalyptic Lyric*. New Haven, CT: Yale University Press, forthcoming.

Carter, J. Kameron. "An Unlikely Convergence: W. E. B. Du Bois, Karl Barth, and the Problem of the Imperial God-Man." *CR: The New Centennial Review* 11, no. 3 (2011): 167–224.

Carter, J. Kameron. "The White Messianic: Rethinking Race and Religion." Panel on Race and Religion beyond the State. Paris, Sciences Po–CERI, June 10, 2021.

Castells Ballarin, Pilar. "La Santa Muerte y La Cultura de los Derechos Humanos." *Liminar: Estudios sociales y humanísticos* 6, no. 1 (2008): 13–25.

Cavanaugh, William T. *Migrations of the Holy: God, State, and the Political Meaning of the Church*. Grand Rapids, MI: William ZB. Eerdmans, 2011.

Cavanaugh, William T., and Vincent Lloyd "Why Does Political Theology Matter? William Cavanaugh and Vincent Lloyd in Conversation." Political Theology Network, November 2, 2022. https://politicaltheology.com/what-is-the-state-of-political-theology-today-a-conversation-with-paul-heck-william-cavanaugh-and-vincent-lloyd/.

Chacón, Justin Akers. *The Border Crossed Us: The Case for Opening the U.S.-Mexico Border*. Chicago: Haymarket Books, 2021.

Chang, Arturo. "Restoring Anáhuac: Indigenous Genealogies and Hemispheric Republicanism in Postcolonial Mexico." *American Journal of Political Science* 67 (September 2021): 718–31.

SOURCES

Center for Biological Diversity. Press release. October 9, 2018. https://www.biologicaldiversity.org/news/press_releases/2018/border-wall-10-09-2018.php.

Center for Constitutional Rights. "Guantanamo." Accessed August 26, 2024. https://ccrjustice.org/home/what-we-do/issues/guantanamo.

Center for Constitutional Rights and Rule of Law Clinic at Yale Law School. "Window Dressing the Muslim Ban: Reports of Waivers and Mass Denials from Yemeni-American Families Stuck in Limbo." June 2018. Accessed August 26, 2024. https://ccrjustice.org/window-dressing-Muslim-ban-waivers-yemen-american-report.

Center for Land Use Interpretation. "The Forty-Fifth Parallel." Chap. 3 in *United Divide: A Linear Portrait of the USA/Canada Border*, Center for Land Use Interpretation Research Project (2014–15). https://clui.org/projects/united-divide/45th-parallel.

Cervantes, Antonio, Jr. "Santa Muerte: Threatening the U.S. Homeland." Master of military studies thesis, US Marine Corps Command and Staff College, Marine Corps University, 2011.

Chidester, David. *Empire of Religion: Imperialism and Comparative Religion*. Chicago: University of Chicago, 2013.

Chishti, Muzaffar, and Jessica Bolter. "The Travel Ban at Two: Rocky Implementation Settles into Deeper Impacts." Migration Policy Institute, January 31, 2019. https://www.migrationpolicy.org/article/travel-ban-two-rocky-implementation-settles-deeper-impacts.

Chung, Andrew. "U.S. Supreme Court Spurns Challenge to Arkansas Law against Contractors Boycotting Israel." Reuters, February 21, 2023. https://www.reuters.com/legal/us-supreme-court-spurns-challenge-arkansas-law-against-contractors-boycotting 2023-02-21.

Clark, T.J. *Farewell to an Idea: Episodes from a History of Modernism*. New Haven, CT: Yale University Press, 1999.

Coates, Benjamin Allen. *Legalist Empire: International Law and American Foreign Relations in the Early Twentieth Century*. Oxford: Oxford University Press, 2016.

Coerver, Don M. "Treaty of 1884." Handbook of Texas Online, August 19, 2023. Texas State Historical Association. https://www.tshaonline.org/handbook/entries/treaty-of-1884.

Cole, Brendan. "Evangelical Pastor Robert Jeffress Defends Trump's Border Wall: 'Heaven Itself is Going to Have a Wall Around It.'" *Newsweek*, January 10, 2019. Accessed August 30, 2024. https://www.newsweek.com/evangelical-pastor-robert-jeffress-defends-trumps-border-wall-heaven-itself-1286249.

Congressional Research Service. "The 574 Federally Recognized Indian Tribes in the United States." CRS Report R47414. Washington, DC, February 8, 2023. Updated January 18, 2024. https://crsreports.congress.gov/product/pdf/R/R47414.

Cosa v. Mukasey. 543 F.3d 1066 (9th Cir. 2008). https://casetext.com/case/cosa-v-mukasey.

Crisp, Jeff. "What Is Externalization and Why Is It a Threat to Refugees?" Chatham House Expert Comment, London, October 14, 2020. https://www.chathamhouse.org/2020/10/what-externalization-and-why-it-threat-refugees.

Crosson, J. Brent. *Experiments with Power: Obeah and the Remaking of Religion in Trinidad*. Chicago: University of Chicago Press, 2020.

Cuban American Bar Ass'n, Inc. v. Christopher. 43 F.3d 1412 (11th Cir. 1995). https://casetext.com/case/cuban-american-bar-assn-inc-v-christopher.

Cunningham, Hilary. "Sanctuary and Sovereignty: Church and State along the U.S.-Mexico Border." *Journal of Church and State* 40, no. 2 (Spring 1998): 371–86.

Cunningham, Hilary. *God and Caesar at the Rio Grande: Sanctuary and the Politics of Religion*. Minneapolis: University of Minnesota Press, 1995.

Curtis, Edward. "The Black Muslim Scare: The History of State Islamophobia and Its Post-9/11 Variations." In *Islamophobia in America: The Anatomy of Intolerance*, edited by Carl Ernst, 75–102. New York: Palgrave Macmillan, 2013.

Daily Dish. "The HIV Travel Ban." *Atlantic*, December 5, 2006. https://www.theatlantic.com/daily-dish/archive/2006/12/the-hiv-travel-ban/232005/.

Dalsheim, Joyce. *Israel Has a Jewish Problem: Self-Determination as Self-Elimination*. Oxford: Oxford University Press, 2019.

Darweesh v. Trump. 17 Civ. 480 (AMD), WL 388504 (E.D.N.Y. Jan. 28, 2017).

Davis, Emma. "Faking Remembrance: Anti-Semitism, Holocaust Memory, and the Liberal International Order." Unpublished manuscript.

Davis, Emma. "International Relations and the Jewish Question: Reconsidering Self-Determination." Unpublished manuscript.

Davis v. State. 329 S.W.3d 798 (Tex. Crim. App. 2011). https://casetext.com/case/davis-v-state-560.

Dayan, Hilla, and Yolande Jansen. "Antisemitism, Anti-Palestinian racism, and Europe: A Plea for a Critical and Democratic Debate." *Eurozine*, February 21, 2024. https://www.eurozine.com/antisemitism-anti-palestinian-racism-and-europe.

de Hinojosa, Alana. "'El Chamizal Is Ours Forever:' Rumor, Time, and the Law in El Paso's Settler Society." *Environment and Planning D: Society and Space* 42, no. 1 (2024): 91–113.

Delaney, Erin. "Immigration in the Age of Trump: Extremism vs. Exceptionalism." President Trump's First 100 Days: A Symposium. *Illinois Law Review*, April 29, 2017. https://illinoislawreview.org/symposium/first-100-days/immigration-in-the-age-of-trump/.

Deleuze, Gilles, and Félix Guattari. *A Thousand Plateaus: Capitalism and Schizophrenia*. Minneapolis: University of Minnesota Press, 1987.

Deleuze, Gilles, and Félix Guattari. *What Is Philosophy?* New York: Columbia University Press, 1996.

Diaspora Alliance official website. Accessed May 23, 2024. diasporaalliance.co.

Doan, Daniel. *Indian Stream Republic: Settling a New England Frontier, 1785–1842*. Lebanon, NH: University Press of New England, 1997.

Dougherty, John. "One Nation, Under Fire." *High Country News*, February 19, 2007. https://www.hcn.org/issues/issue-340/one-nation-under-fire/.

Downes v. Bidwell. 182 U.S. 244, 21 S. Ct. 770 (1901). https://casetext.com/case/samuel-downes-v-george-bidwell.

Dreher, Rod. "Santa Muerte and the Spiritual Realities of the Drug War." *American Conservative*, November 25, 2022. https://www.theamericanconservative.com/santa-muerte-the-spiritual-realities-of-the-drug-war/.

Dubnov, Arie. "Israel's Jewish and Democratic Balance: A Historian Reflects on the Nation-State Law." *Fathom*, December 2018. https://fathomjournal.org/the-long-read-israels-jewish-and-democratic-balance-a-historian-reflects-on-the-nation-state-law/.

Durbin, Sean. *Righteous Gentiles: Religion, Identity, and Myth in John Hagee's Christians United for Israel*. Leiden, Netherlands: Brill, 2019.

Eddington, Patrick. "Is the Black Identity Extremist Label Still in Use?" *Antiwar.com*. November 30, 2022. https://original.antiwar.com/Patrick_Eddington/2022/11/29/is-the-fbis-black-identity-extremist-label-still-in-use/.

Edmondson, Catie. "House Approves $1 Billion for the Iron Dome as Democrats Feud over Israel." *New York Times*, September 21, 2021. https://www.nytimes.com/2021/09/23/us/politics/israel-iron-dome-congress.html.

Elbit Systems. "Elbit Systems U.S. Subsidiary Awarded Additional $26 Million Contract to Provide Integrated Fixed Towers System in Arizona." Press release. Haifa, Israel, June 26, 2019. https://elbitsystems.com/pr-new/elbit-systems-u-s-subsidiary-awarded-additional-26-million-contract-to-provide-integrated-fixed-towers-system-in-arizona.

Emmons, Alex. "Commander in Chief Trump Will Have Terrifying Powers. Thanks, Obama." *Intercept*, November 11, 2016. https://theintercept.com/2016/11/11/commander-in-chief-donald-trump-will-have-terrifying-powers-thanks-obama/.

Epstein, Mara, and Sarah McFarland Taylor, eds. *Selling the Sacred: Religion and Marketing from Crossfit to QAnon*. New York: Routledge, 2024.

Espejo, Paulina Ochoa. *On Borders: Territories, Legitimacy, and the Rights of Place*. Oxford: Oxford University Press, 2020.

Evans, Richard Kent. *MOVE: An American Religion*. Oxford: Oxford University Press, 2020.

Fallas, Amy. "El Pueblo de Israel: Latino Evangélicos and Christian Zionism." *Revealer*, September 9, 2021. https://therevealer.org/el-pueblo-de-israel-latino-evangelicos-and-christian-zionism/.

Farah, Kirby. "Day of the Dead: From Aztec Goddess Worship to Modern Mexican Celebration." *Conversation*, October 28, 2019. https://theconversation.com/day-of-the-dead-from-aztec-goddess-worship-to-modern-mexican-celebration-124962.

Fassin, Didier. "The Precarious Truth of Asylum." *Public Culture* 25, no. 1 (2013): 39–63.

Felbab-Brown, Vanda, and Elisa Norio. "What Border Vigilantes Taught U.S. Right-Wing Armed Groups." *Mexico Today*, March 12, 2021. https://mexicotoday.com/2021/03/12/opinion-what-border-vigilantes-taught-u-s-right-wing-armed-groups/.

Fiddian-Qasmiyeh, Elena. "The Faith-Gender-Asylum Nexus: An Intersectionalist Analysis of Representations of the 'Refugee Crisis.'" In *The Refugee Crisis and Religion: Secularism, Security and Hospitality in Question*, edited by Luca Mavelli and Erin K. Wilson, 207–22. New York: Rowman and Littlefield, 2017.

Fisher, Max. "In Era of Hardening Identities, Trump Order on Jews Kindles Questions Old and New." *New York Times*, December 15, 2019. https://www.nytimes.com/2019/12/15/world/americas/trump-jews-executive-order.html.

Flaherty, Joseph. "Arizona Tribe Expands High-Tech IDs to Ease Border Crossing." *Phoenix New Times*, July 11, 2017. https://www.phoenixnewtimes.com/news/yaqui-tribe-expands-high-tech-ids-9477002.

Fontana, Bernard L. "Pilgrimage to Magdalena." *American West*, September/October 1981. Accessed August 26, 2024. http://padrekino.com/index.php/khs_home/kino-heritage/kino-magdalena-pilgrimage.

Fox, Porter. *Northland: A 4,000-Mile Journey along America's Forgotten Border*. New York: W. W. Norton, 2018.

Frank, Jason. "The Democratic Sublime: On Aesthetics and Popular Assembly." Lecture, Northwestern University, November 12, 2021.

Frank, Jason. *The Democratic Sublime: On Aesthetics and Popular Assembly*. Oxford: Oxford University Press, 2021.

Franks, Mary Ann. "Guantanamo Forever: United States Sovereignty and the Unending State of Exception." *Harvard Law & Policy Review* 1, no. 259 (2007): 259–66.

Freese, Kevin. "The Death Cult of the Drug Lords Mexico's Patron Saint of Crime, Criminals, and the Dispossessed." Fort Leavenworth, KS: Foreign Military Studies Office, United States Army, 2005. Accessed August 26, 2024. https://community.apan.org/wg/tradoc-g2/fmso/m/fmso-monographs/247308.

French, Rebecca. "The Anthropology of Religion and Law." *Religious Studies Review* 45, no. 2 (July 2019): 153–61.

Frost, Robert. "Mending Wall." In *The New Poetry: An Anthology*, edited by Harriet Monroe. New York: Macmillan, 1917, 404.

Garcia-Navarro, Lulu. "In America, We Trust the Wrong People." *First Person* (podcast). *New York Times*, March 9, 2023. https://www.nytimes.com/2023/03/09/opinion/refugees-credibility-george-santos.html.

Gardner, Lauren, Daniel Lippman, and Andy Blatchford. "Border Stops for People of Iranian Descent Spark Outrage." *Politico*, January 5, 2020. https://www.politico.com/news/2020/01/05/reports-detaining-iranian-descent-backlash-094415.

Gessen, Masha. "In the Shadow of the Holocaust." *New Yorker*, December 9, 2023. https://www.newyorker.com/news/the-weekend-essay/in-the-shadow-of-the-holocaust.

Gessen, Masha. "The Real Purpose of Trump's Executive Order on Anti-Semitism." *New Yorker*, December 12, 2019. https://www.newyorker.com/news/our-columnists/the-real-purpose-of-trumps-executive-order-on-anti-semitism.

Goldmacher, Shane. "Ron Lauder Pledges $25 Million for Campaign Against Anti-Semitism." *New York Times*, December 10, 2019. https://www.nytimes.com/2019/12/09/us/politics/ron-lauder-anti-semitism.html.

Goldstein, Brandt. *Storming the Court: How a Band of Yale Law Students Sued the President and Won.* New York: Scribner, 2005.

Goldstein, Eric L. *The Price of Whiteness: Jews, Race, and American Identity.* Princeton, NJ: Princeton University Press, 2006.

Goodman, J. David. "Texas Patrols Its Own Border, Pushing Legal Limits." *New York Times*, May 9, 2023. https://www.nytimes.com/2023/05/09/us/texas-border-enforcement-abbott.html.

Gordon, Neve. "Antisemitism and Zionism: The Internal Operations of the IHRA Definition." *Middle East Critique*, March 2024: 1–16.

Gorski, Philip S., and Samuel L. Perry. *The Flag and the Cross: White Christian Nationalism and the Threat to American Democracy.* Oxford: Oxford University Press, 2022.

Graber, Jennifer. *The Gods of Indian Country: Religion and the Struggle for the American West.* Oxford: Oxford University Press, 2018.

Grandin, Greg. *The End of the Myth: From the Frontier to the Border Wall in the Mind of America.* New York: Metropolitan Books, 2019.

Grassiani, Erella. "Commercialised Occupation Skills: Israeli Security Experience as an International Brand." In *Security/Mobility: Politics of Movement*, edited by Matthias Leese and Stef Wittendorp, 57–73. Manchester, UK: Manchester University Press, 2017.

Graziano, Michael. "Race, the Law, and Religion in America." *Oxford Research Encyclopedia of Religion*, September 2017, 1–30.

Green, Mark A. "The US Exports More to Mexico Than to All EU Countries Combined." *Stubborn Things* (blog), Wilson Center, July 12, 2022. https://wilsoncenter.org/blog-post/us-exports-more-mexico-all-eu-countries-combined.

Gregory, Gladys, and Sheldon B. Liss. "Chamizal Dispute." Handbook of Texas Online, September 5, 2022. Texas State Historical Association. https://www.tshaonline.org/handbook/entries/chamizal-dispute.

Griffith, James S. "Pilgrimage to Magdalena and The Festival de San Francisco." Kino Historical Society. Accessed August 26, 2024. http://padrekino.com/index.php/khs_home/kino-heritage/kino-magdalena-pilgrimage.

Grubb, Patrick. "Source Provides Directive Telling CBP Officers to detain Iranian-Born Travelers." *Northern Light*, January 29, 2020. https://www.thenorthernlight.com/stories/source-provides-directive-telling-cbp-officers-to-detain-iranian-born-travelers,9315.

Hacking, Ian. *Historical Ontology*. Cambridge, MA: Harvard University Press, 2002.

Hadley, Diana. "Border Boomtown—Douglas, Arizona, 1900–1920." *Cochise Quarterly* 17, no. 3 (Fall 1987): 2–47.

Handelman, Kali, and Elayne Oliphant. "On France, Violence, and Religious Media." *Revealer*, November 12, 2020. Accessed August 30, 2024. https://therevealer.org/on-france-violence-and-religious-media/.

Hansen, Jonathan M. *Guantánamo: An American History*. New York: Hill and Wang, 2011.

Hauerwas, Stanley. *War and the American Difference: Theological Reflections on Violence and National Identity*. Grand Rapids, MI: Baker Academic, 2011.

Hawaii v. Trump. 241 F. Supp. 3d 1119 (D. Haw. 2017); aff'd, 859 F.3d 741, 756 (9th Cir. 2017).

Hayes, Kelly E. *Holy Harlots: Femininity, Sexuality, and Black Magic in Brazil*. Berkeley: University of California Press, 2011.

Heer, Jeet. "Don't Just Impeach Trump. End the Imperial Presidency." *New Republic*, August 12, 2017. https://newrepublic.com/article/144297/dont-just-impeach-trump-end-imperial-presidency.

Hennessy-Fiske, Molly. "It's Illegal to Destroy Saguaro Cactuses. So Why Are They Being Removed for Trump's Border Wall?" *Los Angeles Times*, February 26, 2020. https://www.latimes.com/world-nation/story/2020-02-26/border-wall-saguaro-cactus.

Historical Marker Database. "San Bernardino Ranch." June 4, 2020. https://www.hmdb.org/m.asp?m=28301.

Holy Land USA website. Accessed July 28, 2023. https://www.holylandwaterbury.org/about.

Howe, Cymene, Susanna Zaraysky, and Lois Ann Lorentzen. "Devotional Crossings: Transgender Sex Workers, Santisima Muerte, and Spiritual Solidarity in Guadalajara and San Francisco." In *Religion at the Corner of Bliss and Nirvana: Politics, Identity, and Faith in New Migrant Communities*, edited by Lois Ann Lorentzen, Joaquin Jay Gonzalez III, Kevin M. Chun, and Hien Duc Do. Durham, NC: Duke University Press, 2009, 3–38.

Howe, Nicholas. *Landscapes of the Secular: Law, Religion, and American Sacred Space*. Chicago: University of Chicago Press, 2016.

Hughes, Jennifer Scheper. *The Church of the Dead: The Epidemic of 1576 and the Birth of Christianity in the Americas*. New York: New York University Press, 2021.

Hughes, Richard T. *Christian America and the Kingdom of God*. Urbana: University of Illinois Press, 2009.

Human Rights Watch. "US: States Use Anti-Boycott Laws to Punish Responsible Businesses." April 23, 2019. https://www.hrw.org/news/2019/04/23/us-states-use-anti-boycott-laws-punish-responsible-businesses.

Hummel, Daniel G. *Covenant Brothers: Evangelicals, Jews, and U.S.-Israeli Relations*. Philadelphia: University of Pennsylvania Press, 2019.

Hurd, Elizabeth Shakman. *Beyond Religious Freedom: The New Global Politics of Religion*. Princeton, NJ: Princeton University Press, 2015.

Hurd, Elizabeth Shakman. "Border Religion." In Hurd and Sullivan, *At Home and Abroad*, 228–45.

Hurd, Elizabeth Shakman. "Narratives of De-secularization in International Relations." *Intellectual History Review* 27, no. 1 (January 2017): 97–113.

Hurd, Elizabeth Shakman. *The Politics of Secularism in International Relations*. Princeton, NJ: Princeton University Press, 2008.

Hurd, Elizabeth Shakman, and Winnifred Fallers Sullivan, eds. *At Home and Abroad: The Politics of American Religion*. New York: Columbia University Press, 2021.

Hurd, Elizabeth Shakman, and Winnifred Fallers Sullivan. "Introduction: Religion, Law, and Politics, American-Style." In Hurd and Sullivan, *At Home and Abroad*, 1–16.

Hurd, Ian. *How to Do Things with International Law*. Princeton, NJ: Princeton University Press, 2017.

Hussin, Iza. "'The New Global Politics of Religion': Religious Harmony, Public Order, and Securitisation in the Post-colony." *Journal of Religious and Political Practice* 4 (2018): 93–106.

Huq, Aziz. "The Future of Constitutional Discrimination Law after *Hawai'i v. Trump*." *Take Care*, June 26, 2018. https://takecareblog.com/blog/the-future-of-constitutional-discrimination-law-after-hawai-i-v-trump.

Immerwahr, Daniel. "The Greater United States: Territory and Empire in U.S. History." *Diplomatic History* 40, no. 3 (2016): 373–91.

Immerwahr, Daniel. *How to Hide an Empire: A History of the Greater United States*. New York: Farrar, Straus and Giroux, 2019.

Indian Removal Act (1830). Library of Congress Primary Documents in American History. Accessed January 4, 2024. https://guides.loc.gov/indian-removal-act.

Ingram, Brannon. *How Islam Became a Religion*. Unpublished manuscript.

International Boundary and Water Commission, United States and Mexico. "About Us." https://www.ibwc.gov/about-us/. Accessed August 26, 2024.

International Boundary Commission de la Frontière Internationale, Canada and United States. "The Boundary and You." Accessed August 29, 2023. https://internationalboundarycommission.org/en/the-boundary-and-you.php.

Int'l Refugee Assistance Project v. Trump. 241 F. Supp. 3d 539 (D. Md. 2017), aff'd, 857 F.3d 554, 572 (4th Cir. 2017).

Jansen, Yolande, Robin Celikates, and Joost de Bloois. *The Irregularization of Migration in Contemporary Europe*. London: Rowman and Littlefield International, 2005.

Jerusalem Declaration on Antisemitism. Accessed August 31, 2023. https://jerusalemdeclaration.org/wp-content/uploads/2021/03/JDA-1.pdf.

JewBelong. "Antisemitism Cheat Sheet: 10 Facts to Help You Cut Through the BS." Accessed January 28, 2024. https://www.jewbelong.com/more/jewbelong-cheat-sheet/.

Johnson, Greg. "At Home and Abroad: Greg Johnson on Indigenous Hawaiian Repatriation." *Interactions* (podcast). Center for the Study of Law and Religion, Emory University, May 17, 2023.

Johnson, Greg. "Domestic Bones, Foreign Land, and the Kingdom Come: Jurisdictions of Religion in Contemporary Hawaii." In Hurd and Sullivan, *At Home and Abroad*, 148–66.

Johnson, Greg. *Sacred Claims: Repatriation and Living Tradition*. Charlottesville: University of Virginia Press, 2007.

Johnson, Jenna. "Trump Calls for 'Total and Complete Shutdown of Muslims Entering the United States.'" *Washington Post*, December 7, 2015. https://www.washingtonpost.com/news/post-politics/wp/2015/12/07/donald-trump-calls-for-total-and-complete-shutdown-of-muslims-entering-the-united-states/.

Johnson, Paul Christopher. "Book Review: Sovereignty and the Sacred: Secularism and the Political Economy of Religion by Robert A. Yelle." *Sociology of Religion* 81, no. 2 (Summer 2020): 240–42.

SOURCES

Johnson, Paul Christopher, Pamela E. Klassen, and Winnifred Fallers Sullivan. *Ekklesia: Three Inquiries in Church and State*. Chicago: University of Chicago Press, 2018.

Johnson, Sylvester, and Steven Weitzman, eds. *The FBI and Religion: Faith and National Security Before and After 9/11*. Berkeley: University of California Press, 2017.

Jones, Eddie. "There's No Invasion at Our Southern Border. I Know. I Design Ports of Entry." AZ-Central. May 24, 2024. Accessed August 29, 2024. https://www.azcentral.com/story/opinion/op-ed/2024/05/24/border-ports-entry-designed-orderly-immigration/73807938007/.

Jones Studio. "Mariposa Land Point of Entry." Accessed August 26, 2024. https://jonesstudioinc.com/project/mariposa-land-port-of-entry/.

Jordan, Miriam. "U.S. Born Children, Too, Were Separated from Parents at the Border." *New York Times*, April 11, 2023. https://www.nytimes.com/2023/04/11/us/migrant-family-separations-citizens.html.

Justo, Nathalia. "The Global Politics of Citizenship: Producing and Protecting the 'Deserving' Subject." PhD diss., Department of Political Science, Northwestern University, 2023.

Just Vision. "Anti-Boycott Legislation Tracker." Accessed August 26, 2024. https://justvision.org/boycott/legislation-tracker.

Kaell, Hillary. *Walking Where Jesus Walked: American Christians and Holy Land Pilgrimage*. New York: New York University Press, 2014.

Kagan, Michael. "Refugee Credibility Assessment and the Religious Imposter Problem: A Case Study of Eritrean Pentecostal Claims in Egypt." *Vanderbilt Journal of Transnational Law* 43 (2010): 1179–233.

Kahn, Paul W. *Political Theology: Four New Chapters on the Concept of Sovereignty*. New York: Columbia University Press, 2011.

Kang, S. Deborah. *The INS on the Line: Making Immigration Law on the US-Mexico Border, 1917–1954*. Oxford: Oxford University Press, 2017.

Kanno-Youngs, Zolan. "Trump Administration Adds Six More Countries to Travel Ban." *New York Times*, January 31, 2020. https://www.nytimes.com/2020/01/31/us/politics/trump-travel-ban.html.

Kanno-Youngs, Zolan, Mike Baker, and Mariel Padilla. "U.S. Stops Dozens of Iranian-Americans Returning from Canada." *New York Times*, January 5, 2020. https://www.nytimes.com/2020/01/05/us/politics/iranian-americans-border.html.

Kantorowicz, Ernst. *The King's Two Bodies: A Study in Medieval Political Theology*. Princeton, NJ: Princeton University Press, 2016.

Kaplan, Amy. *Our American Israel: The Story of an Entangled Alliance*. Cambridge, MA: Harvard University Press, 2018.Kappler, Charles J. "1904 - Indian Affairs - Laws and Treaties, Treaties Vol II, Charles J. Kappler" (2019). US and Indian Relations. 62. https://digitalcommons.csumb.edu/hornbeck_usa_2_e/6.

Karaim, Reed. "Mariposa Land Point of Entry, Designed by Jones Studio." *Architect: Journal of the American Institute of Architects*, October 27, 2014. https://www.architectmagazine.com/design/buildings/mariposa-land-port-of-entry-designed-by-jones-studio_o.

Katyal, Neal. "*Trump v. Hawaii*: How the Supreme Court Simultaneously Overturned and Revived *Korematsu*." *Yale Law Journal* 128 (2018–19). https://www.yalelawjournal.org/forum/trump-v-hawaii.

Kaufman, Ellie. "Cubans Still Reside on Guantánamo Bay Base Decades after US-Cuba Relations Deteriorated." CNN.com, September 12, 2021. https://www.cnn.com/2021/09/12/politics/cubans-who-live-at-guantanamo-bay-naval-base/index.html.

Keane, Webb. *Christian Moderns: Freedom and Fetish in the Mission Encounter.* Berkeley: University of California Press, 2007.

Kim, Jaeeun. "Between Sacred Gift and Profane Exchange: Identity Craft and Relational Work in Asylum Claims-Making on Religious Grounds." *Theory and Society* 51 (2022): 303–33.

Kirk, Mimi. "Christian Zionist Cowboys: American and Israeli Affinities Laid Bare." Al Jazeera, January 19, 2024. https://www.aljazeera.com/opinions/2024/1/19/christian-zionist-cowboys-american-and-israeli-affinities-laid-bare.

Khalidi, Dima. "Expert Q&A: Trump's Executive Order on Campus Antisemitism." Institute for Middle East Understanding, December 18, 2019. https://imeu.org/article/expert-qa-trumps-executive-order-on-campus-antisemitism.

Khosravi, Shahram, and Mahmoud Keshavarz. "The Magic of Borders." *e-flux Architecture*, May 2020. https://www.e-flux.com/architecture/at-the-border/325755/the-magic-of-borders/.

Kino Border Initiative official website. Accessed August 26, 2024. https://www.kinoborderinitiative.org.

Knesset (Israeli parliament). "Basic Law: Israel as the Nation-State of the Jewish People." Enacted July 19, 2018. Accessed August 26, 2024. chrome-extension://efaidnbmnnnibpcajpcglclefindmkaj/https://www.adalah.org/uploads/uploads/Final_2_pager_on_the_JNSL_27.11.2018%20.pdf.

Kobes de Mez, Kristin. *Jesus and John Wayne: How White Evangelicals Corrupted a Faith and Fractured a Nation.* New York: Liveright, 2020.

Koenig, Sarah, and Dana Chivvis. "The Special Project." *Serial* (podcast), season 4: Guantánamo, episode 2. *New York Times*, March 21, 2024. https://www.nytimes.com/interactive/2024/podcasts/serial-season-four-guantanamo.html.

Korematsu v. United States, 323 U.S. 214 (1944).

Kramer, Paul. "A Border Crosses." *New Yorker*, September 20, 2014. https://www.newyorker.com/news/news-desk/moving-mexican-border.

Kramer, Paul. "A Useful Corner of the World: Guantánamo." *New Yorker*, July 31, 2013. https://www.newyorker.com/news/news-desk/a-useful-corner-of-the-world-guantnamo.

Kubzansky, Caroline. "Man Accused of Human Smuggling Near U.S.-Canada Border Is Arrested at O'Hare." *Chicago Tribune*, February 23, 2024. https://www.chicagotribune.com/2024/02/23/man-accused-of-human-smuggling-near-canadian-border-arrested-at-ohare/.

La Pierre, Alex & Jerry Haas, dirs. *The Pilgrimage to Magdalena*. Tupac, AZ. National Park Service, 2021.

Lalami, Laila. "The Border Is All Around Us, and It's Growing." *New York Times*, April 25, 2017. https://www.nytimes.com/2017/04/25/magazine/the-border-is-all-around-us-and-its-growing.html.

LeMire, Jonathan, Lisa Mascaro, and Jill Colvin. "White House Considering Dramatic Expansion of Travel Ban." AP News, January 10, 2020. https://apnews.com/753968e412fab06e6fb8180e7ac98d47.

Léon, Luis D. "Metaphor and Place: The U.S.-Mexico Border as Center and Periphery in the Interpretation of Religion." *Journal of the American Academy of Religion* 67, no. 3 (September 1999): 541–71.

Leza, Christina. "What Is the U.S.-Mexico Border to Indigenous Peoples Who Have Lived There?" *Yes!*, July 7, 2020. https://www.yesmagazine.org/opinion/2020/07/07/mexico-border-indigenous-leaders.

Li, Darryl. "Who's Afraid of the Big Bad Anti-Boycott Laws?" *Allegra Lab*, June 2023. https://allegralaboratory.net/whos-afraid-of-the-big-bad-anti-boycott-laws.

Li, Darryl. *The Universal Enemy: Jihad, Empire, and the Challenge of Solidarity*. Stanford, CA: Stanford University Press, 2019.

Lieber, Robert J. *Indispensable Nation: American Foreign Policy in a Turbulent World*. New Haven, CT: Yale University Press, 2022.

Lipman, Jana K. *Guantanamo: A Working-Class History between Empire and Revolution*. Berkeley: University of California, 2008.

Litman, Leah. "Unchecked Power Is Still Dangerous No Matter What the Court Says." *New York Times*, June 26, 2018. https://www.nytimes.com/2018/06/26/opinion/travel-ban-hawaii-supreme-court.html.

Lloyd, Dana. *Land Is Kin: Sovereignty, Religious Freedom, and Indigenous Sacred Sites*. Foreword by Judge Abby Abinanti. Studies in US Religion, Politics, and Law. Kansas City: University Press of Kansas, 2023.

Lloyd, Vincent, and Jonathan Kahn, eds. *Race and Secularism in America*. New York: Columbia University Press, 2016.

Loera, Javier, War Captain of the Ysleta del Sur Pueblo Tribal Council. "The Boundary." Interview with the National Park Service. Chamizal National Monument, National Park Service Accessed August 29, 2024. https://www.nps.gov/media/video/view.htm?id=6F691100-AD6F-F095-93B357C7A1DE0EB9.

Lofton, Kathryn. *Consuming Religion*. Chicago: University of Chicago Press, 2017.

Logan, Dana W. *Awkward Rituals: Sensations of Governance in Protestant America*. Chicago: University of Chicago Press, 2022.

Lomnitz, Claudio. *Death and the Idea of Mexico*. Cambridge, MA: Zone Books, 2005.

Long, Burke O. *Imagining the Holy Land: Maps, Models, and Fantasy Travels*. Bloomington: Indiana University Press, 2003.

Long, Trish. "El Pasoans Escaped Dry Times during Prohibition at 'Holes in the Wall' along Rio Grande." *El Paso Times*, January 28, 2021. https://www.elpasotimes.com/story/news/local/el-paso/2021/01/28/el-pasoans-mum-prohibition-era-hole-wall-tales-from-the-morgue-trish-long/4285853001/.

Lorentzen, Lois Ann. "Saint of the Dispossessed, Enemy of Church and State." *States of Devotion: Religion, Neoliberalism, Biopolitics* 13 (2016). https://hemisphericinstitute.org/en/emisferica-13-1-states-of-devotion.html.

Luiselli, Valeria. *Tell Me How It Ends: An Essay in 40 Questions*. Minneapolis, MN: Coffee House Press, 2017.

Machado, Daisy, Bryan S. Turner, and Trygve Wyller, eds. *Borderland Religion: Ambiguous Practices of Difference, Hope and Beyond*. London: Routledge, 2018.

Mack, Stephen. "A:cim O'odham (We the O'odham): The Himdag Ki: and the Tohono O'odham Community." Copyright 2018, Himdag Ki:. http://www.himdagki.org/wp-content/uploads/2018/12/AcimOodham.pdf.

Magid, Shaul. *American Post-Judaism: Identity and Renewal in a Postethnic Society*. Bloomington: Indiana University Press, 2013.

Magid, Shaul. "The Enforcers." *Tablet*, July 13, 2021. https://www.tabletmag.com/sections/community/articles/enforcers-anti-zionists.

Magid, Shaul. "The Judeo-Christian Tradition." In *Theologies of American Exceptionalism*, edited by Winnifred Fallers Sullivan and Elizabeth Shakman Hurd. Bloomington: Indiana

University Press, 2019. https://publish.iupress.indiana.edu/read/theologies-of-american-exceptionalism/section/0bebab72-c6b6-4839-a58a-4c86ea2fc977.

Magid, Shaul. *The Necessity of Exile: Essays from a Distance*. New York: Ayin Press, 2023.

Maldonado Rivera, David. "'A Perfect, Irrevocable Gift': Recognizing the Proprietary Church in Puerto Rico," in Hurd and Sullivan, eds. *At Home and Abroad*, 37–50.

Manrique, Carlos A. "Foucault's Political Theologies and the Traces of Liberation Theology in Latin America." *Political Theology* 22, no. 1 (2021): 75–82.

Manrique, Carlos A., Alhena Caicedo, and Elizabeth Shakman Hurd, eds. "Religiosidades Insumisas, Protestas Sociales y Democracias Hoy." Unpublished manuscript.

Mansour, Sanya. "Laws Preventing Boycotts of Israel Are Sweeping the U.S. This New Documentary Chronicles the Fight." *Time*, March 3, 2023. https://time.com/6260083/israel-boycott-documentary-eliminate-act/.

Manuel, Kate M. "Executive Authority to Exclude Aliens: In Brief." CRS Report R44743, January 23, 2017. https://fas.org/sgp/crs/homesec/R44743.pdf.

Marchbanks, Rachel. "The Borderline: Indigenous Communities on the International Frontier." *Journal of American Indian Higher Education* 26, no. 3 (2015). https://tribalcollegejournal.org/borderline-indigenous-communities-international-frontier/.

Marcus, Kenneth L. "Time for Biden to Issue Executive Order on Antisemitism." *Hill*, June 22, 2021. https://thehill.com/blogs/congress-blog/politics/559729-time-for-biden-to-issue-executive-order-on-antisemitism.

Martín, Desirée A. *Borderlands Saints: Secular Sanctity in Chicano/a and Mexican Culture*. New Brunswick, NJ: Rutgers University Press, 2013.

Martinson, Mattias. *Sekularism, Populism, Xenofobi: En Ess Om Religionsdebatten*. Malmé: Eskaton, 2017.

Marizco, Michael. "Tohono O'odham's San Miguel Gate May Be Closing." *AZPM*, December 9, 2016. https://www.azpm.org/s/38099-native-american-mexico-border-crossing-threatened/.

Marzouki, Nadia. "Conversion as Statelessness: A Study of Contemporary Algerian Conversions to Evangelical Christianity." *Middle East Law & Governance* 4 (2012): 69–105.

Marzouki, Nadia. *Islam: An American Religion*. New York: Columbia University Press, 2017.

Mauléon, Emmanuel. "It's Time to Put CVE to Bed." Just Security, November 2, 2018. https://www.justsecurity.org/61332/its-time-put-cve-bed/.

Mavelli, Luca, and Erin K Wilson, eds. *The Refugee Crisis and Religion: Secularism, Security and Hospitality in Question*. London: Rowman and Littlefield International, 2016.

Mayblin, Lucy. *Asylum after Empire: Colonial Legacies in the Politics of Asylum Seeking*. London: Rowman and Littlefield International, 2018.

McAlister, Melani. *Epic Encounters: Culture, Media, and U.S. Interests in the Middle East since 1945*. Berkeley: University of California Press, 2005. Originally published 2001.

McCrary, Charles. *Sincerely Held: American Secularism and Its Believers*. Chicago: University of Chicago Press, 2022.

Mead, Sidney E. *The Lively Experiment: The Shaping of Christianity in America*. New York: Harper and Row, 1963.

Mearsheimer, John J., and Stephen M. Walt. *The Israel Lobby and U.S. Foreign Policy*. New York: Farrar, Straus and Giroux, 2007.

Meis, Morgan. "The Philosopher Who Believes in Living Things." *New Yorker*, February 23, 2023. https://www.newyorker.com/culture/annals-of-inquiry/the-philosopher-who-believes-in-living-things.

SOURCES

Mekay, Emad. "UN Report: Soleimani Drone Killing a 'Watershed' for Rule of Law." International Bar Association, August 5, 2020. https://www.ibanet.org/article/45C796CC-3EAD-4F7C-BF63-5CC66C984079.
Mendoza, Jennifer. "The Border Crossed Us: The Tohono O'odham Nation's Divide." *Medium*, May 15, 2018. https://medium.com/race-law-a-critical-analysis/the-border-crossed-us-the-tohono-oodham-s-nation-divide-32c9260f1458.
Meyer, Birgit, ed. *Refugees and Religion: Ethnographic Studies of Global Trajectories*. Repr. ed. New York: Bloomsbury Academic, 2022.
Miera-Rosete, Mixcoatl. "Officers at the Gate: Why *United States v. Medina-Copete* Should Be the Rule and Not the Exception." *New Mexico Law Review* 47, 1 (Winter 2017): 184–208.
Miller, Todd. "After Years of Tribal Resistance, DHS Finishes Its 'Virtual Wall' on the Tohono O'odham Nation." Counterpunch, September 7, 2022. https://www.counterpunch.org/2022/09/07/after-years-of-tribal-resistance-dhs-finishes-its-virtual-wall-on-the-tohono-oodham-nation/.
Miller, Todd. *Empire of Borders: The Expansion of the US Border around the World*. New York: Verso, 2019.
Miller, Todd. "Walls Must Fall: Ending the Deadly Politics of Border Militarization." Transnational Institute webinar. Posted on YouTube, June 17, 2020. https://www.youtube.com/watch?v=T8B-cJ2bTi8.
Mireles v. State. No. 05-12-00040-CR (Tex. App. Jan. 18, 2013). https://casetext.com/case/mireles-v-state.
Miroff, Nick. "Why the U.S. Base at Cuba's Guantanamo Bay Is Probably Doomed." *Washington Post*, May 15, 2015. https://www.washingtonpost.com/news/worldviews/wp/2015/05/15/why-the-u-s-base-at-cubas-guantanamo-bay-is-probably-doomed/.
Mishra, Pankaj. "The Shoah after Gaza." *London Review of Books* 46, no. 6 (March 21, 2024). https://www.lrb.co.uk/the-paper/v46/n06.
Molina, Michelle. *Inventories of Ruin: The Demise of the Mexican Jesuits, in Three Acts*. New York: Fordham University Press, 2025.
Montoya-Galvez, Camilo. "Nearly 80% of Texas' Floating Border Barrier Is Technically in Mexico, Survey Finds." CBS News, August 15, 2023. https://www.cbsnews.com/news/texas-floating-border-barrier-technically-in-mexico-survey-finds/.
Morales, Laurel. "Border Wall Would Cut across Land Sacred to Native Tribe." *Morning Edition*, NPR, February 23, 2017. https://www.npr.org/2017/02/23/516477313/border-wall-would-cut-across-land-sacred-to-native-tribe.
Morley, Anders. "Walking New Hampshire's Northern Border." *New Hampshire Magazine*, September 16, 2016. https://www.nhmagazine.com/walking-new-hampshires-northern-border.
Mullen, Lincoln. *The Chance of Salvation: A History of Conversion in America*. Cambridge, MA: Harvard University Press, 2017.
Musalo, Karen. "Claims for Protection Based on Religion or Belief: Analysis and Proposed Conclusions." *International Journal of Refugee Law* 16 (2004): 165–226.
Nadler, Congressman Jerry, New York, 12th District. "Congressman Nadler's Floor Speech Condemning Worldwide Explosion of Antisemitism and Calling out House GOP's Intentional Divisiveness." Jerry Nadler Newsroom, Floor Statement, December 5, 2023. https://nadler.house.gov/news/documentsingle.aspx?DocumentID=395107.
Najafi v. I.N.S.. 104 F.3d 943 (7th Cir. 1997). https://casetext.com/case/najafi-v-ins.
Nañez, Dianna M. "A Border Tribe, and the Wall That Will Divide It." *USA Today*, A Special

Report: "The Wall," 2018. https://www.usatoday.com/border-wall/story/tohonooodham-nationarizona-tribe/582487001/.
National Commission on Terrorist Attacks upon the United States (9/11 Commission). *9/11 Commission Report: Final Report of the National Commission on Terrorist Attacks upon the United States.* Washington, DC, July 22, 2004. https://www.govinfo.gov/app/details/GPO-911REPORT/.
National Congress of American Indians. "Homeland Security." Accessed August 30, 2024. https://archive.ncai.org/policy-issues/tribal-governance/homeland-security.
National Cowboy & Western Heritage Museum (Oklahoma City, Oklahoma) website. Accessed August 30, 2024. https://nationalcowboymuseum.org.
National Park Service. Chamizal: National Memorial Texas. "Where History and Culture Come to Life." Last updated April 5, 2024. https://www.nps.gov/cham/index.htm.
National Park Service. "A Little Black Box." Chamizal National Memorial. Updated January 6, 2022. https://www.nps.gov/cham/learn/historyculture/bb.htm.
National Park Service. "Quitobaquito Springs." Organ Pipe Cactus National Monument. Accessed May 23, 2023. https://www.nps.gov/orpi/learn/historyculture/quitobaquito-springs.htm.
National Park Service. "San Bernardino Ranch." Accessed June 28, 2023. https://www.nps.gov/places/san-bernardino-ranch.htm.
Nayeri, Dina. *The Ungrateful Refugee.* New York: Catapult, 2019.
New York Times. "The Guantánamo Docket." Updated August 7, 2024. https://www.nytimes.com/interactive/2021/us/guantanamo-bay-detainees.html.
New York University. "NYU to Create Center for the Study of Antisemitism." News release, November 15, 2023. https://www.nyu.edu/about/news-publications/news/2023/november/nyu-to-create--center-for-the-study-of-antisemitism-.html.
Nijhawan, Michael. *The Precarious Diasporas of Sikh and Ahmadiyya Generations: Violence, Memory, and Agency.* New York: Palgrave Macmillan, 2016.
Nixon, Ron. "U.S. Expands Restrictions on Visa-Waiver Program for Visitors." *New York Times,* February 18, 2016. https://www.nytimes.com/2016/02/19/us/politics/us-expands-restrictions-on-visa-waiver-program-for-visitors.html.
Ngai, Mae. *Impossible Subjects: Illegal Aliens and the Making of Modern America.* Princeton, NJ: Princeton University Press, 2004.
Nongbri, Brent. *Before Religion: A History of a Modern Concept.* New Haven, CT: Yale University Press, 2013.
Office of the United States Trade Representative. Executive Office of the President. "Israel Free Trade Agreement." Accessed February 21, 2024. https://ustr.gov/trade-agreements/free-trade-agreements/israel-fta. Full text available at https://ustr.gov/sites/default/files/files/agreements/FTA/israel/Israel%20FTA.pdf.
Oglala Sioux Tribe. "Statement of Oglala Sioux Tribal President Frank Star Comes Out Responding to S.D. Governor Kristi Noem's Border Address to the Joint Session of the South Dakota Legislature." Office of the President Frank Star Comes Out. Pine Ridge, South Dakota, February 2, 2024.
Omer, Atalia. *Days of Awe: Reimagining Jewishness in Solidarity with Palestinians.* Chicago: University of Chicago Press, 2019.
Oraby, Mona. "Law, the State, and Public Order: Regulating Religion in Contemporary Egypt." *Law & Society Review* 52, no. 3 (September 2018): 574–602.
Orsi, Robert A. *History and Presence.* Cambridge, MA: Belknap, 2016.
Oxford English Dictionary. 2nd ed. Oxford: Oxford University Press, 2023.

Palestine Legal. "Ten Things to Know about Anti-Boycott Legislation." July 14, 2020. https://palestinelegal.org/news/2016/6/3/what-to-know-about-anti-bds-legislation.

Pan v. Holder. 132 S. Ct. 555, 181 L. Ed. 2d 397, 80 U.S.L.W. 3134, 80 U.S.L.W. 3277 (2011). https://casetext.com/case/pan-v-holder.

Panduranga, Harsha, and Faiza Patel. *Stronger Rules against Bias: A Proposal for a New DHS Nondiscrimination Policy*. New York University School of Law, Brennan Center for Justice. September 15, 2022. https://www.brennancenter.org/our-work/policy-solutions/stronger-rules-against-bias.

Pansters, Wil G., ed. *La Santa Muerte in Mexico: History, Devotion, and Society*. Albuquerque: University of New Mexico Press, 2019.

Parrish, Will. "The U.S. Border Patrol and an Israeli Military Contractor Are Putting a Native American Reservation under 'Persistent Surveillance.'" *Intercept*, August 25, 2019. https://theintercept.com/2019/08/25/border-patrol-israel-elbit-surveillance/.

Patel, Faiza. "The Fight against Trump's Muslim Ban Isn't Over." Brennan Center for Justice, January 25, 2019. https://www.brennancenter.org/our-work/analysis-opinion/fight-against-trumps-muslim-ban-isnt-over.

Perez, Thomas E., assistant attorney general, to Assistant Secretary for Civil Rights Russlyn H. Ali. "Re: Title VI and Coverage of Religiously Identifiable Groups." September 8, 2010. US Department of Justice, Civil Rights Division. https://www.justice.gov/sites/default/files/crt/legacy/2011/05/04/090810_AAG_Perez_Letter_to_Ed_OCR_Title%20VI_and_Religiously_Identifiable_Groups.pdf.

Philbin, Patrick F., Deputy Assistant Attorney General. Memorandum for William J. Haynes II, General Counsel, Department of Defense. "Re: Possible Habeas Jurisdiction over Aliens Held in Guantanamo Bay, Cuba." US Department of Justice, Office of Legal Counsel. Washington, DC, December 28, 2001, 1–9. https://nsarchive2.gwu.edu/torturingdemocracy/documents/20011228.pdf.

Posner, Sarah. "The Army of Prayer Warriors Fighting Trump's Impeachment." *Huffington Post*, December 19, 2019. https://www.huffpost.com/entry/white-evangelicals-trump-impeachment_n_5df950c6e4b08083dc5ae146.

Preston, Andrew. "Monsters Everywhere: A Genealogy of National Security." *Diplomatic History* 38, no. 3 (2014): 477–500.

Prospectus of the Jerusalem Exhibit Company. St. Louis: Jerusalem Exhibit, 1903.

Pulso staff. "The Border Is Alive!" *Pulso Podcast*, season 3, episode 23, October 11, 2022. https://projectpulso.org/2022/10/11/ep23-border-is-alive/.

Ramsey, Kate. *The Spirits and the Law: Vodou and Power in Haiti*. Chicago: University of Chicago Press, 2011.

Rajah, Jothie. *Discounting Life: Necropolitical Law, Culture, and the Long War on Terror*. New York: Cambridge University Press, 2023.

Rasul v. Bush. 542 US 466 (2004). https://casetext.com/case/rasul-v-bush.

Ravid, Barak. "Ex-Israeli Intel Chief Admits Role in Assassination of Iran's Qassem Soleimani." *Haaretz*, December 20, 2021. https://www.haaretz.com/israel-news/israeli-intel-chief-takes-responsibility-for-assassination-of-iran-s-soleimani-1.10481220.

Raz-Krakotzkin, Amnon. "Religion and Nationalism in the Jewish and Zionist Context." In *When Politics Are Sacralized: Comparative Perspectives on Religious Claims and Nationalism*, edited by Nadim N. Rouhana and Nadera Shalhoub-Kervorkian, 33–53. Cambridge: Cambridge University Press, 2021.

Reed, Isaac Ariail. "The King's Two Bodies and the Crisis of Liberal Modernity." *Hedgehog Review* 21, no. 3 (Fall 2019). https://hedgehogreview.com/issues/eating-and-being/articles/the-kings-two-bodies-and-the-crisis-of-liberal-modernity.

Richland, Justin B. *Cooperation without Submission: Indigenous Jurisdictions in Native Nation-US Engagements*. Chicago: University of Chicago Press, 2021.

Ríos, Alberto. "Border Lines." 2003. Accessed August 30, 2024. https://www.public.asu.edu/~aarios/fox/page2.html.

Rivera, Mark. "Chicago-Area College Protest Organizers Push Back against Accusations of Antisemitism." May 4, 2024. ABC7chicago.com.

Rodriguez, Joshua, and Jeanne Batalova. "Ukrainian Immigrants in the United States." Migration Policy Institute, June 22, 2022. https://www.migrationpolicy.org/article/ukrainian-immigrants-united-states.

Roldan, Rione. "Homeland Security Report: Tensions Rising in Overcrowded Migrant Detention Facilities." *Texas Tribune*, July 2, 2019. https://www.texastribune.org/2019/07/02/tensions-rising-overcrowded-texas-migrant-facilities-report-says/.

Rose, Lena. "Nazareth Village and the Creation of the Holy Land in Israel-Palestine: The Question of Evangelical Orthodoxy." *Current Anthropology* 61, no. 3 (June 2020): 335–55.

Rose, Lena, and Zoë Given-Wilson. "What Is 'Truth?' Negotiating Christian Convert Asylum Seekers' Credibility." *Annals of the American Academy of Political and Social Science* 697, no. 1 (2021): 221–35.

Rose, Nikolas. *Inventing Our Selves: Psychology, Power, and Personhood*. Cambridge: Cambridge University Press, 1996.

Rosen, Deborah A. *Border Law: The First Seminole War and American Nationhood*. Cambridge, MA: Harvard University Press, 2015.

Rosenberg, Carol. "The Cost of Running Guantánamo Bay: $13 Million per Prisoner." *New York Times*, September 16, 2019. https://www.nytimes.com/2019/09/16/us/politics/guantanamo-bay-cost-prison.html.

Rosenfeld, Arno. "Behind the TV Ads against Antisemitism: A Fortune Assembled Under Apartheid." *Forward*, February 22, 2023. https://forward.com/news/536949/antisemitism-tv-ads-apartheid-south-africa-shine-a-light-natie-kirsh/.

Rosenfeld, Arno. "Robert Kraft Will Spend $25 Million Running Ads against Antisemitism. Is This the Right Way to Protect Jews?" *Forward*, March 27, 2023. https://forward.com/news/541111/robert-kraft-antisemitism-advertising-campaign-foundation/.

Rosenfeld, Arno. "Ronald Lauder Pledged $25 Million to Fight Antisemitism. Where Did the Money Go?" *Forward*, September 18, 2023. https://forward.com/news/561313/ronald-lauder-pledged-25-million-to-fight-antisemitism-where-did-the-money-go/.

Rossinow, Doug. "'The Edge of the Abyss': The Origins of the Israel Lobby, 1949–1954." *Modern American History* 1 (2018): 23–43.

Roush, Laura. "Santa Muerte, Protection, and *Desamparo*: A View from a Mexico City Altar." *Latin American Research Review* 49 (2014): 129–48.

Rudalevige, Andrew. *The New Imperial Presidency: Renewing Presidential Power after Watergate*. Ann Arbor: University of Michigan Press, 2006.

Sale v. Haitian Ctrs. Council, Inc. 509 U.S. 155, 113 S. Ct. 2549 (1993). https://casetext.com/case/sale-v-haitian-ctrs-council-inc.

Salyer, Lucy. *Laws Harsh as Tigers: Chinese Immigrants and the Making of Modern Immigration Law*. Chapel Hill: University of North Carolina Press, 1995.

Samahon, Tuan N. "The Religion Clauses and Political Asylum: Religious Persecution Claims and the Religious Membership-Conversion Imposter Problem." *Georgetown Law Journal* 88 (2000): 2211–38.

Sanders, Seth. "Despite Conflation of Israel with Judaism, Anti-Zionism Is More Kosher Than You Think." Religion Dispatches, January 14, 2024. https://religiondispatches.org/despite-the-conflation-of-israel-with-judaism-anti-zionism-is-more-kosher-than-you-think/.

Santner, Eric L. *The Royal Remains: The People's Two Bodies and the Endgames of Sovereignty.* Chicago: University of Chicago Press.

Schaeffer, Felicity Amaya. *Unsettled Borders: The Militarized Science of Surveillance on Sacred Lands.* Durham, NC: Duke University Press, 2022.

Schmiedel, Ulrich, and Hannah Strømmen. *The Claim to Christianity: Responding to the Far Right.* London: SCM, 2020.

Scherer, Matthew. *Beyond Church and State: Democracy, Secularism, and Conversion.* Cambridge: Cambridge University Press, 2013.

Schermerhorn, Seth. "Pilgrimage to Magdalena." Interview by Spencer Dew and Elizabeth Shakman Hurd. Annual Conference of the American Academy of Religion, Denver, CO, November 2022.

Schermerhorn, Seth. *Walking to Magdalena: Personhood and Place in Tohono O'odham Songs, Sticks, and Stories.* Lincoln: University of Nebraska Press, 2019.

Schermerhorn, Seth, and Lillia McEnaney. "Through Indigenous Eyes: A Comparison of Two Tohono O'odham Photographic Collections Documenting Pilgrimages to Magdalena." *Religious Studies and Theology* 36, no. 1 (2017): 21–54.

Schonthal, Benjamin. *Buddhism, Politics and the Limits of Law: The Pyrrhic Constitutionalism of Sri Lanka.* Cambridge: Cambridge University Press, 2016.

Schwab, Stephen Irving Max. *Guantánamo, USA: The Untold History of America's Cuban Outpost.* Lawrence: University Press of Kansas, 2009.

Scott, James C. *The Art of Not Being Governed: An Anarchist History of Upland Southeast Asia.* New Haven, CT: Yale University Press, 2010.

Shabad, Rebecca. "South Dakota Tribe Bans Gov. Kristi Noem from Reservation." NBC News, February 5, 2024. https://www.nbcnews.com/politics/politics-news/south-dakota-tribe-bans-gov-kristi-noem-reservation-rcna137248.

Shachar, Ayelet. *The Shifting Border: Legal Cartographies of Migration and Mobility, Ayelet Shachar in Dialogue.* Manchester, UK: Manchester University Press, 2020.

Shaka King et al., *Judas and the Black Messiah.* Burbank, CA, Warner Bros. Home Entertainment, 2021.

Shane, Peter M. *Madison's Nightmare: How Executive Power Threatens American Democracy.* Chicago: University of Chicago Press, 2009.

Shapira, Harel. *Waiting for José: The Minutemen's Pursuit of America.* Princeton, NJ: Princeton University Press, 2018.

Sherwood, Harriet. "Refugees Seeking Asylum on Religious Grounds Quizzed on 'Bible Trivia.'" *Guardian*, June 7, 2016. https://www.theguardian.com/uk-news/2016/jun/07/refugees-asylum-religious-grounds-quizzed-on-bible-trivia.

Shortall, Sarah. *Soldiers of God in a Secular World: Catholic Theology and Twentieth-Century French Politics.* Cambridge, MA: Harvard University Press, 2021.

Sideris, Lisa H. "American Techno-Optimism." In *Theologies of American Exceptionalism*, edited by Elizabeth Shakman Hurd and Winnifred Fallers Sullivan. Bloomington: Indiana University Press, 2019.

Siegelbaum, Lewis. "On Anti-Zionism and Antisemitism: A 'Non-Jewish' Jewish perspective." *Nation*, November 24, 2023. https://www.thenation.com/article/world/antisemitism-palestine-israel-gaza/.

Silliman, Daniel. "The Holy Land Experience Never Made It to the Financial Promised Land." *Christianity Today*, August 10, 2021. https://www.christianitytoday.com/news/2021/august/holy-land-experience-closes-sells-tbn-adventist-rosenthal.html.

Singh, Simran Jeet. "Expanded Travel Ban Gives World's Democracies More Cover for Anti-Muslim Measures." Religion News Service, January 28, 2020. https://religionnews.com/2020/01/28/expanding-travel-ban-trump-provides-cover-for-anti-muslim-measures/.

Slahi, Mohamedou Ould *Guantánamo Diary*. Edited by Larry Siems. New York: Little, Brown, 2015.

Smith, Matt. "Modern-Day Witch Trials: Law Enforcement Target Mexican Folk Religion." *Reveal*, October 16, 2015. https://revealnews.org/article/modern-day-witch-trials-law-enforcement-target-mexican-folk-religion/.

Sostaita, Barbara Andrea. Sanctuary Everywhere: The Fugitive Sacred in the Sonoran Desert. Durham, NC and London: Duke University Press, 2024.

Sostaita, Barbara Andrea. "'Water, Not Walls': Toward a Religious Study of Life that Defies Borders." *American Religion* 1, no. 2 (2020): 74–97.

St. John, Rachel. *Line in the Sand: A History of the Western U.S.-Mexico Border*. Princeton, NJ: Princeton University Press, 2012.

Stack, Megan K. "Let's Not Pretend We're Keeping Our Promises on Asylum." *New York Times*, July 2, 2022. https://www.nytimes.com/2022/07/02/opinion/asylum-refugees-immigration.html.

Statista. "Agent Staffing of the U.S. Border Patrol from FY 1992 to 2020." Accessed May 9, 2023. https://www.statista.com/statistics/455866/us-border-patrol-agent-staffing/.

Steele, Jeannette. "Where Mail Is the Lifeblood: Naval Station Guantanamo Bay to Open New Post Office." Office of Corporate Communications, NAVSUP FLC Jacksonville. August 23, 2022. https://cnrse.cnic.navy.mil/News/News-Detail/Article/3136670/where-mail-is-the-lifeblood-naval-station-guantanamo-bay-to-open-new-post-office/.

Steller, Tim. "Prayerful Pilgrimage." *Arizona Daily Star*, October 4, 1998.

Stephanson, Anders. *Manifest Destiny: American Expansion and the Empire of Right*. New York: Hill and Wang, 1996.

Stern, Kenneth. "I Drafted the Definition of Antisemitism. Rightwing Jews Are Weaponizing It." *Guardian*, December 13, 2019. https://www.theguardian.com/commentisfree/2019/dec/13/antisemitism-executive-order-trump-chilling-effect.

Stevenson, Jill. *Sensational Devotion: Evangelical Performance in Twenty-First-Century America*. Ann Arbor: University of Michigan Press, 2013.

Storm, Jason Ānanda Josephson. *The Invention of Religion in Japan*. Chicago: University of Chicago Press, 2012.

Strømmen, Hannah M. *The Bibles of the Far Right*. Oxford: Oxford University Press, 2024.

Sturm, Mark. "Wild Matters: The Organ Pipe Cactus Wilderness." National Park Service. January 5, 2012. https://www.nps.gov/orpi/learn/news/wild-matters.htm.

Stutman, Gabe. "'Completely Wrongheaded': Local Jewish Studies Profs Skewer Trump's Order Targeting Campus Anti-Semitism." *Jewish News of Northern California*, December 19, 2019. https://www.jweekly.com/2019/12/19/completely-wrongheaded-local-jewish-studies-profs-skewer-trumps-title-vi-executive-order/.

Sullivan, Winnifred Fallers. *Church State Corporation: Construing Religion in US Law*. Chicago: University of Chicago Press, 2020.
Sullivan, Winnifred Fallers. *The Impossibility of Religious Freedom: New Edition*. Princeton, NJ: Princeton University Press, 2018.
Sullivan, Winnifred Fallers. *Prison Religion: Faith-Based Reform and the Constitution*. Princeton, NJ: Princeton University Press, 2009.
Sullivan, Winnifred Fallers. "'... You're Doing It Right Now': Aaron Bushnell and Legal Pluralism." Sightings, Martin Marty Center, University of Chicago Divinity School, March 6, 2024. https://martycenter.org/sightings/youre-doing-it-right-now-aaron-bushnell-and-legal-pluralism.
Supangat v. Holder. 735 F.3d 792 (8th Cir. 2013). https://casetext.com/case/supangat-v-holder.
Tafjord, Bjørn Ola. "Santa Negrita." Unpublished manuscript.
Taussig-Rubbo, Mateo. "Sacred Property: Searching for Value in the Rubble of 9/11." In *After Secular Law*, edited by Winnifred Fallers Sullivan, Robert Yelle, and Mateo Taussig-Rubbo, 322–40. Stanford, CA: Stanford University Press, 2011.
Taylor, Chelsea. "American Christians and the Holy Land: Pilgrimage, Tourism, and Replicas." Religion, Race and Politics: Imperial and Global Perspectives graduate seminar paper, Northwestern University, March 2019.
Texas Office of the Attorney General. "Supporting Texas' Efforts to Secure the Border." Letter from twenty-eight state attorneys general to President Joseph R. Biden Jr. and DHS secretary Alejandro Mayorkas, January 29, 2024. https://www.texasattorneygeneral.gov/sites/default/files/images/press/AGs%20Letter%20Supporting%20Abbott%20and%20Paxton.pdf.
Thebault, Deborah, and Lena Rose. "What Kind of Christianity? *A v Switzerland*." *Oxford Journal of Law and Religion* 7, no. 3 (2018): 543–50.
Timmons, Patrick. "Trump's Wall at Nixon's Border." *North American Congress on Latin America (NACLA) Report on the Americas* 49, no. 1 (2017): 15–24.
Tohono O'odham Legislative Council. "Border Security and Immigration Enforcement on the Tohono O'odham Nation." Resolution No. 17-053. February 8, 2017. http://www.tonation-nsn.gov/wp-content/uploads/2017/02/17-053-Border-Security-and-Immigration-Enforcement-on-the-Tohono-Oodham-Nation.pdf.
Tohono O'odham Nation Cultural Center & Museum. "About." Accessed August 26, 2024. http://www.himdagki.org/about/.
Tohono O'odham Nation website. "11 Tohono O'odham Nation Districts." Accessed June 27, 2023. http://www.himdagki.org/guests-of-the-tohono-oodham-nation/.
Tohono O'odham Nation website. "History and Culture." Accessed June 21, 2023. http://www.tonation-nsn.gov/history-culture/.
Tohono O'odham Nation website. "No Wall." Accessed June 21, 2023. http://www.tonation-nsn.gov/nowall/.
Topol, Sarah A. "The America That Americans Forget." *New York Times*, July 9, 2023. https://www.nytimes.com/2023/07/07/magazine/guam-american-military.html.
Torbati, Yeganeh. "Exclusive: Only 6 Percent of Those Subject to Trump Travel Ban Granted Waivers." Reuters, April 4, 2019. https://www.reuters.com/article/us-usa-immigration-visas-exclusive/exclusive-only-6-percent-of-those-subject-to-trump-travel-ban-granted-u-s-waivers-idUSKCN1RG30X.
Tracey, Caroline. "Checkpoint Dreams." *New York Review of Books*, March 23, 2024. https://www.nybooks.com/online/2024/03/23/checkpoint-dreams-arizona-border/.

Trump v. Hawaii 585 U.S. 667 (2018). https://www.supremecourt.gov/opinions/17pdf/585us2r70_jgkn.pdf.

Trump v. Int'l Refugee Assistance Project. 137 S. Ct. 2080, 2086–88 (2017) (per curiam).

Trump v. Int'l Refuge Assistance Project. 138 S. Ct. 353 (2017).

United Nations Refugee Agency (UNHCR). "Guidelines on International Protection No. 6: Religion-Based Refugee Claims under Article 1A (2) of the 1951 Convention and/or the 1967 Protocol Relating to the Status of Refugees." UN Doc. HCR/GIP/04/06 (April 28, 2004). http://www.unhcr.org/en-us/publications/legal/40d8427a4/guidelines-international-protection-6-religion-based-refugee-claims-under.html.

United Nations Refugee Agency (UNHCR). "Note on Burden and Standard of Proof in Refugee Claims," December 16, 1998. http://www.unhcr.org/refworld/pdfid/3ae6b3338.pdf.

United Nations Refugee Agency (UNHCR). "What Is Asylum?" Accessed 8/29/23. https://help.unhcr.org/usa/applying-for-asylum/what-is-asylum/.

United States v. Abbott. 1:23-CV-853-DAE (W.D. Tex. Apr. 26, 2024). https://casetext.com/case/united-states-v-abbott-60.

United States v. Goxcon-Chagal, 886 F. Supp. 2d 1222 (D.N.M. 2012). https://casetext.com/case/united-states-v-goxconchagal-2.

United States v. Medina-Copete. 757 F.3d 1092 (10th Cir. 2014). https://casetext.com/case/united-states-v-medina-copete.

U.S. v Favela-Lujan. No. CR 10-3232 RB (D.N.M. Jan. 21, 2011). https://casetext.com/case/us-v-favela-lujan.

United States v. Holmes. No. 13-1660 (8th Cir. May. 12, 2014) https://casetext.com/case/united-states-v-holmes-39.

Upholt, Boyce. "Saguaro, Free of the Earth." *Emergence Magazine*, March 31, 2022. https://emergencemagazine.org/essay/saguaro-free-of-the-earth/.

Urry, Amelia. "'Come and See Me—My Grave Is Open': Finding Life after Deportation in Nogales, Sonora." *Pacific Standard*, June 10, 2019. https://psmag.com/social-justice/come-and-see-me-my-grave-is-open-finding-life-after-deportation-in-nogales-sonora.

US Army Corps of Engineers. "Section 10 of the Rivers & Harbors Act." Los Angeles District Website. Accessed August 30, 2024. https://www.spl.usace.army.mil/Missions/Regulatory/Jurisdictional-Determination/Section-10-of-the-Rivers-Harbors-Act/.

US Citizenship and Immigration Services. "Uniting for Ukraine." Accessed May 8, 2023. https://www.uscis.gov/ukraine.

US Congress. United States Code: Immigration and Nationality, 8 U.S.C. §§ 1104-1401 (Suppl. 2 1964). https://www.loc.gov/item/uscode1964-016008006/.

US Congress. Combating BDS Act of 2017. S. 170, 115th Congress (2017). https://www.congress.gov/bill/115th-congress/senate-bill/170.

US Congress. Combating BDS Act of 2023. S. 1637, 118th Congress (2023). https://www.congress.gov/bill/118th-congress/senate-bill/1637.

US Congress. "Strongly Condemning and Denouncing the Drastic Rise of Antisemitism in the United States and around the World." H. Res. 894, 118th Congress (2023). https://www.congress.gov/bill/118th-congress/house-resolution/894.

US Congress. Immigration and Nationality Act of 1952 (McCarran-Walter Act). Pub. L. 82-414, 66 Stat. 182 (1952).

US Congress. REAL ID Act of 2005. H.R. 418, 109th Congress (2005). https://www.congress.gov/bill/109th-congress/house-bill/418.

SOURCES

US Customs and Border Protection. "Air and Marine Operations Operating Locations." November 17, 2023. https://www.cbp.gov/border-security/air-sea/oam-operating-locations.
US Customs and Border Protection. "CBP, Princess Cruise Line Introduces Facial Biometrics at Port of San Francisco." Press release, October 11, 2022. https://www.cbp.gov/newsroom/national-media-release/cbp-princess-cruise-line-introduces-facial-biometrics-port-san.
US Customs and Border Protection. "CBP Attaches." May 9, 2023. https://www.cbp.gov/border-security/international-initiatives/cbp-attaches.
US Customs and Border Protection. "Did You Know . . . Massive Flood in 1864 Altered Course of Rio Grande Resulting in Border Dispute?" Last modified, December 20, 2019. https://www.cbp.gov/about/history/did-you-know/flood.
US Customs and Border Protection. "International Operations." January 24, 2023. https://www.ice.gov/about-ice/homeland-security-investigations/international-operations.
US Customs and Border Protection. "Iranian Supreme Leaders Vows Forceful Revenge after US Kills Maj. General Qassim Suleimani in Baghdad—Threat Alert High." Office of Field Operations. Tactical Analytical Unit—Seattle Field Office. UPDATED PROCEDURES (Best Practices Learned in Last 24 Hours). Seattle, WA, January 2020.
US Customs and Border Protection. "Jefferson Davis Milton a.k.a Jeff Milton 1861–1947." Last modified November 9, 2015. https://www.cbp.gov/about/history/timeline/timeline-date/jefferson-davis-milton-aka-jeff-milton-1861-1947.
US Customs and Border Protection. "National Standards on Transport, Escort, Detention, and Search." Washington, DC, October 2015. https://www.cbp.gov/sites/default/files/assets/documents/2020-Feb/cbp-teds-policy-october2015.pdf.
US Customs and Border Protection. "Say Hello to the New Face of Security, Safety and Efficiency: Introducing Biometric Facial Comparison." Accessed January 28, 2024. https://biometrics.cbp.gov.
US Customs and Border Protection. *2022–2026 U.S. Border Patrol Strategy*. CBP Publication No. 1678-0222. Washington, DC, February 2022.
US Department of Commerce. "U.S. Trade with Israel." Office of Technology Evaluation. Washington, DC, 2021. https://www.bis.doc.gov/index.php/documents/technology-evaluation/ote-data-portal/country-analysis/2989-2021-statistical-analysis-of-u-s-trade-with-israel/file.
US Department of Energy. "President Biden Invokes Defense Production Act to Accelerate Domestic Manufacturing of Clean Energy." Washington, DC, June 6, 2022. https://www.energy.gov/articles/president-biden-invokes-defense-production-act-accelerate-domestic-manufacturing-clean.
US Department of Health and Human Services. "Operational Challenges within ORR and the ORR Emergency Intake Site at Fort Bliss Hindered Case Management for Children." Office of the Inspector General. OEI-07-21-00251, September 27, 2022. https://oig.hhs.gov/oei/reports/OEI-07-21-00251.asp. Full report: https://oig.hhs.gov/oei/reports/OEI-07-21-00251.pdf.
US Department of Homeland Security. "Management Alert—DHS Needs to Address Dangerous Overcrowding and Prolonged Detention of Children and Adults in the Rio Grande Valley (Redacted)." Office of the Inspector General. Washington, DC, July 2, 2019. https://www.oig.dhs.gov/sites/default/files/assets/2019-07/OIG-19-51-Jul19_.pdf.
US Department of the Interior. Memorandum: "Entitlements to Water under the Southern Arizona Water Rights Settlement Act (SAWRSA)." Office of the Solicitor. M-36982,

Washington, DC, March 30, 1995. https://www.doi.gov/sites/doi.opengov.ibmcloud.com/files/uploads/M-36982.pdf.

US Department of Justice. "Guidance for Federal Law Enforcement Agencies Regarding the Use of Race, Ethnicity, Gender, National Origin, Religion, Sexual Orientation or Gender Identity." Washington, DC, December 2014. https://www.dhs.gov/sites/default/files/publications/use-of-race-policy_0.pdf.

US Department of State. *Boundary: Solution of the Problem of the Chamizal*. Chamizal Convention of 1963: Convention between the United States of America and Mexico. Signed at Mexico City, August 29, 1963. Washington, DC: US Government Printing Office, 1963. https://www.ibwc.gov/wp-content/uploads/2022/11/ChamizalConvention1963.pdf.

US Department of State. The Immigration Act of 1924 (The Johnson-Reed Act). Office of the Historian. Accessed August 30, 2024. https://history.state.gov/milestones/1921-1936/immigration-act.

US Department of State. *Papers Relating to the Foreign Relations of the United States, with the Annual Message of the President Transmitted to Congress December 3, 1907, (In two parts), Part II*. Office of the Historian. https://history.state.gov/historicaldocuments/frus1907p2/d230.

US Department of State. "U.S. Security Cooperation with Ukraine: Fact Sheet." Bureau of Political-Military Affairs. Washington, DC, August 22, 2023. https://www.state.gov/u-s-security-cooperation-with-ukraine/.

US National Archives and Records Administration. Chinese Exclusion Act (1882). Last updated January 17, 2023. https://www.archives.gov/milestone-documents/chinese-exclusion-act.

US National Archives and Records Administration. Platt Amendment (1903). Last updated February 8, 2022. https://www.archives.gov/milestone-documents/platt-amendment.

US Navy. "History." NS Guantanamo Bay. https://cnrse.cnic.navy.mil/Installations/NS-Guantanamo-Bay/About/History/.

US Navy. "Installation Guide." NS Guantanamo Bay. https://cnrse.cnic.navy.mil/Installations/NS-Guantanamo-Bay/About/Installation-Guide/.

US Senate Select Committee on Intelligence. *The Senate Intelligence Committee Report on Torture (Torture Report)*. New York: Melville House, 2014.

U.S. v. Pena-Ponce. 588 F.3d 579 (8th Cir. 2009). https://casetext.com/case/us-v-pena-ponce.

Vaca, Daniel. *Evangelicals Incorporated: Books and the Business of Religion in America*. Cambridge, MA: Harvard University Press, 2019.

Valdemar, Richard. "Patron Saints of the Mexican Drug Underworld." PoliceMag.com, June 2, 2010. https://www.policemag.com/blogs/gangs/blog/15318211/patron-saints-of-the-mexican-drug-underworld-part-1-of-2.

Van der Veer, Peter. *The Value of Comparison*. Durham, NC: Duke University Press, 2016.

Vanderwood, Paul J. *Juan Soldado, Rapist, Murderer, Martyr, Saint*. Durham, NC: Duke University Press, 2006.

Vargas González, Alberto. "¡Oh, Muerte Sagrada, Reliquia de Dios! La Santa Muerte: Religiosidad Popular en la Ribera de Pátzcuaro." *La Palabra y el Hombre*, no. 130 (2004): 101-122.

Vatter, Miguel. *Divine Democracy: Political Theology after Carl Schmitt*. Oxford: Oxford University Press, 2020.

Vatter, Miguel. *Living Law: Jewish Political Theology from Hermann Cohen to Hannah Arendt*. Oxford: Oxford University Press, 2021.

Velikov, Kathy, and Geoffrey Thün. "How the Rio Grande Came to Separate the U.S. and Mexico." *Architect's Newspaper*, July 31, 2018. Accessed August 30, 2024. https://www.archpaper.com/2018/07/politics-etched-concrete-el-paso-ciudad-juarez-rio-grande-border/.

Viefhues-Bailey, Ludger H. *No Separation: Christians, Secular Democracy, and Sex*. New York: Columbia University Press, 2023.

Vitalis, Robert. *Oilcraft: The Myths of Scarcity and Security That Haunt U.S. Foreign Policy*. Stanford, CA: Stanford University Press, 2020.

Walia, Harsha, ed. *Undoing Border Imperialism*. Oakland, CA: AK Press/Institute for Anarchist Studies, 2013.

Ward, Eric K. "Skin in the Game: How Antisemitism Animates White Nationalism." Political Research Associates, June 29, 2017. https://politicalresearch.org/2017/06/29/skin-in-the-game-how-antisemitism-animates-white-nationalism.

Ward, Myah, and Dan Levin. "Anti-Semitism or Free Speech? College Students Cheer and Fear Trump Order." *New York Times*, December 15, 2019. https://www.nytimes.com/2019/12/15/us/trump-anti-semitism-order-college-students.html.

Washington v. Trump. Case No. C17-0141JLR, WL 462040 (W.D. Wash. Feb. 3, 2017).

Weinberger, Sharon, and Jana Winter. "The FBI's New U.S. Terrorist Threat: 'Black Identity Extremists.'" *Foreign Policy*, October 6, 2017. https://foreignpolicy.com/2017/10/06/the-fbi-has-identified-a-new-domestic-terrorist-threat-and-its-black-identity-extremists/.

Weiner, Isaac, and Joshua Dubler, eds. *Religion, Law, USA*. New York: New York University Press, 2019.

Welke, Barbara Young. *Law and the Borders of Belonging in the Long Nineteenth Century*. Cambridge: Cambridge University Press, 2010.

Wessler, Seth Freed. "The Border Where Different Rules Apply." *New York Times*, December 6, 2023. https://www.nytimes.com/2023/12/06/magazine/us-coast-guard-children-detained.html.

Wheatley, Jeffrey. *American Fanatics: Spirited Rebellion and the Policing of Religion*. New York: New York University Press, forthcoming.

Wheeler, Mark. "Shadow Wolves." *Smithsonian Magazine*, January 2003. http://www.smithsonianmag.com/people-places/shadow-wolves-74485304.

Whitlock, Monica. "Legal Limbo of Guantanamo's Prisoners." BBC News, May 16, 2003. Accessed September 5, 2024. http://news.bbc.co.uk/2/hi/americas/3034697.stm.

Whitt, Jacqueline E. "Empire, Religion, and the United States Military." *American Religion* 3, no. 2 (Spring 2022): 117–24.

Wiles, Tay. "A Closed Border Gate Has Cut Off Three Tohono O'odham Villages from Their Closest Food Supply." *Pacific Standard*, February 7, 2019) https://psmag.com/social-justice/a-closed-border-gate-has-cut-off-three-tohono-oodham-villages.

Winter, Jana, and Sharon Weinberger. "The FBI's New U.S. Terrorist Threat: 'Black Identity Extremists.'" *Foreign Policy*, October 6, 2017. https://foreignpolicy.com/2017/10/06/the-fbi-has-identified-a-new-domestic-terrorist-threat-and-its-black-identity-extremists/.

Winters, Joseph. "Race and Religion beyond the State." Webinar. Sciences Po-CERI, Paris, June 10, 2021.

Winston, Susanna E., and Curt G. Beckwith. "The Impact of Removing the Immigration Ban on HIV-Infected Persons." *AIDS Patient Care and STDs* 25, no. 12 (December 2011): 709–11.

White House, President Donald J. Trump. "Protecting the Nation from Foreign Terrorist Entry into the United States." Executive Order No. 13769. 82 Fed. Reg. 8977 (February 1,

2017). https://www.federalregister.gov/documents/2017/02/01/2017-02281/protecting-the-nation-from-foreign-terrorist-entry-into-the-united-states.

White House, President Donald J. Trump. "Enhancing Vetting Capabilities and Processes for Detecting Attempted Entry into the United States by Terrorists or Other Public-Safety Threats." Proclamation No. 9645, 82 Fed. Reg. 45161 (September 24, 2017). https://www.federalregister.gov/documents/2017/09/27/2017-20899/enhancing-vetting-capabilities-and-processes-for-detecting-attempted-entry-into-the-united-states-by.

White House, President Donald J. Trump. "Combating Anti-Semitism." Executive Order No. 13899. 84 Fed. Reg. 68779 (December 11, 2019). https://www.federalregister.gov/documents/2019/12/16/2019-27217/combating-anti-semitism.

White House, President Joseph R. Biden Jr. "Memorandum on Presidential Determination Pursuant to Section 303 of the Defense Production Act of 1950, as Amended." Presidential Determination No. 2022–11 (2022-07421). 87 Fed. Reg. 19775 (April 6, 2022). https://www.federalregister.gov/documents/2022/04/06/2022-07421/presidential-determination-pursuant-to-section-303-of-the-defense-production-act-of-1950-as-amended.

White House, President Joseph R. Biden Jr. "U.S.-Canada/Canada-U.S. Supply Chains Progress Report." Washington, DC, June 2022. https://www.whitehouse.gov/wp-content/uploads/2022/06/CANADA-U.S.-SUPPLY-CHAINS-PROGRESS-REPORT.pdf.

White House, President Joseph R. Biden Jr. "Fact Sheet: Biden-Harris Administration Releases First-Ever National Strategy to Counter Antisemitism." Briefing Room press release, Washington, DC, May 25, 2023. https://www.whitehouse.gov/briefing-room/statements-releases/2023/05/25/fact-sheet-biden-harris-administration-releases-first-ever-u-s-national-strategy-to-counter-antisemitism/.

White House, President Joseph R. Biden Jr. "The U.S. National Strategy to Combat Antisemitism." Washington, DC, May 2023. https://www.whitehouse.gov/wp-content/uploads/2023/05/U.S.-National-Strategy-to-Counter-Antisemitism.pdf.

White House, President Joseph R. Biden Jr. "Fact Sheet: President Biden's Budget Strengthens Border Security, Enhances Legal Pathways, and Provides Resources to Enforce Our Immigration Laws." Briefing Room press release, Washington, DC, March 9, 2023. https://www.whitehouse.gov/briefing-room/statements-releases/2023/03/09/fact-sheet-president-bidens-budget-strengthens-border-security-enhances-legal-pathways-and-provides-resources-to-enforce-our-immigration-laws.

White House, President Joseph R. Biden Jr. "Proclamation on Ending Discriminatory Bans on Entry to the United States." Proclamation 10141 (2021-01749). 86 Fed. Reg. 7005 (January 25, 2021). https://www.federalregister.gov/documents/2021/01/25/2021-01749/ending-discriminatory-bans-on-entry-to-the-united-states.

Yadgar, Yaacov. "On the Uses and Abuses of Tradition: Zionist Theopolitics and Jewish Tradition." In *When Politics Are Sacralized: Comparative Perspectives on Religious Claims and Nationalism*, edited by Rouhana and Shalhoub-Kervorkian, 88–112. Cambridge: Cambridge University Press, 2021.

Yadgar, Yaacov. *Sovereign Jews: Israel, Zionism, and Judaism*. Binghamton: State University of New York Press, 2017.

Yale Law School. "Agreement between the United States and Cuba for the Lease of Lands for Coaling and Naval Stations; February 23, 1903." Avalon Project: Documents in Law, History and Diplomacy. Accessed July 14, 2023. https://avalon.law.yale.edu/20th_century/dip_cuba002.asp.

Yao, Joanne. *The Ideal River: How Control of Nature Shaped the International Order*. Manchester, UK: Manchester University Press, 2022.

Yelle, Robert A. *Sovereignty and the Sacred: Secularism and the Political Economy of Religion*. Chicago: University of Chicago Press, 2019.

Yuhas, Alan. "It's Time to Revisit the Satanic Panic." *New York Times*, March 31, 2021. https://www.nytimes.com/2021/03/31/us/satanic-panic.html.

Yick Wo v. Hopkins. 118 U.S. 356, 6 S. Ct. 1064 (1886). https://casetext.com/case/yick-wo-v-hopkins-wo-lee-v-same.

Yeh, Rihan. *Passing: Two Publics in a Mexican Border City*. Chicago: University of Chicago Press, 2018.

Yourish, Karen, Danielle Ivory, Jennifer Valentino-DeVries, & Alex Lemonides. "How Republicans Echo Antisemitic Tropes Despite Declaring Support for Israel." *New York Times*, May 9, 2024. https://www.nytimes.com/2024/05/09/us/antisemitism-republicans-trump.html.

Zakzok v. Trump. Amended Complaint for Declaratory and Injunctive Relief. Civil Action No. 17-cv-02969-TDC. US District Court for the District of Maryland. October 6, 2017.

Zolberg, Aristide R. *A Nation by Design: Immigration Policy in the Fashioning of America*. Cambridge, MA: Harvard University Press, 2008.

Zonszein, Mairav. "Christian Zionist Philo-Semitism Is Driving Trump's Israel Policy." *Washington Post*, January 28, 2020. https://www.washingtonpost.com/outlook/2020/01/28/trump-thinks-supporting-israel-means-letting-it-do-whatever-it-wants/.

Index

Page numbers in italics refer to figures.

Abbott, Greg (Texas governor), 95, 177n33; and Operation Lone Star, 125–26
abject, the: defined, 89; Jews and, 94–95, 104; loved by Santa Muerte, 135
abortion, 31
Administrative Procedures Act (APA) (1946), 15
Adolfo López Mateos River Channel, 175
Africa, 136
Africa, John, 71–72
African Americans: as Christians on Palestine, 116n110; discrimination against, 76n78; religiosity of, 71
Agamden, Giorgio: on AmericaIsrael, 99; on *homo sacer*, 89
Agrama, Hussein, 41
Ahmadi Muslims, as asylum seekers, 37–38. *See also* Muslims
AIPAC, 106
Albright, Madeleine, 98n26
Ali, Muhammad, 116n110
Allhallowtide, 141n56. *See also* Christianity; religion
Almonte, Robert, 146n72; as expert witness in *US v. Medina-Copete*, 147–51
Alt-Right, anti-Semitism of, 117
America. *See* USA
"AmericaIsrael": and borders' ambivalence, 98–102; criticism of, 107; cultural politics of, 102–7; flags of, 96–97, *96*; as Holy Land(s), 93–94, 100, 102–7; hybrid sovereignty of, 95–96, *96*; and "othering" of Jews, 115; as sacred "supra-nation," 24; spirit of, 107; suppressing criticism of, 108–9; US after, 119–21; variety of opponents of, 107–8; variety of supporters of, 100, 101–102, 106–7; white supremacy in, 117–18. *See also* Israel
American Civil Liberties Union (ACLU): on Fourth Amendment and border zones, 15–16; on Palestinians' First Amendment rights, 113; stats on GTMO detainees, 85–86; on US border restriction zone, 4
American Conservative, 143
American Council for Judaism (ACJ), as anti-Zionist, 105, 110
American Indians. *See* Native Americans
American Israel Public Affairs Committee (AIPAC), 106
American Jewish Committee, 114
"Americanness": as goal of refugees, 47; and religion, 28–47; tradition of perceived, 76
American Revolution, founding of Israel compared to (Uris), 107n66
America-Ukraine, and AmericaIsrael, 99
Antebi, Nicole, 177; discovers/studies "meander maps" of Mississippi River, 168, *169*, 170
Antichrist, in premillennial dispensationalist theology, 92–93n3
"antinomian sacred," 45
anti-Semitism: of Alt-Right, 117; AmericaIsrael and, 95; criticism of Israel as, 108, 112, 114–15, 119; defined by IHRA (2016), 115, 120n128; fused with anti-Zionism, 24, 108–15; Israel gives rise to, 105; legislation opposing (US), 111; non-Zionists and, 107, 111; organizations combatting, 109–11; tropes of perpetuated in AmericaIsrael, 115–17; Trump/Biden oppose, 113–14; two types of, 117–18
Anti-Semitism Accountability Project (ASAP), 109

anti-Zionism: defined, 108–9; fused with anti-Semitism, 24, 108–15; Jewish, 107–8, 111; legislation opposing (US), 111; non-Jewish, 97, 105; organizations combatting, 109–11; proponents of, 110–11; suppressing expression of, 109–11
Anzaldúa, Gloria, 151–52
Apaches (Native Americans), 162; El Chamizal stolen from, 172n15; oppose ranchers' land grabs, 55, 57–58. *See also* Indigenous peoples; Native Americans; *and individual tribes and nations*
apartheid, 110. *See also* racism
Arendt, Hannah, 70
Aristide, Jean-Bertrand, 41, 83
Arizona Daily Star, 159
Arkansas Times, 120n129
Armageddon: Israel and, 105; in premillennial dispensationalist theology, 92–93n3
Asad, Talal, 17n82
assimilation, AmericaIsrael and, 94–95
Associated Press (AP), 65
asylum, religious: basics of, 28–34; critics of adjudication process, 36–37; defined, 28; evolving, 29n7, 71; "eye of the persecutor" and, 36–37, 40, 41; Iranian child receives, 27; as paradoxical, 28; questions asked of applicants, 27–28, 30–35; and US border, 22, 26–47. *See also* asylum seeking; refugees; religion
asylum seeking: and freedom, 45–46; goals of, 47; as liturgical, 40–47; as theological/religious politics, 42–43. *See also* asylum, religious
Axelman, Eric, 120n130
Aziz v. Trump, 63n25

Bacha, Julia, 95
Bagram Air Force Base, 86
Baha'i, 59
Baldwin, James, 116
Barnett, George, *162*
Barth, Karl, 46n76
Bartlett, John Russell, 157–58
Basic Law, on Jewish supremacy in Israel, 118
Baudrillard, Jean, 12
Bay of Pigs debacle (1961), 82
Bayoumi, Moustafa, 72
Beckwith, Kurt G., 83n17
Bender, Courtney, 100–101n38
Berger, Benjamin, 93–94n8
Berlit, Uwe, 33
Berridge, Elizabeth, 33
Berzon (judge), 32n15
Bible, use by far right, 74. *See also individual books*
Biden, Joseph, President, 3, 64, 125; augments Trump's EO on anti-Semitism, 113; policies toward Ukraine, 99
Biden-Harris Fact Sheet, combats anti-Semitism, 113–14

Bigliardi, Stephano, 133
BIRAX: the British Israel Research and Academic Exchange Partnership, 110
black sites, as ambiguous ("limbos"), 87. *See also* Guantánamo Bay naval station
Blumenthal, Sidney, 98n26
Board of Immigration Appeals, 29, 31n13
"body natural"/"body politic," 17–18
Bonhoeffer, Dietrich, 115
borderlessness, 24, 45; AmericaIsrael and, 94; and discrimination against Native Americans, 50; Santa Muerte and, 129–30; US capitalists enact at Mexican border, 54–58
borders, human: "antinomian sacred" and, 45; as brokers of abjection, 89; ideal, 178; as magical spaces, 20; as meaningless, 152–53; policy/politics of, 19–20, 178. *See also* borders, US
borders, US: ambiguity of, 178; AmericaIsrael's ambivalent, 98–102, 107; Arizona's with Sonora, 156; boundaries of, 4, 5, 15, 153–54; capitalists circumvent, 54–58; "Constitution-free," 15; "ideal," 178; meaningless to O'odhams, 161–63, *162*; paradoxical "experience" of, 12–15, 16–17, 22; and political/religious objects, 16–17; refusal of, 128–29, 151–54; regulation along waters, 11–12; and religious asylum, 22, 28; and sovereignty, 19; spread and fortification of, 5–6; surveillance of all, 166; suspension of, 93; as temporary, 152; worldwide enforcement regimes, 4. *See also* borders, human; US-Canada borderlands; US-Mexico borderlands
border security: defiance of, 24; as discriminatory, 72, 76, 124, 125–27; impairs Native American mobility, 52–54; supply store serving, 3
Boumediene, Lakhdar, 87–88
Boumediene v. Bush, 87–88
Boyarin, Daniel, 110
Boycott (film), 112, 120n129
Boycott, Divestment, Sanctions movement (BDS), 108, 109; defined, 111–12; efforts to criminalize, 112
Branch Davidians, 139
Brewer, Megan, 33
Breyer, Stephen (Supreme Court justice), 66, 75
Brown, Bobby, 166
Bunker, Pamela, 138–39
Bunker, Robert, 138–39
Bureau of Alcohol, Tobacco, Firearms, and Explosives, 139
Bush, George H. W., President, 41
Bush, George W., President: Secure Fence Act (2006), 163; Special Registration program, 72
Butler, Judith, 28n2; anti-Zionism of, 110

"Cactus Curtain," 82
Calderón, Felipe, 137
Calvo-Quirós, William, 132, 133, 134n27, 150

INDEX

Cantú, Francisco, 15, 126
Carlos III (king of Spain), 158
Carnegie, Andrew, 49n6
Carter, J. Kameron, 46; on "abject," 89; on borderlessness, 129; on Whiteness, 94, 115–16
Castañeda, Katia Perdigón, 131
Castells Ballarin, Pilar, 129n4, 129n8, 135
Castro, Fidel, on GTMO station, 81
Catholic Church, 90n43; and Santa Muerte cult, 137. *See also* Catholicism
Catholicism: and Chinese woman's claim, 30–31; Mexican, 132; O'odham Sonoran, 133, 159; Santa Muerte's associations with, 130, 131, 133, 141–42, 150, 154; and support for Israel, 106. *See also* Christianity
Cázares-Kelly, Gabriella, 165–66
Center for Constitutional Rights (CCR), on GTMO detainees, 26n85
Central Intelligence Agency (CIA), 82
Cervantes, Antonio, Jr., thesis on Santa Muerte, 144–45
Chace, James, 98n26
Chamizal Convention (1963), relocates Rio Grande into channel, 172–76, *174*, 176. *See also* US-Mexico borderlands
Chamizal dispute over shifts in US-Mexico border, 171–72, 175
Chang, Arturo, 132
Chavez, Arsenio, in lawsuits Santa Muerte worship, 145n71, 146–47, 149–50
Chestnut, Andrew, 128
children: death of unsuccessful immigrant, 11–12n44; detained in cages, 24, 123–24; footprints of, 7, 8; imprisoned at GTMO, 85; Iranian immigrants as, 27; mistreated migrant, 25; unaccompanied migrant, 11n43, 123–24
China, refugee from, 30–31
Chinese Exclusion Act, 51
Chomsky, Noam, anti-Zionism of, 110
"chosenness," American/Canadian, 93–94n8
Christianity: and asylum seeking, 29–34, 46; in court proceeding, 148; Holy Land as "headquarters" of, 105; and pagan *do ut des*, 143; as requirement for asylum, 27, 30n12; spread of, 139; Tohono O'odham Nation and, 160; universal/secular, 46. *See also* conversion, religious; *and individual denominations*
Christians United for Israel (CUFI), and eschatology, 105, 106
Christian Zionism, 103–5; first support for Israel, 106; questioning, 107; and white evangelicalism, 92–93. *See also* anti-Zionism; Zionism
citizenship, "liturgy" into, 40–46. *See also* asylum, religious; asylum seeking
Ciudad Juárez, Mexico, on US-Mexico border, 168, 175, *177*. *See also* US-Mexico borderlands

civil rights, US violates, 60. *See also* discrimination; persecution; protest
Civil Rights Act, on anti-Semitism (Title VI), 113, 114
Clark, T. J., 68
Clinton, Bill, President, DoJ on Haitian refugees, 84
C/O Futures, LLC, 139–40
Cohen, Hermann, 110
Cold War, 105
colleges and universities: anti-Semitism alleged at, 109, 114; as censoring pro-Palestinian demands, 114n101; pro-Palestinian protests, 108. *See also individual campuses*
Combating BTS Act (2019, 2023), 112
conservatives, political/religious, 17
Constitution, Cuban, on Guantánamo Bay, 78–81
Constitution, US: border-relevant exemptions from, 15–16; First Amendment, 30, 37, 40, 60, 63n25, 65, 71; Fourteenth Amendment, 76n78, 84; Fourth Amendment, 15; suspension clause, 88
conversion, religious: and asylum seeking, 31–36, 42, 44–45; from Islam to Christianity, 46. *See also* religion
corporate nationality, and Mexican citizenship, 54
corporate personhood, overrides Mexican sovereignty, 54
Cosa v. Mukasey, 39n53
Council of Trent (1570), 137
Council on American-Islamic Relations (CAIR), on Palestinians' First Amendment rights, 113
COVID-19 pandemic, 109n76
criminality, Santa Muerte worship and, 137–51. *See also* drug trade
Crosson, J. Brent, 135–36
Crum, Bartley, 117
Cuba: refugees' treatment by US, 84–85; relations with US (re GTMO), 78–82
Cuban American Bar Ass'n v. Christopher, 84n21
Cuban Missile Crisis, 173
Cunningham, Hilary, 128
Cuomo, Andrew (New York governor), 95
Curtis, Edward, 71

Darweesh v. Trump, 63n25
David, Nellie Jo, 166
Davies, Myles, 44
Dayan, Hilla, 108–9
Day of the Dead, 140
death: obsession with, 144; Santa Muerte and, 134. *See also* Santa Muerte
Defense Production Act (DPA) (2022), 11
Deleuze, Gilles, 20
Democrats block anti-BDS legislation, 112
Department for Encouragement of Pilgrimage, 106
Department of Homeland Security Western Hemisphere Travel Initiative (WHTI), 52–53

Desert Land Act (1877), 55
Detainee Treatment Act (2005), 88
Dew, Spencer, 128n2
Díaz-Ordaz, Gustavo, President, 175
discrimination: anti-Semitism as, 113; against inhabitants of US territories, 75–76; against Muslims, 16n74, 19, 64–76; against Native Americans, 50–54, 56, 58, 126. *See also* persecution; racism
Doerig, Harold, 33
Dominican Republic, US invades and occupies (1916), 81
Downes v. Bidwell, 89–90
drug trade: anti-smuggling force, 52, 53; Jésus Malverde and, 148; Santa Muerte and, 134, 137, 144–51; suspicion of, 163, 165; trial for, 145–51; at US-Mexico border, 24, 130. *See also* Santa Muerte
Du Bois, W. E. B., 46n76, 94, 115
due process, granted to detainees, 84. *See also* Constitution, US
Duvalier, Jean-Claude, 41

Eilertsen, Sam, 120n130
Einstein, Albert, opposes idea of Jewish State, 105
ekklesia, Indigenous/Catholic, defined, 154, 154n104
Elbit Systems, 25; surveils Tohono O'odham reservation, 166
El Paso, TX, on US-Mexico border, 2, 53, 168, 170, 174–77
Ephesians, Epistle to the, 6:10–12, 141
Epstein, Maria, 134n26
Eric Supangat v. Holder, 39
eschatology, Israel and, 105. *See also* religion; theology
Esposito, Robert, 18n85
Establishment Clause, 37, 63n25, 65, 71. *See also* Constitution, US
European Union (EU), on refugee religious claims, 33–34
Eusebio Francisco Kino (Catholic priest), 155–58
evangelicalism, white, 92–93. *See also* religion; *and individual denominations*
executive branch (of US government), sovereignty of, 68–72
extremism, categories for analysis, 138–40

facial biometrics, at US borders, 124–25
Fallas, Amy, 105, 106
Farah, Kirby, 141n56
Fassin, Didier, 28n3, 29n7, 39n51, 42
Federal Bureau of Investigation (FBI): on Black religiosity, 71; and drug smuggling at US-Mexico border, 52n19; on extremism, 74n71; on religion and criminality, 139
Federal Circuit Court of Appeals, 29–30

Federal Rules of Evidence, 38n49, 148–49, 150
feminism, imperial, as justification for Muslim ban, 63
Fiddian-Qasmiyeh, Elena, 34
Fiesta de San Francisco, 157
First Amendment, 30, 37, 40, 60, 63n25, 65, 148; boycotts protected under, 112, 113, 120n129; rights denied, 71–72; subordinate to national security, 71. *See also* Constitution, US
Fisher, Max, 114
Fisk, Harold, drew Mississippi River "meander maps," 168, *169*
Flowers, Brandon, 155n2
footprints: of Indigenous children, 7, *8*; of O'odham ancestors, 162–63
Forward, The, 109n76
Foundation to Combat Anti-Semitism (FCAS), 109
Fox, Vicente, President, 137
Franciscan monks, 155, 158
Francis of Assisi, Saint, 158
Francis Xavier, Saint, 155–58, *157*
Frank Star Comes Out (president of Oglala Sioux), 126
freedom, defined, 45–46
Free Exercise and Establishment Clauses, 37. *See also* Constitution, US
Freese, Kevin, 143
free speech. *See* First Amendment
Front de Libération de Quebec, 122n1
Frost, Robert, "Mending Wall," 3, 175
Fuller, Melville Weston (Supreme Court justice), 90

Gadsden Purchase/Treaty of La Mesilla (1853), 50, 55, *162*
Garcia-Navarro, Lulu, 27
Gaza: Israeli invasion of (2023), 24, 108n71; Israeli mass killings in, 108, 120; Israeli war in, 94, 97; US desert as, 98. *See also* Israel; Palestine
Geertz, Clifford, 17n82
Geneva Conventions (1951), 28–29n5, 85
Geronimo, opposes conquest of Native American lands, 55
Gessen, Masha, 114–15
Ghazvinian, John, 60
Ginsburg, Ruth Bader (Supreme Court justice), 71
Given-Wilson, Zoë, 39n51
Global Entry program, 122, 124
Golan Heights, 96
Golden Land, AmericaIsrael as, 94
Goldstein, Brandt, 83n18
Goldstein, Eric, 116
Gómez, Juan Gualberto, 79
Gordon, Neve, 120n28
Goxcon-Chagal, Rafael, on trial for Santa Muerte prayer, 145–51
Grandin, Greg, 16

INDEX   215

Grant, Ulysses S., President, 50–51
Graziano, Michael, 76
Greco, John, 102n43
Gregg and Viesca (law firm), 48, 54
Gruzinski, Sergei, 132
Guantánamo Bay naval station (GTMO): Haitian/Cuban immigrants detained, 83–85; history of, 78–82; judged "not US territory," 83–84, 85, 88, 89–90; post office serving, 90, 91; terms of US occupation, 81–82; unlawful combatants imprisoned, 85–86
Guardian, The, 33
Guatemala, border agents for, 4
Guattari, Félix, 20

habeas corpus rights, 85; extended to GTMO detainees, 87–89
Hacking, Ian, 25
Hagee, John, 106
Haiti: refugees' treatment by US, 83–85; as site of "bad" religion, 142; "sorcery" of as rebellion, 136; US invades and occupies (1915), 81
Hamdan v. Rumsfeld, 88
Hawaii v. Trump, 64n26
Haynes, William, 85
Hegel, Georg Wilhelm Friedrich, 69–70
Heine, Heinrich, 119
Helms, Jesse (US senator), 83n16
himdag, 162; encompasses Christian practices, 160
Hinojosa, Alana de, 168, 170, 171, 172n15
HIV, disqualifies refugees from US, 83
Hohokam tribe (Native Americans), 50. *See also* Indigenous peoples; Native Americans
Holocaust, 93, 117
Holy Land: AmericaIsrael as, 93–94; American fascination with, 102–4; cultural politics of, 102–7; as headquarters for Christianity, 105; theme parks, 102–3. *See also* AmericaIsrael; Israel; USA
Holy Land Experience, 102–3
Holy Land USA, 102
Homeland Security Act (2002), 52
Homeland Security Investigations (HSI), locations of, 5, 52n19. *See also* US Department of Immigration and Customs Enforcement
Homestead Act (1862), 55
homo sacer, 89
House of Representatives, US, funding of Israel, 97
Howe, Cymene, 131
humans: Deleuze and Guattari on, 20; philosopher-theologians on, 21
Huq, Aziz, 67
Hutcheson, Joseph C., Jr. (judge), 105

ID cards, Enhanced Tribal, insufficient to cross US-Mexican border, 52–53, 53. *See also* passports

ID cards, forged, 30
I'itoi (O'odham god), 160
Ikuta (judge), 32n15
Immerwahr, Daniel, 76
immigrants, undocumented: Operation Lone Star opposes, 125–26; US government search for, 4. *See also* asylum, religious; children; refugees
immigration and border enforcement: defiance of, 24; as discriminatory, 75–76; paradoxical in US, 12–15; religion and, 23; US budget for, 3–4. *See also individual locations*
Immigration and Nationality Act (INA) (1980), 29, 30, 83n17
Immigration and Naturalization Service (INS), 5, 15, 37n41, 84
immigration judges: decisions on asylum, 27–28; eccentricities of adjudications, 39; religion-based decisions by, 30–32, 34; as "saviors" of asylum seekers, 46. *See also names of individual judges*
"impostorhood": detected at US border, 124, 125; detecting religious, 31–32, 40, 42
Indigenous peoples: on religion and governance, 142–43; worship of Kino/Saint Francisco, 155–67; worship of Santa Muerte et al., 140–41, 143. *See also Native Americans; and individual tribes and nations*
Insular Cases (1921–22), 75–76, 89–90
Intelligence Reform and Terrorism Prevention Act (2004), WHTI and, 52–53
International Boundary and Water Commission, 171n13, 172–73, 175, 177
International Boundary Commission, on controversy of US-Mexico border, 171
International Boundary Commission de la Frontière Internationale, 171
International Holocaust Remembrance Alliance (IHRA), definition of anti-Semitism, 115, 120n28
international law, US national security violates, 61
internment of Japanese (WWII), 66
Int'l Refugee Assistance Project v. Trump, 64n26
Iran: and Israel, 93; refugees from, 27, 31–32, 34n26; US detains Iranians after assassination, 59–60
Iron Dome missile defense system, 97
Iroquois tribal nation, 161
Isaiah 10:20–23, 93n3
Islam, expansion of, 138–39. *See also* Muslims
Islamophobia, 73. *See also* Muslim ban; Muslims
Israel: Basic Law of, as discriminatory, 118; as Christian nation-state, 115–16; discriminatory hierarchy in, 117; expels Iraqi Jews, 120; founders compared to American Revolutionaries, 107n66; invasion of Gaza (2023), 24, 120; Jewish Americans and, 116, 119–20; Judaism collapsed into, 100, 103; opposition to, 107–8, 120–21; punishing boycotts of, 112–13; and Second Coming, 106; US commitment to, 92–119; US

Israel (cont.)
    support for as an ideal, 100–101. See also AmericaIsrael; anti-Zionism; Gaza; Zionism
Israel Anti-Boycott Act (2018), 112
Israelism (film), 120n130

Jackley, Marty, 126
Jackson, Robert (Supreme Court justice), 66
James, Letitia, 95n15
Jansen, Yolande, 108–9
Jeffress, Robert, 178
Jerusalem: exhibition recreates, 103–4; recreated at theme park, 102. See also Holy Land; Israel
Jesuit order, 158. See also Catholicism
Jesus Christ: portrayed at theme park, 102; in premillennial dispensationalist theology, 92–93; Second Coming of, 106. See also Christianity
JewBelong, 109–10
Jewish Americans: "dual loyalties" of (Trump), 116; as "others," 24, 116–17; support for Israel, 93. See also AmericaIsrael; Jews; Zionism
Jewish diaspora, relocating/isolating, 117. See also Jews
Jewishness: ambivalence toward, 116; Germans reinterpret, 118; and Whiteness, 115–16. See also Jews; Judaism
Jewish Voice for Peace, 119
Jews: as belonging in Israel, 103; in Middle East society, 103n46; opposed to Israel, 107–8 (see also anti-Zionism); "othering" of, 115; in premillennial dispensationalist theology, 92–93. See also AmericaIsrael; Israel
John, gospel of, 14:6, 46
Johnson, Greg, 129n7, 152
Johnson, Lyndon B., President, 172n19, 175
Johnson, Paul, 32, 45, 154n104
Johnson, Sterling, Jr., 84
Jones, Eddie, 6, 7
Jones Studio, 6–7
Jose, Kendall, 161
Juan Bautista de Anza National Historic Trail, 155, 156
Juárez, Mexico, on US-Mexico border, 168, 175, 177. See also US-Mexico borderlands
Judaica, sold in theme park, 103
Judaism: collapsed into Israel, 100, 103; connection to Zionism, 114; distinguished from Israel, 105; pluralistic traditions in, 108, 118–20. See also AmericaIsrael; Jewish Americans; Jews
Jude, Saint, 150. See also Catholicism
Justo, Nathalia, 32

Kaell, Hillary, 92–93n3, 104–5, 106n64
Kagan, Michael, 35–36, 37
Kahn, Paul, 16n78, 17n81, 136n40
Kang, S. Deborah, 15
Kantorowicz, Ernst, 17–18, 68–69
Kaplan, Amy, 94, 105, 107; and premillennial dispensationalism, 92n1, 92–93n3
Katyal, Neal, 65, 67
Kaufman, Ellie, 82
Keane, Webb, 45–46, 144–45
Kennedy, Anthony (Supreme Court justice), 75
Kennedy, John F., President, 173
Khalidi, Dima, 114n101
Kickapoo, 52. See also Indigenous peoples; Native Americans
kings: and "body natural"/"body politic," 17–19, 68–69; and popular sovereignty, 68
Kirsh, Natie, 110–11
Klassen, Pamela E., 154n104
Knesset, 118. See also AmericaIsrael; Israel
Koh, Harold Hongju, 83n18
Korean Chinese asylum seekers, "migration industry" and, 34–35. See also asylum, religious; refugees
Korematsu v. United States, 66
Kraft, Robert, 109, 110–11
Kramer, Paul, 78, 84, 85, 170, 176, 178
Kushner, Jared, 115

Lalami, Laila, 4
Laporte, Pierre, 122n1
Latin America, 105n55
Lauder, Ronald S., 109, 110–11
Left Behind book series, 92–93
legislation, environmental, and wall and fence construction, 9–10
Léon, Luis, 152–53
LGBTQ+ populations: claim to be Muslim, 34; Santa Muerte and, 134
Li, Darryl: on anti-boycott legislation, 112–13; on US torture sites worldwide, 86–87
liberals/progressives: on criticism of Israel, 119; disdain support for Israel, 106
limbo: at border, 176; defined, 77n1, 87; Santa Muerte embraces, 134
Lindsay, Hal, 106
liturgy: of asylum, 40–46; etymology/definition of, 43–44. See also religion
Lloyd, Vincent, on American political theology, 99–100n36, 136n40
Loera, Javier, 152
Lofton, Kathryn, 61
Lomnitz, Claudio, 132
Long, Burke, 94, *Imagining the Holy Land*, 102–3
Lopez, Roberto, 159
Lorentzen, Lois, 130–31
Löwith, Karl, 69–70
Lucero, Carlos F. (judge), 149
Luiselli, Valeria, 25
Luxemburg, Rosa, 119

Madsen, Kenneth, 165
Magdalena de Kino, Mexico, as religious destination, 25, 155–67, *156*
Magid, Shaul, 110, 111
Malverde, Jésus, 128, 138; and drug trafficking, 148
mandas, 160
manifest destiny, 98
Mann, Thomas C., 172, 174
Mariposa, AZ, as utopian winter produce entry point, 6–9
mariposa, meanings of, 9
Mariposa Land Port of Entry, awarded for renovations, 6–7, *8*
Martin, Desirée, 131–32, 134, 143
Marx, Karl, 119
Marzouki, Nadia, 73
Mauritanian, The (film), 77n3
Mayblin, Lucy, 32
Mayorkas, Alejandro (DHS secretary), 99n34, 125
Mbembe, Achille, 87n35
McAlister, Melani, 94
McCalla, Bowman H., 78
McEnaney, Lillia, 133
Medina-Copete, Maria Vianey, on trial for Santa Muerte prayer, 145–51
Metcalfe, David, 138
Mexican Revolution (1910–1920), 56
Mictecacihuatl, 140–41
Miera-Rosete, Mixcoatl, 147n77
Military Commissions Act (MCA) (2006), 88
Miller, Todd, 4, 161
Milton, Jefferson Davis, 51
Milton, Jim, 58
Milton, John, 51
Minutemen border militia, 3, 94n11, 96–97, 125; on Israel, 97–98
Mireles, Christian Ramiro, 150–51
Mishra, Pankaj, 116
Mississippi River, meanders/avulsions of, 168–70, *169*
Moore, Allison, 7
Morley Gate, 2, 3, 4
Mountford, Lydia, Madame, 104, 121
MOVE community, denied First Amendment protection, 71–72
Mullen, Lincoln, 39–40, 46
Munguia, Manuel, 172
Musalo, Karen, 30, 36
Muslim ban (2017), 19, 23, 61, 63; plenary power and, 69, 71; Tea Party and, 73–74. *See also* discrimination; Muslims; persecution; Presidential Proclamation 9645; religion
Muslims: civil rights violated, 60; conversion to Christianity, 46; and discrimination, 16n74, 19, 64–68, 72–73; EO-1 discriminates against (2017), 63; LGBTQ+ asylum applicants as, 34; portrayed at theme park, 104; Shia, 59, 65, 140. *See also* discrimination; Islam; Muslim ban; Presidential Proclamation 9645

Nadler, Jerry (US representative), 111
Nakba (1948), 108–9. *See also* Gaza; Palestine
narcocultura, 153
"narco-saint," 147, 148, 150–51n89, 151
National Archives, US, 79
National Council of American Indians, 52
National Cowboy & Western Heritage Museum, honors Slaughter, 57
National Park Service (NPS), 175–76; and Border Patrol, 53–54, 57
National Public Radio (NPR), interviews immigrant child, 27
national security, US: racism and violence against Middle Easterners/Muslims, 59–76; religion and, 23; Santa Muerte threatens Mexican and, 141–42
National Strategy to Counter Antisemitism (2023), 113
Native Americans: protective legislation circumvented, 9–10; US government and, 10. *See also* Indigenous peoples; *and individual tribes and nations*
Navafi v. INS, 34n26
Nayeri, Dina, 27, 35–36, 42
Nazis: desire to relocate Jews, 117; Israeli policy said to resemble, 115
"necropolitical law," 87
Netanyahu, Benjamin, 96n19, 116
New York Times, 16, 85n26, 95, 109, 142n58
New York University (NYU), Jewish students sue for anti-Semitism, 114
Nijhawan, Michael, 37–38
9/11: detritus of as sacred, 101; executive power expanded after, 70, 75n75; Magdalena pilgrims obstructed since, 163
9/11 Commission Report, 4
Noem, Kristi (South Dakota governor), barred from Pine Ridge Reservation, 126
Nogales, AZ, 2, 3, 4, *131*, 155
non-Jewish Israelis, 97
non-Zionism: diverse forms of, 110–11; suppression of, 109–10. *See also* anti-Zionism
Northwestern University, pro-Palestinian encampment at, 108
NYU Center for Study of Antisemitism, 114

Obama, Barack, President: administration and Civil Rights Act Title VI, 113n94; Visa Waiver Program as discriminatory, 65
obeah, 135–36
Oglala Sioux, bars governor from lands, 126. *See also* Indigenous peoples; Native Americans

Omer, Atalia, 117
O'odham: divisions of, 50, 161, 165; history of, 50–52; hybrid Christianity of, 159; landowners obstruct pilgrimages, 163–67, *164*; Mexican/US governments dispossess for ranchers, 56; pilgrimages by, 155, 158, 160–61; protest against border obstruction, 54, *164*, 164–65; Sonoran Catholicism, 133, 159; US control over homelands, 50–54; along US-Mexico border, 22, *162*, *164*. *See also* Indigenous peoples; Native Americans; Tohono O'odham Nation
Operation Global Reach, 5
Operation Lone Star, 125–26
Organ Pipe Cactus National Park, 49, 51, 53–54
Orsi, Robert, 142
Ortega, David, 167n49
Orthodox Judaism, anti-Zionism of ultra-, 110, 111. *See also* anti-Zionism
"other(s)": African religion as, 136; Americans as opposed to, 44, 47, 73; asylum and, 22; Hispanics and Indigenous people as, 172n15; immigrants as, 27, 28, 43; Jewish Americans as, 24, 116–17; Jews as, 114, 115; Santa Muerte embraces, 134
Our Lady of Guadalupe, 153

Palestine, 97, 107; campus protests supporting, 108; defenders as alleged anti-Semites, 112; Jewish domination of, 118–20. *See also* anti-Zionism; Boycott, Divestment, Sanctions movement; Gaza
Palestine Legal, on Palestinians' First Amendment rights, 113
Palestinian Arabs, Israel's discrimination against, 118. *See also* Palestine
Palmore, W. B., 104
Panama Canal, 98
pandemic (COVID-19), 109n76
Pansters, Wil G., 133
Pan v. Holder, 39
Papago, 51, 56. *See also* Indigenous peoples; Native Americans; Tohono O'odham Nation
paro/parar, applications to Santa Muerte, 133
Parrish, Will, 166
Pascua Yaqui, *53*. *See also* Indigenous peoples; Native Americans
passports: and reentry to US from Canada or Mexico, 52–53; required by Israel, 107; required by Mexico for crossing border, 53; required of pilgrims to Magdalena, 163; Soviet, treat Judaism as nationality, 114
Patel, Faiza, 75n75
Patriot Act of 2001, and GTMO, 89n41
Paul E. Singer Foundation, 110n78
Pax Americana, 98
Pena, Leo, 151

Pentecostal church, Eritrean government and, 36. *See also* Christianity
Perez, Thomas E., 113
persecution: adjudication of can be arbitrary, 39; asylum on basis of, 38–39; asylum seekers must prove, 29, 37–38; against Muslims (EO-1), 63; religious/political distinction difficult, 39. *See also* asylum, religious; civil rights, US violates; discrimination; Muslim ban
Philippines, 85n25
Philos Latino, 105n55
Pierce, Franklin, 161
pilgrims: to Israel, 104–5; to Magdalena de Kino, 155–67, *156*
Platt, Orville (US senator), 79
Platt Amendment (1903), 79–81, *80*
plenary power, 68–74; executive immunity and, 67–69
political morality, and political theology, 99–100n36
political theology: national security and, 62; and political morality, 99–100n36; of sovereignty, 68–72. *See also* theology
polytheism, 143. *See also* religion
Pomba Gira, 130
popular sovereignty: complete as impossible, 68; king's "second body" and, 18, 68–69; pressures of, 72–76. *See also* sovereignty
Presbyterians, 44. *See also* Christianity
Presidential Proclamation 9645 ("Muslim ban") (2017, 2020), 23, 63; discriminates against Muslims, 65–67, 72–76; states banned from entry by, 64; third iteration of, 64n30; visas rejected, 64–65n31. *See also* discrimination; Muslim ban; *Trump v. Hawaii*
Preston, Andrew, 61
Princess Cruise Lines, CBP works with, 125
Proctor & Gamble, as satanic, 141–42n58
Prohibition, "watering holes" during, 2, 172
Promised Land: AmericaIsrael as, 94; Israel as, 106. *See also* AmericaIsrael; Holy Land; Israel
protest: over anti-Muslim animus, 73–76; on behalf of white supremacy (Charlottesville), 95; Cubans' against US presence, 82; Haitians' against HIV exclusion, 83; against Israeli brutality in Gaza, 108; against O'odham border obstruction, 165, 166–67; against Platt Amendment, 79; against *Trump v. Hawaii* decision, 66–67. *See also* civil rights, US violates; discrimination; persecution
Protestantism: evangelical, in USA, 47, 92–93; liberal, 143; and support for Israel, 106. *See also* Christianity
Protocol of New York (1967), 28–29n5
Puerto Rico, as "shadowed" US possession, 90

Quitobaquito Springs, Native Americans and wildlife desecrated in, 10

racial profiling, permitted by CBP and DHS, 16. *See also* racism
racism: anti-Semitism conflated with anti-Zionism, 110–11; and executive plenary power, 67–68, 72, 73; Israel accused of, 115; against Jews, 116; and religion, 136; Santa Muerte worship and, 143; in Western religion, 136. *See also* discrimination; persecution
Rajah, Jothie, 87
Ramsey, Kate, 136
Rapture, the, 92–93n3, 106
Rasul v. Bush, 88
Real ID Act (1996), 9n32
refugees: defined, 28–29n5, 29; Haitian et al. (at sea) barred from US, 41, 85n22. *See also* asylum, religious; immigrants, undocumented
refugee status determination (RSD), 29; can become religious trial, 37–38. *See also* asylum, religious
religion: adjudicating where disestablished (USA), 38; African, 136; and Americanness, 28–47; Aztec as vulnerable to obsessions, 144, and borders, 17, 98–102, 153–54, 155–67, 156 (*see also* AmericaIsrael); as choice, in USA, 39–40; European and Native American fused, 153–54; as "exit sign," 45; and extremism, 138–40; fused with politics, 99, 104, 106, 107; "good," 140–42; Indigenous and governance, 142–43; liberal/progressive disdain for, 106; and 9/11 detritus, 101; and racism, 136; Santa Muerte worship as "bad," 137, 140–42; "submerged," 32; "true" and asylum seeking, 43; undefined, 30; upsets disciplinary boundaries, 47; verifying affiliations, 29–34, 30n12, 32n15, 32n17; Yelle on, 98–99. *See also* asylum, religious; Magdalena de Kino, Mexico, as religious destination; Santa Muerte; *and individual religions and dominations*
religious freedom: AmericaIsrael and, 100; American as exclusive, 136; asylum system and, 22, 43, 46; and religious asylum, 36; right to, 39–40, 163. *See also* civil rights, US violates; Muslim ban; persecution; Presidential Proclamation 9645; protest
Report of the National Commission on Terrorist Attacks upon the United States (9/11 Commission Report), 4
Republicans, ambivalence of toward Jews, 95
Republic of Indian Stream, 10–11
Richland, Justin, 152
Rio Grande/Rio Bravo del Norte: as "ideal border," 25, 178; meanderings/avulsions shift US-Mexico border, 168–71, 169; militarized, 177; as temporary border, 152

Ríos, Alberto, "Border Lines," 6
Rivas, Ofelia, 165–67
river, ideal, at borders, 178
Rivers & Harbor Act (RHA), 177
Roa, Raúl, 82
Roberts, John (Supreme Court justice): defends Proclamation 9645, 74; on *Trump v. Hawaii*, 70
Robertson, Pat, 106
Robles, John, 159
Romo, David, 128
Roosevelt, Franklin, President, 51; Platt Amendment repealed under (1934), 81
Root, Elihu, 79
Rose, Lena, 34, 37, 39n51
Rose, Nikolas, 20
Rosenfeld, Arno, 110n78
Rosenthal, Marvin, 102
Rosenwald, Lessing, 105
Rosenzweig, Franz, 110
Roush, Laura, 130
Rubio, Marco (US senator), 112
Rumsfeld, Donald, 83

saguaro cacti, 49
saints, Catholic: excluded from Santa Muerte worship, 140–41; as "legitimate," 150. *See also* Catholicism; *and individual saints' names*
Sale v. Haitian Ctrs. Council, Inc., 83n18
Samahon, Tuan, 37
Samaritans, 159
San Bernardino Land Grant, 55
Sanctuary of Holy Death, 137. *See also* Santa Muerte
Sanders, Bernie (US senator), 119–20
San Miguel (Wo'osan) Gate, obstructs O'odham pilgrims, 163–66, *164*
San Pascual Bailon, 132
Santa María Magdalena, as pilgrimage destination, 155
Santa Muerte, 127; as agent of borderlessness, 24, 153–54; as agent of solidarity, 153–54; associations of, 130–32; commercialized, 134; criminalized, 137–51; dark side of, 134–35; and drug trade, 134, 137, 144–51; as equalizer, 134; fear of, 141–42, 145, 153; human sacrifice to, 140–41; and idol worship, 140–41; Indigenous peoples and, 133–34, 140–41, 143, 153–54; and mainstream Christianity, 143; many names of, 130n9, 146; in Mexican history, 131–33; police belief in, 141–42; popularity of, 128; prayers to, 133, 135n34, 145–46; publications on, 140; racist denigration of, 135, 143; as superstition, 137, 142; as travel goddess, 145–46; worship of, 128–54
Santa Muerte Universal (SMU), 137
Santner, Eric, 17, 74; on popular sovereignty, 18–19, 68–69; on "surplus immanence," 18n85
Satanic panic (1980s), 141–42

Satmar Hasidic Jews, 111. *See also* anti-Zionism; Jews; Judaism
Sauter, Rodney, 173–74
Schaeffer, Felicity Amaya, 9–10, 162
Schermerhorn, Seth, 133, 159–60, 162
Schmitt, Carl, 45, 62
Schusterman Family Philanthropies, 110n78
Scott, James, 32, 129
Second Coming, 92
secularism, 21, 41–42n62
Secure Fence Act (2006), 163
Shadow Wolves, 51–52
Shakman, Stephen, 122
Shane, Peter, 70
Shapira, Harel, 3, 126; interviews Minuteman, 97–98
Sherman, R. E. (El Paso mayor), 172
Shine a Light, 109–10
Shortall, Sarah, 62
siakam, 160–61
Singer, Paul, 105n55
Slahi, Mohamedou Ould: *Guantánamo Diary*, 77–78, 86; tortured at GTMO, 86
Slaughter, John H. (Texas sheriff), 51; landholdings span US-Mexico border, 55–58; memorialized in Southwest, 57–58
Slaughter Ranch Museum, 57
Small Wars Journal, 138–39
Smith, Matt, 138
Soldado, Juan, 128, 133, 138
Soleimani, Qasim (major general), US government assassinates, 59, 61, 96
sorcery, African practices as, 135–36
Sotomayor, Sonia (Supreme Court justice), on Muslim ban, 66, 71
sovereignty: American, and religion, 22; material science of, 19; O'odham claims to, 161–62; and political theology, 68–72; and sacrality, 101; Santa Muerte cult challenges, 128–30, 134; transcending, 120–21. *See also* popular sovereignty
Spanish Inquisition, asylum regimes and, 41–42
Spanish-American War, 76, 78
Special Registration, as discriminatory against Muslims, 72. *See also* discrimination; Muslim ban; Muslims
Spinoza, Baruch, 119
"spiritual insurgency," 128–29
state of exception, 89n41
Stern, Kenneth, 114
St. John, Rachel, 2n3, 12, 51, 54, 56; on Slaughter takeover of Tohono O'odham/Yaqui lands, 55–56
St. Louis Mirror, 104
Stop the Wall, 166
Storey, Hugo, 33
Storm, Jason Ānanda Josephson, 137

Strømmen, Hannah, 74
Stutman, Gabe, 115
Sullivan, Winnifred Fallers, 72, 153, 154n104; on obstacles to consulting religion experts in RSD, 38; on state power and the church, 19
superstition: criminalizing, 142; Santa Muerte worship as, 137

Tafjord, Bjørn Ola, 143
Taussig-Rubbo, Mateo, 101
Taylor, Chelsea, 102–3
Taylor, Sarah McFarland, 134n26
Tea Party, opposes "threatening minority," 73–74
Tello, Manuel, 172
terrorism, criticism of Israel as, 112
Texas, controversies over border, 125–26, 177. *See also* El Paso, TX, on US-Mexico border; Rio Grande/Rio Bravo del Norte
Texas State Historical Association, on "law of accretion," 171
Thebault, Deborah, 34, 37
theology: in court's reasoning, 148–49, 150; law enforcement and, 143; political, 99, 104; premillennial dispensationalist, 92–93n3. *See also* political theology
Thün, Geoffrey, 171
Tohono O'odham Nation: border divides, 25, 161–63, *162*; and Christianity, 160; Cultural Center and Museum (Himdag Ki), 48–49, 54; demographics of, 50; Mexican/US governments dispossess, 56, 58; militarization of lands, 166–67; pilgrimages by, 159; protest against US policing of border, 54. *See also* Indigenous peoples; Native Americans; O'odham
Tonantzin (Nahuatl deity), 153
torture, by US, of unlawful detainees, 86–87. *See also* Guantánamo Bay naval station; persecution
Toufighi (Iranian refugee), 32n15
Traditional Apostolic Catholic Church Mexico-USA, 137. *See also* Santa Muerte
Treaty of 1884, 170
Treaty of Guadalupe Hidalgo (1848), 50; border provided by, 157, 161, 169–70
Treaty of Paris (1898), 78, 79
Trillo, Maria Eugenio, 2
Trinity Broadcasting Network, 102
Trotsky, Leon, 119
Trump, Donald, President: and border wall construction, 9; EO 13769 overruled by courts, 63; EO on anti-Semitism and Civil Rights Act, 113–15; on Jews who vote Democratic, 116n111; and Muslim ban, 63, 66, 72; on Netanyahu, 96n19, 116
Trump v. Hawaii, 23, 63, 65–67, 70, 74n74, 75
Trump v. Int'l Refugee Assistance Project, 64n26

INDEX

UJA-Federation of New York, 110n78
Ukraine, and US political morality, 99
UN Convention Relating to the Status of Refugees, 29
UN Educational, Scientific and Cultural Organization (UNESCO), 51
United Kingdom (UK), asylum seekers and, 32–33
United Nations (UN), condemns Soleimani assassination, 61
United States v. Bastanipour, 31–32
United States v. Goxcon-Chagal, 147–48
University of Chicago, Jewish students oppose Gaza invasion, 108
UN Protocol Relating to the Status of Refugees (1967), 29n6
UN Refugee Agency (UNHCR), 28, 33; on assessing refugee religious claims, 33–34
UN Refugee Convention (1951), 29
Uris, Leon, 107
Urry, Amelia, 3
USA: after AmericaIsrael, 119–21; asylum and religion in, 26–47; as "chosen nation," 104; commitment to Israel, 92–119; hegemonic aspirations of, 7, 61, 98, 99; as kingdom of God, 46; most states oppose BDS, 112–13; paradox of borderlands of, 12–15; sovereign exceptionalism of, 98–99; as temporary overseer of borderlands, 152; treatment of borders and "secular *corpus mysticum*," 18. *See also* AmericaIsrael; Israel
US Army Corps of Engineers, 168, 169, 177n33
US-Canada borderlands: commission created to oversee (1908), 171; controversies at/over, 11n42, 122n1; human smuggling along, 11–12n44; Iranians detained at WA crossing, 59–60; Native Americans and blurriness of, 10–11
US CPB Air and Marine Operations Assets, 6
US-Cuba (non)borderlands, hazy enforcement at GTMO, 23
US Customs and Border Protection (CBP), 51, 122–23, 129; budget for, 3–4, 5–6; facial recognition kiosks at borders, 124–25; locations of, 4–5; on national security threats, 61, 72; orders Iranians/Iranian Americans detained, 59; prerogatives of, 4; problems at Texas border, 125–26; violates sanitation standards, 123–24;
US Department of Defense (DoD), redacted diary, 77–78
US Department of Education (DoE), and Civil Rights Act Title VI, 113n94, 114
US Department of Homeland Security (DHS), 5–6, 24; denies refugees appeal to, 29; interviews refugee applicants, 29; Investigations Tactical Patrol, 52; Office of the Inspector General (IG), 123–24; powers of Secretary of, 9n32; report on children in cages, 123–24

US Department of Immigration and Customs Enforcement (ICE), 52; budget for, 3–4, 6; DHS report on, 123–24
US Department of Justice (DoJ), on Haitian refugees, 84
US Fish and Wildlife Service, 57
US Foreign Military Studies Office, 128, 143
US Immigration Service Border Patrol, 51, 52; ignores obstruction at O'odham border, 164–65; obstructs/harasses Magdalena pilgrims, 163; surveils Tohono O'odham lands, 166; works with NPS, 53–54, 57
US-Israel Free Trade Agreement (FTA) (1985), 99
US-Mexico borderlands: barriers to crossing (O'odham Nation et al.), 52–54, 163–67, 177–78; illegal immigration opposed at, 125–26; irrelevant to O'odham people, 161–63, 162; Native American territories along, 10, 22–23; nineteenth-century exceptions allowed, 22–23; sanctity threatened by meanderings of Rio Grande, 168, 169, 170–71; towns along as Prohibition-era "watering holes," 2; Ukrainians crossing, 99n34; US capitalists seize from Native Americans, 54–58; as "vast zone of exception," 15. *See also* borders, US; *and individual place names*
US Supreme Court, 120n129; ruling on discrimination case, 65–66; ruling on Real ID waiver, 9–10; supports national security (Muslim ban), 63, 75–76. *See also individual cases and justices*
US v. Favela-Lujan, 148n79
US v. Holmes, 150–51n89
US v. Medina-Copete, 145–51
US v. Pena-Ponce, 148n79

Valdemar, Richard, on Indigenous "idol worship," 140–41
Van der Veer, Peter, 43
Vargas Gonzalez, Alfredo, 131n12, 132
Vatter, Miguel, 69–70
Velikov, Kathy, 171
Venn diagram, 99
Virgin Mary, 133n24
Visa Waiver Program Improvement and Terrorist Travel Prevention Act (2015), discriminates against Muslims, 65
voudou, 136; Santa Muerte worship resembles, 143

walking, for pilgrimages, 159–60. *See also* pilgrims
Washington v. Trump, 63n25
Watergate scandal, 70
Weber, Max, 45
Welke, Barbara Young, 72
Wessler, Seth Freed, 85n22

West, Noel, 82–83
white nationalists, racism against Jews, 116–17. *See also* racism
Whiteness: religion of, 94–95, 115–16; question of Jewish, 116
white supremacy, 3; in AmericaIsrael, 117–18; Border Patrol and, 16; Israel embodies (Baldwin), 116; protest on behalf of (Charlottesville), 95; US and, 46n76. *See also* discrimination; racism
Wicca, Santa Muerte worship resembles, 143
Wiles, Tay, 165
Wilson, Woodrow, President, 51
Winston, Susanna E., 83n17
World Jewish Congress, 109
World's Fair of 1904, Holy Land exhibition, 103–4
World Trade Organization (WTO), on America-Israel "borders," 99
Wynter, Sylvia, 94

Yadgar, Yaacov, 118–19
Yao, Joanne, 178
Yaqui, 158, 159; Mexican/US governments dispossess, 56. *See also* Indigenous peoples; Native Americans
Yelle, Robert, 20; on "*antinomian sacred*," 45; on religion, 98–99, 100–101
Yoo, John, 85, 85n25

Zahrani, Yasser Talal Al, 85
Zakzok v. Trump, 63n24, 64n26, 73–74n70
Zaraysky, Susanna, 131
Zionism: Christian and Jewish, 93; Christian in Latin America, 105n55; Judaism's connection to, questioned, 114, 118; misconceived, 103n46; opposed, 105, 119; in theme park, 103; varieties of in AmericaIsrael, 95, 117, 119–20. *See also* anti-Semitism; anti-Zionism
Zuley, Richard ("Captain Collins"), 86

www.ingramcontent.com/pod-product-compliance
Lightning Source LLC
Chambersburg PA
CBHW022053290426
44109CB00014B/1078